GW00361242

Hello!

Welcome to the world of the iPod. In the seven years since Apple unveiled this remarkable device, it has changed beyond all recognition. The first models were mono-screened, chunky, heavy lumps of metal that did little more than play your music.

The latest models in the line-up couldn't be more different if they tried. They still play music, but supplement this with audio books, podcasts and even video. They are slimmer, and now boast colour screens. The iPod touch – king of the pride – will even let you browse the web wirelessly, send and receive emails and manage your calendar.

A whole world of accessories has grown up alongside the iPod, meaning you now no longer have to listen through the bundled white headphones, iconic though they may be. Now you can share your music with the world by plugging in to a massive choice of speakers, or broadcast on FM for listening in the car.

In this guide we'll highlight some of the best features in every iPod, and show you how to do more with your chosen gadget than just play music on the move. We'll be retrieving our tracks from an iPod after losing them on our computer, downloading free applications to run on the iPod touch and checking out alternatives to the iTunes Store. We'll connect our iPods to the hi-fi and TV, create compilation CDs from iTunes and build smart playlists that keep themselves up to date without us doing any work ourselves.

To help you navigate this book, we have colour-coded the edges of the pages. Product reviews, including the complete iPod line-up and chosen add-ons, have a yellow edge. Features are blue, and in between the two you'll find our workshops, each of which is carefully written to help you get the most out of your iPod.

These, too, are colour-coded, on the basis of technical requirement. Green ones are easy, amber are a little more technical and red are advanced, so pick up from wherever you feel most comfortable.

Happy reading... and perhaps more importantly, happy listening!

Nik Rawlinson

P.S. If you have an iPhone too, check out *The Independent Guide to the iPhone 3G* at www.macuser.co.uk/iphone

The Ultimate iPod Guide

EDITORIAL
FAX 020 7907 6369
EMAIL *mailbox@macuser.co.uk*

EDITOR Nik Rawlinson
DESIGN Stephen Savage, Camille Neilson
PRODUCTION Jon Lysons, Kate MacWhannell, Stephen Savage

DEPUTY EDITOR Kenny Hemphill
CONTRIBUTORS Ian Betteridge, Christopher Brennan, Ross Burridge, Chris Cain, Will Head, Kenny Hemphill, Niall Magennis, Keith Martin, Christopher Phin, Nik Rawlinson,
IMAGES Danny Bird, Nickan Arzpeyma, Jamie McGowan, John Reynolds, Chris Robson, Chip Wass, Robert Wilson, Lee Woodgate, Aston Leach

ADVERTISING
020 7907 6000, Fax 020 7907 6600
ads.macuser@dennis.co.uk
ACCOUNT MANAGER Alexandra Skinner 020 7907 6623
ACCOUNT MANAGER Guy Scott-Wilson 020 7907 6651
AD PRODUCTION EXEC Anisha Mogra 020 7907 6067

INTERNET
ONLINE EDITOR Nik Rawlinson 020 7907 6361
ACCOUNT MANAGER Gary Rayneau 020 7907 6661
MANAGING DIRECTOR Pete Wootton 020 7907 6299

PUBLISHING & MARKETING
020 7907 6000, fax 020 7907 6122
BOOKAZINE MANAGER Dharmesh Mistry 020 7907 6100
MARKETING MANAGER Claire Childs 020 7907 6113
MANAGING DIRECTOR Ian Westwood 020 7907 6355
RESEARCH DIRECTOR Lesley Muir 020 7907 6110
ASSOCIATE PUBLISHER Paul Rayner 020 7907 6663
LIST RENTAL EXECUTIVE John Perry 020 7907 6151
CIRCULATION MANAGER Kate Du Cros

DENNIS PUBLISHING LTD
DIRECTOR OF ADVERTISING Julian Lloyd-Evans
NEWSTRADE DIRECTOR Martin Belson
FINANCE DIRECTOR Brett Reynolds
GROUP FINANCE DIRECTOR Ian Leggett
CHIEF EXECUTIVE James Tye
CHAIRMAN Felix Dennis

Distribution Seymour Distribution 020 7396 8000

MacUser, incorporating *Apple User*, *DTP*, *MacShopper* and *MacBuyer*, is published fortnightly by Dennis Publishing Ltd, 30 Cleveland Street, London W1T 4JD, a company registered in England number 1138891. Entire contents © 2008 Dennis Publishing Ltd licensed by Felden. *MacUser* is an independent journal, not affiliated with Apple Computer Inc. 'Apple' and the Apple logo, 'Macintosh', 'Mac', the Mac logo and 'MacUser' are the trademarks of Apple Computer Inc.

HOW TO CONTACT US
MAIL MACUSER, 30 Cleveland Street, London, W1T 4JD
EMAIL *mailbox@macuser.co.uk* Web *www.macuser.co.uk*
PHONE 020 7907 6000 Fax 020 7907 6369
EMAIL AND WEB
To contact the editorial team *mailbox@macuser.co.uk*

Note: some accessories reviewed in this guide will not work with all models of the iPod. Please check compatibility with your player before making a purchase.

Ultimate Guide

007   **iPod introduction**
Choosing the right iPod for you

010   **iPodtastic**
Apple's latest players take centre stage

018   **iPod touch vs iPhone**
Choosing between these two devices

021   **Nike+**
Testing the Apple and Nike running gadget

024   **iPod accessories**
Six pages of add-ons for your iPod

031   **Online applications**
The best iPod touch-compatible apps

036   **What is iTunes?**
iTunes for beginners

041   **Ripping**
Adding your CD collection to your library

044   **Playlists**
Putting your songs in order the easy way

050   **iTunes Store alternatives**
The low-down on other great music stores

054   **Podcasts**
Subscribing to podcast feeds

056   **Connect your iPod to a hi-fi**
Get in the party mood by sharing your playlists

059   **Creating a compilation CD**
Burn your favourite songs to disc

063   **Application highlights**
The best software downloads for the iPod touch

068   **Applying parental controls to an iPod**
Prevent your kids from downloading adult content

070   **Using the iTunes Equaliser**
Making the most of your sounds

072   **Smart playlists**
Let iTunes do all the hard work for you

075   **Digitise your vinyl**
Turning vinyl tunes into digital format

082   **Optimise your data**
Synchronising your iPod with your computer

086   **iTunes plug-ins**
Our pick of the best plug-ins

092   **Ripping music out**
Transferring music from your iPod to your computer

094   **Encoding video for iPods**
Nine simple steps to converting videos

097   **Better audio encoding**
Getting the best out of your MP3 encoder

102   **iTunes servers**
Sharing your library across several computers

106   **Autocue masterclass**
Creating a speech autocue using QuickTime Pro

112   **Podcasting for profit**
Find out who's making money on podcasts

116   **DJing with your iPod**
Ditch the vinyl and go digital with these decks

120   **Who really created the iPod?**
The brains behind the gadget

126   **iPod evolution**
How the iPod came into being

130   **Where next for the iPod?**
What lies ahead for future iPod designs

132   **Buying and selling secondhand**
Comparing costs secondhand market

134   **Best iPod websites**
Sites offering info, humour and advice

138   **iPod Q&A**
Solutions to your queries

140   **iPod troubleshooting**
What to do when it all goes wrong

144   **Glossary**
Understanding iPod terms

Read me fi

All the information you need to decide which iPod is right for you

PAGE 008
Choosing an iPod

Not sure if you need a shuffle or a nano, iPhone or touch? Help is here with our simple flowchart.

Do not disconnect.

PAGE 140
Troubleshooting

From a frozen iPod to problems sharing music between computers, we answer all your queries and offer solutions.

PAGE 010
iPodtastic

The latest range of revamped iPods come complete with a host of new technologies, so get the ultimate lowdown on the shuffle, nano, classic and the touch before you make your purchase.

This is it, *The Ultimate iPod Guide* is back for the fourth edition. We take you through everything to do with the iPod, from essential advice to all the useful handy hints that you could possibly wish to know about this amazing device from Apple.

PAGE 036
What is iTunes?

If your music is scattered all over your hard drive it might be time to switch to iTunes. It's an easy-to-use piece of free software that will catalogue, track, copy, organise and play your music.

PRODUCTS

All you need to know about your shuffle, nano, classic and touch plus the lowdown on the iPhone 3G. We ask is it really better than the original iPhone? And no matter which iPod you choose we've rounded-up the perfect kit to go with it.

BEGINNERS

Organising your music is a simple task with iTunes. Our easy-to-follow guide shows you how to copy, track and catalogue your favourite tunes, plus advice on ripping CDs, creating playlists, subscribing to podcasts and connecting to a TV or hi-fi.

INTERMEDIATE

Want to control what your children are viewing? Our parental controls masterclass gives tips on enabling download restrictions. Plus steps on converting vinyl tunes into digital format, sychronising your iPod with your computer and a round-up of great iTunes plug-ins

ADVANCED

In this section we offer handy tips on how to convert video so that you can watch clips and movies on your iPod. And if you've ever been lost for words turn to the autocue masterclass. Plus how to get the best quality sound when ripping CDs.

FEATURES

Ever wondered who was the brains behind the iPod? We go behind the scenes and find out the true story. We also take a look ahead and ask whether these tiny iconic devices have reached their technological peak?

Sorry, leather aroma not included in this ad.

Reviews

008 Choosing an iPod

010 iPod review

018 iPod touch vs iPhone

021 Nike+

022 iPhone 3G

024 Add-ons

031 Online applications

Not sure which iPod is right for you? Here's an easy way to find out!

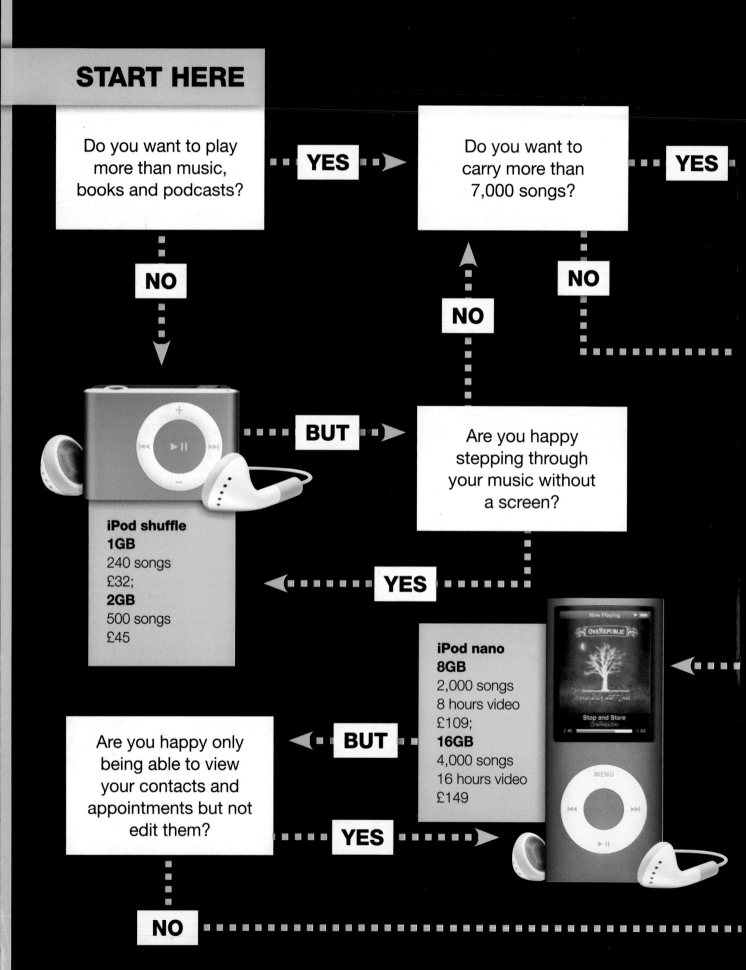

START HERE

Do you want to play more than music, books and podcasts?

YES ▶

NO ▼

Do you want to carry more than 7,000 songs?

YES

NO

NO ▲

BUT ▶

Are you happy stepping through your music without a screen?

YES ◀

iPod shuffle
1GB
240 songs
£32;
2GB
500 songs
£45

iPod nano
8GB
2,000 songs
8 hours video
£109;
16GB
4,000 songs
16 hours video
£149

Now Playing
ONEREPUBLIC
Stop and Stare
OneRepublic

◀ **BUT**

Are you happy only being able to view your contacts and appointments but not edit them?

YES ▶

NO

iPod classic
120GB
30,000 songs
150 hours video
£179

BUT

NO

Are you happy to compromise on capacity for features?

YES

Do you want to watch much video on your iPod?

NO

YES

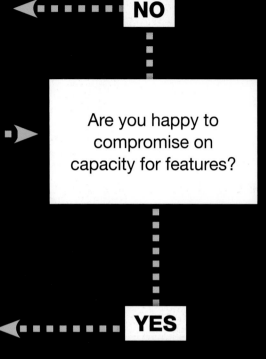

iPhone
From free to £349 depending on capacity. Available in **8GB** and **16GB** versions

So a small screen would be ok?

YES

NO

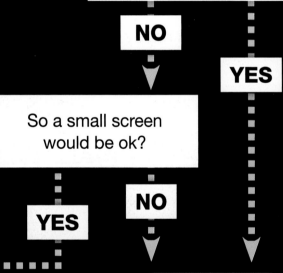

iPod touch
8GB
1,750 songs
10 hours video
£169;

16GB
3,500 songs
20 hours video
£219;

32GB
7,000 songs
40 hours video
£289

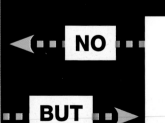

YES

NO

BUT

Would you consider getting a mobile contract and an iPhone instead?

iPodtastic

Apple has completely revamped the iPod, discarding its
iconic white design and adding a host of new technologies.
We examine the ins and outs of Apple's new media players.

Image Getty Images

If you still picture a chunky white brick whenever someone
says 'iPod', you're behind the times. Apple CEO Steve Jobs brought
the all-white era to a close in September 2007 with the introduction
of the iPod classic.

Apple had completely revamped its music player line-up in an
effort to drive ever greater sales. And it worked. Since then, it has
reworked the range once more, and now iPods come in more
colours than ever before, with the iPod nano alone being available in
an unprecedented 11 different finishes.

The iPod has been replaced at the pinnacle of the line-up by the
iPod touch, a widescreen, touch-sensitive, wireless iPod. The touch
takes its cues from the iPhone but completely redefines what

constitutes a portable music player by allowing you to download
music directly from the iTunes Store.

Completing the line-up is the nano and shuffle iPods. The former
has recently returned to its tall, slim format after a bloated year as
a squarer, flatter format. The new nano now has a curved body
and screen, and by borrowing a trick from the touch and iPhone,
can rather cleverly sense its orientation. Flip it on its side and it
knows exactly what you've done, with the screen format changing
to match. The shuffle, meanwhile, is Apple's screen-less low-end
entry device. A masterpiece of minimalism, it does nothing
but play music, either randomly or in order, with trimmed down
controls to match.

iPOD TOUCH

The announcement of the iPod touch in late summer 2007 wasn't exactly a surprise: rumours of a widescreen, touch-sensitive iPod with built-in wifi had been circulating for more than a year. And given that Apple already had the bones of the device in the iPhone, the touch seemed a natural and logical move. Despite the lack of surprise, though, the confirmation of the new iPod was greeted enthusiastically, particularly as it can be used as a mobile web browser and email device wherever there's a wifi network.

The iPod touch features the same multi-touch interface as the iPhone, and includes Cover Flow — Apple's visual metaphor for flipping through record sleeves in a stack. In addition to playing music, it has built-in applications for viewing photos, watching movies, connecting to YouTube, and a version of Safari for web browsing. PDA-type applications include a calendar, contacts book, clock and calculator.

With one push of a button on the touch's screen, users can connect directly to the iTunes Store whenever they're connected to a wireless network. This means that for the first time, iPod users don't need a Mac or PC to download music.

Over the year since then, Apple has released two software updates for the iPod touch, adding new features and giving it access to the iTunes App Store, allowing owners to install third-party applications on the device to plug the rather obvious gaps Apple left in its core feature set. Instant messaging, for example, is an obvious application for an Internet-enabled application, but until the App Store came along it was strictly off limits.

The iPod touch's screen is the same 3.5in widescreen, 480 x 320-pixel display seen on the iPhone. But the device itself is shorter and thinner than the iPhone, presumably due to the absence of a phone and camera inside. The second-generation touch has a more contoured body than the original, making it more comfortable to hold, and now features a built-in speaker for what Jobs called casual listening, acknowledging the fact that it won't rival headphones or dedicated external speakers.

The built-in wifi adaptor supports 802.11b and 802.11g standards but not the draft specification supported by Apple's Macs. This shouldn't be too much of a problem in a handheld device though.

Battery life has been a thorn in Apple's flesh since it shipped the very first iPod. So its reassuring to note that even with such a large screen, Apple quotes 36 hours of playback for music and six hours for video.

The touch, like the iPhone and the nano, uses flash memory. That's why it's so thin and is able to run for a reasonably long time on one charge. But it also seriously limits its capacity. The three available capacities, 8GB, 16GB and 32GB, fall far short of the capacities of the hard disk-based iPod classic. For those of us with large music libraries, who've become accustomed to copying everything from iTunes to the iPod, this presents a problem: either choose a classic with its narrow feature set, or start to be very strict about what music you copy to your iPod and how often you sync it with your Mac or PC.

This dilemma was unavoidable — it wouldn't have made sense for Apple to swap the flash memory for a hard drive: doing so would have meant a fatter case and shorter battery life. Yet there must be thousands of potential touch users who will be put off by the relatively low storage capacity. Storage is even more limited when you consider that one of the touch's main attractions is the ability to play video on a reasonable (for a handheld) sized screen.

Product (Red)

Apple is one of eight high-profile corporations licensing the Product (Red) brand for key members of their product range. Other partners include Microsoft, Dell and American Express.

For every Product (Red) iPod nano, shuffle or gift card purchased, Apple will make a contribution to the Global Fund fighting HIV/Aids in Africa. Ten per cent of all $25 gift cards is contributed to the fund, while the funds given through the purchase of an iPod nano is sufficient to provide 83 single treatments of a drug that helps prevent the transmission of HIV from mother to child. Product (Red) products cost you no more to buy than the regular equivalents in each range, so a (Red) nano is identically-priced to a blue or green one. Likewise the shuffle. The contribution is given by the manufacturer directly to the Global Fund without any further contribution from yourself. This, alone, should be enough to encourage you to at least take a look at the red nano and shuffle. They're really rather nice.

Video Formats

The touch supports the same audio and video formats as other iPods. That means there's still no support for Windows Media Audio or Video. While this is unlikely to be an issue for most Mac users, it remains a bone of contention among consumer groups who believe that the cost to Apple of licensing Windows Media would amount to a few pence per iPod, and that the reason for its exclusion is to lock iPod owners out of the stores that sell music in Windows Media-protected formats.

Supported video formats are H.264 and Mpeg-4, with a maximum resolution of 640 x 480 pixels (which is scaled down to the touch's display resolution of 480 x 320 pixels).

At £169 for the 8GB version, the touch is £60 more expensive than the equivalently-sized nano, but in terms of features and the sheer fun of using it, there's no comparison. If you can live with the higher costs, then the only decision you have to make is whether to buy the 8GB, 16GB or 32GB model.

Ringtones

It was widely expected that Apple would announce the decision to sell downloadable ringtones from the iTunes Store. What wasn't expected was the model Apple would employ to sell them.

Rather than buying just the ringtone, iPhone owners must buy the entire song they want to use as a ringtone, then pay an additional 99 cents for the ringtone itself. This means that buying a ringtone from the iTunes Store costs $1.98. On the plus side, users can edit their ringtones so that any section of the track can be used.

This is how it works: you buy a song from the iTunes Store that has an associated ringtone, or you look through your Purchased playlist in iTunes and pick one that has a ringtone symbol next to it. Then you open the Ringtone Editor in iTunes, choose the section you want to use as your ringtone – which can be up to 30 seconds long – and set the fade in and fade out points and the playback delay. Then click purchase. The ringtone is created and downloaded to iTunes to be synced with your iPhone.

At the time of writing, ringtones were not available for download from the UK iTunes Store. According to Apple, however, the US iTunes Store has half a million songs with ringtones available.

It is possible to create your own ringtones using GarageBand by right-clicking a non-protected track (so not downloaded from the iTunes Store) in the iTunes interface and selecting Show in Finder. Drag it from the Finder window that pops up into a new project in GarageBand, use the Cycle Region tool to define a repeating loop and then from the Share menu pick Send ringtone to iTunes.

Alternatively, you can create a ringtone in a less precise manner using nothing more than iTunes by changing the start and end points of a track through iTunes' Get Info command (accessible when right-clicking on a track). Setting the start and end points close together and then dragging the resulting file to your desktop, changing the name and returning it to iTunes creates the tone. Full details can be found online at *theappleblog.com/2008/08/07*.

iPOD NANO

The new iPod nano's tall, narrow form factor is perhaps an effort by Apple to win back customers who were put off by the square model introduced in 2007. It is a step back towards the form factor of the phenomenally successful original, and makes you wonder why Apple introduced the square edition at all. Logically, you could say that it was so that it could introduce video playback, but this hasn't disappeared with the return to the vertical form-factor; Apple just expects you to turn your player on its side when you want to watch movies.

However, in switching back to this tall casing, we think that rather than creating a more universally appealing device, Apple has come up with something that will polarise users more than ever. Is that why it's chosen to ship it in a choice of nine colours; is it hoping that if it comes in 'your' colour you could overlook the casing?

Perhaps, but we're not so sure. This new form factor isn't flat like the other iPods; it's oval-shaped, with a curved screen. This is a risky move on Apple's part since you can't help but catch reflections from any light source within a 180-degree arc. With a flat screen you could easily tilt the iPod to remove individual reflections from the screen and give you a clear view.

However, casing aside, the nano is still incredibly thin, and its anodised aluminium shell looks every bit as good as it did on any previous generation.

The nano is the smallest iPod to feature a screen, and what a screen it is. Bright and vibrant and with a high resolution it is a joy to look at, but we have some concerns over the Click Wheel used to control the menus and volume. Our test model's wheel was just too clicky, and felt more plasticky and cheap than those on former models. As such, we're not sure we can repeat our earlier claims that this model is 'the most appealing nano Apple has produced so far'.

The nano now comes in capacities of 4GB and 8GB holding 2000 and 4000 tracks respectively. Both capacities come in all available colours, in contrast to earlier versions where the black nano was available only at higher capacities and the silver at lower. The red nano is available only directly from Apple, as part of the proceeds are donated to the Product (RED) charity to fight HIV/Aids in Africa.

Battery life is a reasonable 24 hours for music and four hours for video, according to Apple. Charging the nano fully over USB takes about three hours, while charging to 80 per cent of the battery capacity takes an hour and a half, according to Apple.

As with the classic and touch, the nano supports the Cover Flow interface, which enables you to browse albums by cover art. On the nano and classic, scrolling through albums is done using the Click Wheel, rather than by wiping your finger across the screen, as you do with the touch.

iPOD CLASSIC

The iPod is dead. Long live the classic. Ditching the white iPod made sense for Apple in 2007 as it moved away from white as its favoured colour scheme for consumer products (the MacBook is now the only white Mac in the range).

So why did that colour come back in 2008, when it put in an appearance on both the iPhone 3G and the revamped iPod classic? As with the return of the taller form-factor on the iPod nano, this feels very much like backtracking from a company that wonders whether it went wrong somewhere the year before.

The classic is the only iPod in the range to use a hard drive rather than flash memory for storage. For many users this will be enough to sway the decision of which iPod to buy in its favour. Using a hard drive means that its storage capacity is significantly higher than the flash-based nano and touch.

The classic has storage capacities of 120GB, and is remarkably thin for a hard drive-based device with such a high capacity. It's certainly much thinner than an iPod of comparable

capacity from a couple of years ago, and the capacity is much more realistic for users with large music libraries, and for downloading video content.

Using Apple's own metrics, the 120GB iPod classic can hold up to 30,000 songs in AAC format encoded at 128-kbps, 150

hours of video, or up to 25,000 iPod-viewable photos. Sadly, the classic's screen is nowhere near as good as the touch's for watching video. At 2.5in across its diagonal, it's bigger than the nano's, but well short of the touch. And its 320 x 240-pixel resolution is the same as the nano's.

The interface on both the classic and the nano makes full use of the colour display. In addition to Cover Flow, menu items such as the graphic equaliser look great.

All in all, the iPod classic is a worthy update to the hard disk iPod line.

It will have to compete with the touch and the iPhone for attention, and they both have far more exciting features and an alluring touch-sensitive display, but the classic has plenty of life left in it and could still prove itself to be the iPod for grown-ups.

SHUFFLE

▲ The shuffle and hold buttons on the top look neat.

▲ The headphone jack doubles as a docking port.

If the iPod classic is the iPod for grown-ups, the shuffle is the iPod you can give your kids without worrying too much about them losing it. Its starting price of £32 is hardly pocket money, but it's as close as you'll get in the portable music player market.

The shuffle hasn't changed at all, except in the range of colours available. It now comes in silver, blue, green, purple and the Product Red Special Edition. As with the nano, the red shuffle is available only directly from Apple, with a share of the proceeds going to the Global Fund to help fight HIV/Aids in Africa. As with all previous shuffles, it doesn't have a dock connector. It connects

to its supplied dock through the 3.5mm headphone jack, which also carries data.

The shuffle may be the smallest, and least exciting of the iPods, but that doesn't mean Apple has paid any less attention to the details of its design.

The headphone socket, which bulges from the rear of the case, has been used as a hinge for the clip; an ingenious way of turning a problem into a solution. The Click Wheel is specially designed – as it has been since the first shuffle – to account for the fact that it's too small to operate in the same

way as the Click Wheel on the nano and classic. And the hold and shuffle switches look like tiny chrome rivets.

It comes in two capacities: 1GB and 2GB. Apple says that the lower of those two equates to 240 songs encoded at 128-bit in AAC format.

The capacity of the 2GB model is 500 songs at the same settings. The 20 song discrepancy presumably accounts for the space taken up by the operating system that of course isn't doubled when you double the capacity.

Apple's quoted battery life is 12 hours when full, which takes four hours to charge.

The shuffle isn't for everyone. It's the iPod equivalent of Forest Gump's box of chocolates, but if you like the element of surprise, don't mind syncing regularly and want an inexpensive iPod, it's perfect.

iPod Comparison

	TOUCH 8GB	TOUCH 16GB	TOUCH 32GB
Price inc VAT	£169 (£143 ex VAT)	£219 (£186 ex VAT)	£289 (£246 ex VAT)
Colours	●	●	●
Screen size	3.5in	3.5in	3.5in
Screen resolution	480 x 320 pixels	480 x 320 pixels	480 x 320 pixels
Quoted battery life	Up to 36 hours for music, up to 6 hour for video	Up to 36 hours for music, up to 6 hour for video	Up to 36 hours for music, up to 6 hour for video
Charge time	4 hours (2 hours fast charge to 80% capacity)	4 hours (2 hours fast charge to 80% capacity)	4 hours (2 hours fast charge to 80% capacity)
Size (w x d x h)	110 x 61.8 x 8mm	110 x 61.8 x 8mm	110 x 61.8 x 8mm
Weight	115g	115g	115g

	CLASSIC 120GB	NANO 8GB	NANO 16GB	SHUFFLE 1GB & 2GB
	£179 (£152 ex VAT)	£109 (£93 ex VAT)	£149 (£127 ex VAT)	£32 or £45 (£27 and £38 ex VAT)
	2.5in	2in	2in	n/a
	320 x 240 pixels	320 x 240 pixels	320 x 240 pixels	n/a
	Up to 36 hours for music, up to 6 hours for video	Up to 24 hours for music, up to 4 hours for video	Up to 24 hours for music, up to 4 hours for video	12 hours
	4 hours (2 hours fast charge to 80% capacity)	3 hours (1.5 hours fast charge to 80% capacity)	3 hours (1.5 hours fast charge to 80% capacity)	4 hours (2 hours fast charge to 80% capacity)
	103.5 x 61.8 x 10.5mm	90.7 x 38.7 x 6.2mm	90.7 x 38.7 x 6.2mm	41.2 x 27.3 x 10.5mm
	140g	36.8g	36.8g	15.6g

FINAL REPORTS

iPod touch
★★★★☆

Price £169 (£143 ex VAT) for 8GB;
£219 (£186 ex VAT) for 16GB;
£289 (£246 ex VAT) for 32GB
Contact Apple
Pros Large, wide screen + Wifi + Direct
download from iTunes
Cons Limited capacity + No Bluetooth

iPod classic
★★★★★

Price £179 (£152 ex VAT) for 120GB
Contact Apple
Pros New operating system with Cover
Flow + High capacity + Aluminium front
Cons Slightly sluggish with Cover Flow
switched on

iPod nano
★★★★☆

Price £109 (£93 ex VAT) for 8GB;
£149 (£127 ex VAT) for 16GB
Contact Apple
Pros Looks great + Wafer thin + New
operating system with Cover Flow
Cons Screen too small for video

iPod shuffle
★★★☆☆

Price £32 (£27 ex VAT) for 1GB;
£45 (£38 ex VAT) for 2GB
Contact Apple
Pros Tiny + Good price
Cons Low capacity + Nothing new in
this update

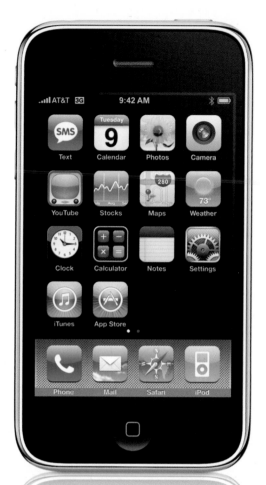

iPod touch vs iPhone

The differences between the iPod touch and iPhone are getting slimmer with every software update.

When Steve Jobs visited London to launch the iPhone in the UK, he called the iPod touch 'training wheels' for the phone. At the time, few understood how right he was. Back then, the iPod touch was seriously hobbled, with no proper email application, which limited its appeal to business users. Now, though, two software updates later, things are very different.

The key difference between the two is that the iPhone can transfer data over the mobile phone network, so doesn't rely on you always having access to a wireless home or office network to keep up to date or browse the web.

However, the iPod touch now boasts the same excellent email application as the iPhone, and so has serious, legitimate business uses.

The iPod touch is thinner and lighter than the iPhone. A key benefit for users on a budget is that while the iPhone incurs a monthly ongoing charge, the iPod touch requires only a one-off up-front payment with no ongoing contracts or fees. For that, you get the same high resolution,

touch-sensitive screen, complete with orientation sensor to switch application layouts to match the orientation of the device itself. This also lets you play many games designed for the iPhone, such as Super Monkey Ball, which racked up impressive sales as soon as Apple opened the App Store.

A wide range of other applications from the Store are also iPod touch-compatible, allowing you to expand its featureset over time.

However, those applications that make use of iPhone specific tools, such as the built-in GPS sensor, will have limited or no functionality. All of the system requirements for each application are detailed at the Store.

Unfortunately, by opting for an iPod touch in preference to the iPhone, you will also lose the latter's built-in camera. If you don't plan on sending multimedia text messages, this may not sound like much of a hardship, but if you want to post blog entries from your iPod touch using the third-party software from Wordpress or Typepad, you will be unable to post photos to your site.

But there is one other important difference between the two: while all iPod

owners get minor software updates for free to keep their devices up to date with the latest security patches and the most current editions of iTunes, iPod touch owners have to pay for major firmware updates that are delivered to iPhone owners free of charge.

The fee is normally fairly small, with the 2.0 software delivered at the same time as the iPhone 3G costing UK users just £5.99, and those in the US $9.99.

This is because of the fact that the iPhone and iPod touch are seen as very different product types for accounting purposes, preventing Apple from giving away the software for free to a non-subscription device.

So the question you have to ask yourself, really, is whether you need data connectivity on the move, a built-in camera, GPS or free system software updates. If you do, then opt for the iPhone over the iPod touch. If not, you can save yourself a not-inconsiderable ongoing cost by sticking with the iPod.

Whichever you choose, much of what follows in this guide remains relevant. The iPhone has excellent music- and video-playback features, which mimic exactly those found on the iPod touch.

 **Apple Store**

H A Harman International Company

Hear us. everywhere.

Plugged

Compatible with:

Introducing JBL Multimedia – Wherever you are, wherever you're headed, you can always enjoy high-performance JBL sound. **JBL Radial™ Micro** and **JBL On Stage™° Micro** are portable, battery-powered sound docks. Compact and extremely lightweight, they're some of the most versatile systems around. **JBL Radial™**, **On Stage™° II** and **JBL On Time™**– can fill any room with accurate, full-spectrum sound. They deliver clean, powerful high- and mid-frequency sound, and plenty of deep, distortion-free bass. JBL On Time is also a time machine that includes a radio, clock and dual alarm. All docking stations are available in white or black.

For more information visit, www.jbl.com. **Tel: 01707 278 100**

ICEMATAUDIO
SIBERIAHEADSET

The Icemat Siberia Headset is glossy white or black and looks like no other headset. The headset is specifically designed for a multitude of uses including gaming, portable MP3 players, HI-FI and IP-telephony

Perfect for MP3 players

Open type headphones

Separate volume regulator

Looks damn cool

www.**ICEMAT**.com/UK

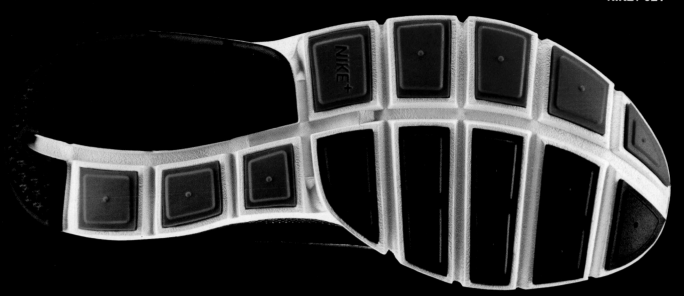

ACCESSORIES

Nike+iPod Sport Kit

★★★★☆

Price £19.99 (£17 ex VAT)

Contact Nike + *nikeplus.com*

Needs iPod nano + iTunes + Nike+ shoes

Pros Cheaper than a personal trainer + Easy to set up and use

Cons Only works with Nike+ shoes + Shouldn't really be playing spoken word tracks

Of all the Bond kit cars that could swim, bracelets that spat poisoned darts, underwater breathing equipment the size of a Mont Blanc pen – the most realistic gadget was the little transmitter that slotted into the heel of his shoe. So, it's not surprising that it's the first one we've seen make the break from the big screen into the real world, in the shape of Apple and Nike's Sport Kit.

Admittedly this smart little two-part combo won't transmit your position to the nearest FBI field station, but it might get you one step closer to a tumble in the hay with Pussy Galore as it helps you stay trim and motivated on your work out.

To put it to the test, we took it to perhaps the most gruelling challenge any mere mortal is likely to undertake in their life – the 1500km hike from Le Puy to Santiago de Compostela – to cover the last six hours of the route.

Set-up is a no-brainer. Unless you're up for hacking a hole in your existing trainers, you need a pair of Nike+ shoes (we picked up a pair of black Air Zoom Moire), which has a small recess under the left-foot insole. This is plugged by a small foam placeholder when it arrives, but once removed perfectly houses the lozenge-shaped transmitter, so that the activation button points down towards the road. The kit's second half is a small receiver, about the size of a postage stamp and slightly

slimmer than a nano, the only iPod with which it will work. Plugging it in adds a new Nike+iPod entry to the menu, through which you select your workout type.

Here, you can customise everything, but there are plenty of presets if you need a quick fix. These range from runs of 20 to 90 minutes, or 3km to a marathon, and fat burning workouts. Pick the one you're after, choose the kind of music you want, either from the album you're already playing, an existing playlist or a random shuffle of your whole library, and head off. For the purists, there's also a 'None' option onto the bottom of the music-picker screens, but that's rather missing the point.

Your progress is tracked both onscreen and through your headphones, with the music dipping wedding-disco style to make way for a calm voice (male or female, it's up to you) to tell you how far you've run, how far you have to go, your pace or how many calories you've lost.

The clever bit comes when you next sync with iTunes. You'll be prompted to register a free account at *nikeplus.com*, where your full workout history will be stored for later analysis. It's entirely flash based and, even on a corporate leased line, ran quite slowly at times, but the stats it spits out are a better motivator than a hastily-hacked training spreadsheet. Here, you can set

cumulative goals, such as running 100 miles over three months, and see how your individual daily workouts chip away at the mountain still to climb. You can also race against other nikeplus members anywhere in the world, setting tasks for each other like being the first to cover a set distance in multiple runs over a certain time. You'll see who is in the lead at any time and, because data can only be entered after syncing with a Nike+iPod equipped nano you can be sure that nobody is cheating.

This could well be a big earner for both companies. Two of the world's coolest brands working together should see Nike selling more shoes and, more importantly, Apple selling more music.

Our only complaint, beyond the fact that you're tied into Nike footwear, no pun intended, is that in our tests it was just as likely to play a chapter from an audiobook as it was to speed us on with one of our favourite tracks. Considering these were tagged with the standard Books & Spoken ID3 tag, as assigned through iTunes' dropdown list of genre types, we're surprised and a little disappointed that Apple didn't tweak the firmware to filter them.

Like the best technological innovations, though, this is a system that will grow as you do. As you become more confident, you'll be trimming the settings so they're calibrated to your stride length and weight for a more precise gauging of your fitness routine.

You can also use the same receiver with more than one sensor, either because you're rich enough to buy several pairs of Nike+ shoes, or you live in a house full of fitness freaks, each with their own pair of iPod-compatible trainers.

So, did we like it? Yes, very much. It didn't make us run any faster, but it did keep us going longer, and in that respect was as close to a personal trainer as you're likely to get for less than £20 an hour.

3G SMARTPHONE

iPhone 3G

★★★★☆

Price 8GB model: £99 with £30 or £35/month contract; free with £45 or £75/month contract
16GB model: £159 with £30 or £35/month contract; £59 with £45/month contract; free with £75/month contract
Contact Apple or O2 + *o2.co.uk*
Needs USB 2 port + Mac OS X 10.4.10 + iTunes 7.7
Pros 3G + Hundreds of third-party applications available + MobileMe syncing over-the-air
Cons No notes or tasks sync

Few Apple products have polarised opinion in the way that the iPhone has since it was first announced back in January 2007. Depending on who you listen to, it's either the most desirable gadget on the planet, or an over-priced, not very clever and fairly ordinary mobile phone.

And despite the fact that it's getting close to a year since it first hit the UK, there's no sign of the breathless blanket coverage slowing down, as you will have noticed if you happened to be browsing practically any technology website.

So is this latest incarnation, the iPhone 3G, worthy of all the attention? Yes. And no. As a piece of hardware, the improvements over the original iPhone – GPS, 3G and an increase in capacity to 16GB – barely merit a mention. But in terms of what it can now do, thanks mostly to the software update to version 2.0, it's a world away from the first iPhone.

And there's the rub. The greatest improvements, the best new features, and the cause of most of the excitement around its launch, are all contained inside the software update, which is free to owners of the first iPhone. This makes the decision about whether or not to upgrade relatively easy. Unless you need the 3G data transfer, or more space for music and movies, don't bother. If you don't already have an iPhone, and have been waiting for a 3G version before buying, then there's no reason for further procrastination.

The iPhone 3G comes in two capacities, 8GB and 16GB, and its most obvious physical difference from the original iPhone is its plastic, curved back. On the 8GB model, the back is black, matching the front of the iPhone, while the 16GB iPhone comes with either a black or white back. Unlike the MacBook, there's no premium for choosing a different colour.

The slight curve on the back makes it more comfortable to hold than the original model. Other than that they're practically identical. Hardware controls are still limited to the on/off switch, home button, hold switch and volume controls, and the screen, while lovely, is still prone to smears. The camera is

stuck at two megapixels, which is something of a bone of contention. There are those who would argue that two megapixels is miserable given that there are phones now available with five megapixel cameras. However, squeezing more pixels onto a tiny CCD means more noise and a lower quality image. And if uploading images to the web or showing them to friends on your phone is all you want to do, two megapixels is plenty. Battery life on 3G is up to five hours of talk or web surfing time, and up to 300 hours standby.

The GPS receiver works in partnership with the Google Maps app to provide data on your current location and the surrounding area. In our tests it worked well, pinpointing our location and plotting it on the map.

Central to the new iPhone software is its link with MobileMe, Apple's replacement for .Mac. You can sync mail with your MobileMe email account, as well as contacts, calendars and bookmarks, all

◄ **The new iPhone features a two-megapixel camera, which is more than enough if you want to upload images to the web for your friends.**

◄ **Despite the appearance of screws on the bottom of the device, the iPhone 3G's battery is not replaceable.**

◄ **If the iPhone has a killer feature, it's the ability to push mail from your MobileMe account, as well as contacts, calendars and bookmarks, while you're on the move.**

over the air. Just set it up, ask it to check for updates automatically every 15 minutes, and you'll never be out of touch, so long as you're in range of O2's 3G network or a wifi hotspot.

If the new iPhone has a killer feature, it's this. Rim built an empire on the back of push email. By building it into the iPhone, albeit with the requirement that you shell out £59 a year for MobileMe, and adding support for Exchange, Apple will grab a big chunk of the BlackBerry's market. It's not perfect, though. There's no way to sync notes from the iPhone's Notes application, and iCal To Dos, which also appear in Mac OS X Mail, don't seem to sync either – although there is a folder for them on the iPhone. And there's no way to view calendars to which you've subscribed on your Mac.

If push email is the most important feature on the 3G iPhone, then the new App Store is the most exciting. On launch day, there were already hundreds of free and paid-for third-party applications on the Store. Some are astonishing, others merely very good. One of the best, and the most popular free application at the time of writing is Remote, from Apple, which allows you to use your iPhone as a remote control for iTunes. It operates over wifi and lets you view your playlists on the iPhone's screen. So if you have a media streaming device, like Airport Express and have your Mac housed in an office or upstairs room, you can now listen to and control your music without leaving the living room.

Other applications range from the frivolous – LightSaber, which emits a Star Wars light saber 'swishing' sound when you wave your iPhone around – to the genuinely useful — phrase books, currency converters and flight checkers are particularly popular.

There's no doubt that the iPhone 3G is a quantum leap ahead of the original iPhone in terms of what it can do. But equally, there's no doubt that the hardware improvements don't really merit paying £99 for the upgrade. The conclusion? If you already have an iPhone, upgrade the software and wait for the next version. If you don't, the only decision to make is which contract to choose: the £35 per month tariff is best value for most users. But if you make lots of calls, you can have an 8GB model for free on a £45 per month deal, and both versions free on a £75 per month contract.

iPOD SPEAKER DOCK
Griffin Evolve

★★★★☆

Price £250 (£213 ex VAT)
Contact AM Micro 01392 426473 + *griffintechnology.com*
Needs Any iPod with Dock connector
Pros Wireless speakers + Charging dock + Mono/stereo switch
Cons Poor remote control + Audio quality could be better + Expensive

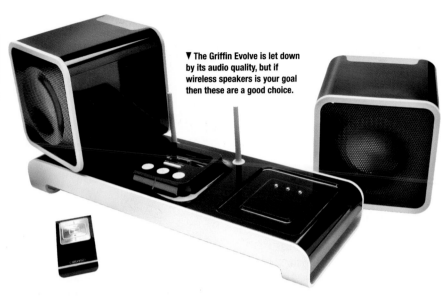

▼ The Griffin Evolve is let down by its audio quality, but if wireless speakers is your goal then these are a good choice.

iPod speaker docks are 10 a penny
these days but Griffin's Evolve is different. Its speakers are completely wireless, which means that they can be placed anywhere within 150ft of the docking station. The speakers measure 140 x 140 x 140mm and each contains an RF module, rechargeable lithium ion battery and 12W amplifier. The battery has a stated life of 10 hours listening at a 'normal listening volume' on a full charge.

The docking unit hosts a Universal Dock, flanked by a couple of RF antennae and the charging stations for the speakers. Apart from an iPod, audio can be fed from any

device with RCA output sockets. And audio can be pushed out from the iPod over the same kind of connector, though that seems a bit of a waste when you have two wireless speakers to hand.

There are also composite and S-video outputs for displaying video and still images from your iPod on a TV.

The remote control enables you to change the volume, step forward and backward, shuffle, repeat and change the equalisation setting. There's no visual

display on the remote though, while changing the EQ had no audible effect.

We were impressed with the build quality of the Evolve – and setting up is simplicity itself. From opening the box to listening to music from an iPod took less than five minutes. It comes with adaptors for most dockable iPods, but there are no additional cables for connecting it to a TV or adding another audio input.

Thanks to the charging station, concerns over battery life are largely redundant, while

EARPHONES
Denon AH-C551

★★★★★

Price £69.99 (£59.57 ex VAT)
Contact Denon 01753 680568 + *denon.co.uk*
Needs 3.5mm socket
Pros Excellent audio quality + Short cable with extension + Aluminium housing
Cons A little expensive

EARPHONES
Denon AH-C351

★★★★☆

Price £39.99 (£34.04 ex VAT)
Contact Denon 01753 680568 + *denon.co.uk*
Needs 3.5mm socket
Pros Excellent audio quality + Short cable with extension
Cons None

It's almost become a cliché to suggest
that the iPod and iPhone are let down by the poor quality of the in-ear headphones that Apple continues to supply. Nevertheless it's absolutely true, so budgeting for a better pair is a necessity if you want half-decent audio. Thankfully there are plenty of well-priced, high-quality alternatives and these two sets from Denon are the latest additions.

As you would expect from a maker with a record of excellence in high-fidelity reproduction both the C551 and C351 are extremely well made and sound great. Each features what Denon calls an Acoustic

Optimizer, which adjusts the sound pressure balance between, in front of and behind the diaphragm to improve audio quality. Both pairs sit in your ear canal, isolating the output from your iPod and keeping background noise to a minimum.

A neat touch, the C551 and C351 have a 0.5m cable, which can be lengthened to 1.3m via the supplied extension. That means that if you habitually carry your iPod or iPhone in a jacket pocket, you won't have a metre's worth of cable dangling from or stuffed in it. However, you still have the option of popping it into a bag or trouser pocket.

▼ The C551 phones have aluminium housings.

▼ The cheaper C351 almost matches its stablemate for sound.

the ability to switch between mono and stereo makes placing speakers in different rooms feasible. The controls are basic though, and the remote control isn't that good: it feels cheap compared to the rest of the unit and the buttons click annoyingly.

Audio quality is average – it lacks presence and could be crisper. Bass is a little muddy and the mid-range and treble frequencies are noticeably soft. It's definitely not the best choice if audio quality is top of your list of priorities.

Griffin has clearly thought about how wireless speakers are likely to be used. In addition to the option to switch to mono, the base unit can transmit audio to multiple pairs of speakers.

When you put a speaker on the charging pod it is paired with the base unit and defined as being either left or right.

If you place two or more pairs on the base unit sequentially, each set of speakers is paired. If preferred, you can then put each pair in a different room and have the same music broadcast to each pairing.

If avoiding wires and being able to move speakers around easily is an important consideration, the Evolve is an excellent choice, if a little expensive.

The C551 and C351 differ in a couple of ways. For instance, the C551 has a wider frequency response range and so can pick out detail at higher frequencies and deliver deeper bass. It can also deal with greater power input without distortion.

The other differences are in the build quality and included accessories. The C351 housings are made of plastic and the supplied case is a soft pouch. The C551s come in aluminium and a hard shell case. Both have gold-plated 3.5mm jacks and three sizes of rubber in-ear fittings. The two of them excel in use. Detail is picked out crisply, while bass is delivered enthusiastically. There's plenty in the mid-range too.

Like all ear-canal type earbuds, both take a bit of getting used to and trial and error to find the right fitting and adjustment. But once they're in you forget they're there.

We were hard pressed to tell the difference in audio quality – in the end despite the extra outlay, our vote went to the C551 for the housings' superior protection against careless handling and mishaps.

The price of both is a concern though. While Sennheiser's CX300 offering may not be quite a match when it comes to listening excellence, it really is tremendous value at less than £20.

DAB RADIO AND iPOD DOCK
Pure Chronos iDock

★★★★★

Price £99.50 (£84 ex VAT) from Argos
Contact Pure + *pure.com*
Needs DAB reception + Optional iPod
Pros Excellent interface + Powerful tuner
Cons Feels cheap + Missing an iPod adaptor or two

DAB is getting a drubbing right now.
Big radio groups like GCap are backtracking on the medium and shutting down stations, both national and local. And prestigious outlets like *The Guardian* and *FT* are casting doubt on the value of the 20-year-old technology. As *MacUser* in late 2008 went to press, there was even talk of a digital radio crisis meeting of all the top broadcasters desperate for something to finally make the public sit up and take notice. We wonder whether Pure was invited along. Probably not – but it should have been. It has long been the UK's top DAB radio maker. It blazed a trail with a strictly limited run of 200 test units at the turn of the century. And these were so well built and ahead of their time that they're still going strong. We know – we've got one.

That model's great-great-grand-offspring is the low-power, eco-friendly Chronos iDock, which sounds far better and feels more plasticky than the pictures would have you believe.

But it's not just a radio: it's an iPod dock and alarm clock too, with first-class menus and a bright, easy-to-read display that's discreet enough to dim to nothing when not in use. There's just one shortcoming as far as we can tell – the absence of adaptors for the iPod touch and third- and fourth- generation nano, as every other Dock insert comes bundled in the box.

Sound quality and reception were both first class, on one condition – that we didn't use it in the office. While testing on an office desk, there was a slight background hiss; however, on a bedside table at home it was crystal clear and picked up stations from well beyond our local area,

despite the aerial being a flimsy-looking black wire that we traced up the wall and stuck up using Blu-tack.

Autotuning was done quickly and simply, and the clock was set as soon as we plugged it in, making this about as no-nonsense as you could want. The menus rival an iPod for simplicity, while setting an alarm requires only that you step through a series of one-line options, picking how you'd like to wake up (DAB, FM, iPod or tone) and, if you chose the radio, opting for either a preset or whatever you were listening to when you last switched it off. The snooze button, a slightly tacky silver bar above the screen, is a little smaller than we're used to but still easily slapped in a morning half-haze.

Sound quality might not be your first thought each day but given that you may want to use this device as a regular radio, it really should be.

The speakers give reasonable separation, being angled outwards on two front corners of the triangular case, and the sound spectrum is broad, with bright highlights and a fair bass. It wouldn't rival a hi-fi with a separate sub-woofer, but then you're not paying enough for that.

If you got the impression we liked the Chronos iDock, you'd be right. We question some of the materials Pure has chosen in its construction, but can't fault the interface, tuning or performance. Bye-bye crackly FM. Good morning crystal clear DAB…

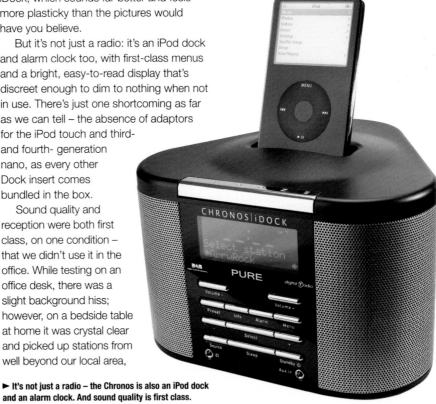

► **It's not just a radio – the Chronos is also an iPod dock and an alarm clock. And sound quality is first class.**

STEREO SPEAKERS

Creative Gigaworks T40

★★★★☆

Price £85.16 (£72.48 ex VAT) from *microwarehouse.co.uk*
Contact Creative + *uk.europe.creative.com*
Needs 3.5mm output jack
Pros Look good + Sound great + Treble and bass controls
Cons Huge + Power switch on rear of speaker

The first thing you'll notice on unpacking these stereo speakers from Creative is their size. Intended as desktop monitors, they rival bookshelf speakers in their dimensions. They sit 30cm above desk level without the included stand, and are 14cm deep with the front grille attached, so you'll need plenty of space to sit them next to your Mac or PC.

They look good, although we prefer them with the grilles removed. Creative says the arrangement of two mid-range drivers on either side of a cloth dome tweeter improves

audio quality significantly and produces a more accurate lower-frequency response. Talking of lower frequencies, there's no sub-woofer in this set-up, and no option to add one.

Instead, Creative has added what it calls BasXPort, which channels sound waves from the inner chamber to improve lower mid-range frequencies. The quoted frequency response is 50Hz – 20KHz and the power rating is 14W RMS per channel.

The front of the right-hand speaker has controls for treble, bass and volume, as well as a 3.5mm headphone jack. At the back is a power switch, input jack, output to the left-hand speaker and a DC input. The power input is supplied by another hefty component, a transformer that is heavy enough to need placing on the floor.

The T40 speakers produce a big, warm, meaty sound. Detail is picked out well and bass is kept to reasonable levels. For a pair of sub-£100 speakers, audio quality doesn't get much better than this.

We have one or two minor criticisms: the stands don't feel as robust or well-made as

► The T40s are large for desktop speakers.

the speakers. The on/off switch on the rear of the right-hand speaker is difficult to reach, and removing the speaker grilles, while easy, can make the rubber plugs that hold them in place come loose and fall off.

These are all relatively minor points, however. Overall, the T40 speakers look good, are well constructed and sound great.

EARPHONES

Q-Jays Dual Micro Armature Earphones

★★★★★

Price £129 (£109.78 ex VAT)
Contact Jays + *jays.se*
Needs 3.5mm headphone jack
Pros Excellent audio reproduction + Lots of extras + Very comfortable
Cons None

We all know that the first thing you should do after buying an iPod is chuck away the included earbuds and buy a decent set instead. And while spending £130 on a pair might seem excessive, the rewards more than justify the wince-inducing expenditure.

Despite the rather odd name, these Q-Jay earbuds are superb. For one thing, they sound fantastic. Bass is reproduced with just the right amount of enthusiasm, the middle ranges are bright and breezy and the treble is crisp and detailed.

The only complaint that you'll have will be that the inbuilt flaws of poorly encoded and compressed tracks housed in your iTunes library, masked by the inadequacy of most earphones, are exposed by the

Q-Jays. However, if you're prepared to pay £130 for a pair of earphones, you're almost certainly the kind of person who cares enough about how your music sounds to make sure that it is encoded at a high bit rate with a decent codec and so won't be troubled by flaws in your favourite songs.

We had no trouble with music that we had ripped from CD ourselves or even tracks which had been bought from iTunes. The Q-Jays come with lots of extras. We love the fact that the cable is only 60cm long and that there are two 90cm extension cables in the box – one with an L-shaped connector and one with a straight plug.

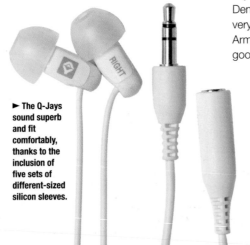

► The Q-Jays sound superb and fit comfortably, thanks to the inclusion of five sets of different-sized silicon sleeves.

◄ The Q-Jays come with two 90cm extension cables (one straight and one angled).

There are also five sets of silicon sleeves of different sizes, meaning the Q-jays should sit snugly in your ear canal no matter how big or small it is. And there are adaptors for aeroplane-style output sockets and for sharing your iPod's music with two sets of earphones. Finally, there's a zip-around leather case to carry the Q-Jays.

There's a great deal of choice in the earphones market and Q-Jays' competition comes from no less well-established brands than Shure, Sennheiser, and Denon. Regardless of that, they are a match for anything in their price bracket.

If we were being really picky, we would say that we prefer the aluminium housing of Denon's AH-C551 (see p24), but that's a very minor point. The Q-Jays Dual Micro Armature Earphones really are very good indeed.

MULTIMEDIA HARDWARE
Apple TV

★★★☆☆

Price 40GB £199 (£169 ex VAT); 160GB £269 (£228 ex VAT)
Contact Apple
Needs High-definition TV capable of 1080p 60/50Hz, 1080i 60/50Hz, 720p 60/50Hz, 576p 50Hz or 480p 60Hz; HDMI or Component input
Pros Buy music and TV shows from your living room + Works seamlessly with or without iTunes
Cons Limited connectivity options + Lacks PVR functionality + Expensive

When Steve Jobs announced that the Apple TV had failed, it was an unusual admission that sometimes Apple doesn't get it right. The first version failed for several reasons, so Apple has re-focused its living-room offering with take two of Apple TV.

If you had invested in a first generation Apple TV, you'll be glad to know that this improved Apple TV is simply a software upgrade, which can be downloaded for free.

Apple TV is an add-on box that allows you to play content from your iTunes Library through your TV. It takes both music and video in its stride, although it can take some time to set up as it synchronises with the library on your Mac or PC.

Physically the Apple TV is the same hardware, with the same ports and disk sizes as the first version.

A 40GB and 160GB model are available for £199 and £269 respectively. However, the Apple TV software has been radically remodelled and now it can be used without the aid of a Mac.

Setup is a breeze and even if you do want to tie your Apple TV to your Mac the process is as simple as it was with the original software.

The main menu has lost the Front Row styling and is simply a table with content

types on the left and the options within these are displayed on the right. The movies option allows you to buy or rent movies from the iTunes Store.

We also get TV shows from a selection of networks in the UK. Navigating the download options is simple and elegant. When you choose a show to download, you're asked for your password and then the transfer begins.

We chose an episode of *The West Wing* and it was ready to watch within a few seconds of the download beginning. That's quite impressive if you bear in mind that this is a 50-minute programme. Image quality is very good, though it's not exceptional; we'd say it's on a par with DVD content – no better no worse.

Buying music on your Apple TV is a great addition to the process. You can navigate through with a selection of hand-picked albums that Apple thinks you'll enjoy.

If Morrissey and the soundtrack to *Juno* aren't to your liking though, you can search for alternatives.This requires that you use the Apple remote to select individual characters but the predictive

search does a good job of narrowing down the choices. We only had to type 'eme' to get to Emerson, Lake and Palmer for instance.

Podcasts, Photos and YouTube navigation are all much the same. The Flickr integration is a nice touch and being able to add multiple contacts increases the appeal of the photo aspect of the Apple TV.

Watching low-resolution video of teenagers dancing to the latest chart topper doesn't yet hold a mass appeal but the Apple TV does offer one of the few good methods of transferring this online technology to the living room. When the quality of the video and the production values improve, however, the YouTube content will be really worthwhile.

We're still a little hesitant to recommend the Apple TV even in this much improved second coming, although the changes to the interface and the ability to purchase music and TV shows is really excellent. The HDMI port can now output at 1080p, and best of all this update was free. However, there are still a few insurmountable failings.

The lack of PVR functionality, or ability to add one is disappointing. The fact that the UK didn't get the price cut, while the US did, is unforgivable.

If this had been the Apple TV take one, there's no doubt we'd have been raving over it but this is the second swing of the bat for Apple and though it's not the miss of Apple TV 1 it's not the home run we wanted either.

▲ Gone is the Front Row styling, replaced with a more simplistic way of accessing content.

Roberts Robi

★★★★☆

Price £50 (£42.55 ex VAT)
Contact Roberts + *robertsradio.co.uk*
Needs iPod with Dock connector
Pros Three devices in one + DAB radio works well
+ RDS support in FM radio
Cons One or two operational glitches

Despite a name that makes us cringe
just to print it, Roberts' Robi is a rather neat
little device. It isn't the first iPod accessory
that's both a radio and remote control, but
it's the first we've seen that includes a DAB
tuner alongside the FM receiver.

The Robi plugs into your iPod's Dock
connector and you plug your earphones
into its headphone jack. It switches on
when you turn on your iPod and starts the
most recently used mode.

In remote mode you play,
pause, step forward and
backward, and control the
volume of your iPod's music.

Pressing the Mode button on
the side of the Robi activates DAB;
press it again and the device becomes
an FM tuner.

The first time you switch to
DAB, hold the forward button for
five seconds and Robi scans the
frequencies to find radio stations. It
displays their names and allows you to step
through them.

When you find one you like, pressing
and holding the button labelled with a heart
symbol on top of the Robi stores it as a
preset. Pressing the button once enables
you to step through those stations that have
been saved as presets.

Scanning FM frequencies is almost as
easy, although you do need to keep holding
the forward button while the Robi carries
out its search. There are two separate
favourites lists held in the device – one for
FM and one for DAB.

We like the Robi a lot. It's a great way of
listening to DAB radio when out and about;
and that it doubles as an iPod remote is
very useful. We also like the fact that when

◀ The Robi is the first of its
genre that we've seen with a
DAB tuner and an FM receiver.

you turn it off by holding the Play/Pause
button, your iPod switches off too.
However, we couldn't get it to switch back
on again without disconnecting it and
reconnecting it, which is a flaw.

AT £50, the Robi is a little expensive. But
then it's one of a kind and if you really want
to listen to DAB on your iPod, you certainly
won't be disappointed.

Gear4 Duo

★★☆☆☆

Price £150 (£128 ex VAT)
Contact Gear4 + *gear4.com*
Needs Fourth generation iPods or later except shuffle
Pros Bass unit with portable speaker + Same inputs on both
parts + Two battery compartments
Cons Bass lacks presence + Counter-intuitive layout of
remote + Sticky control of menus

Behind the minimalist matt black case
and metal-trimmed speaker grille, Gear4's
Duo is distinguished by its speaker, which
detaches into an 18mm-deep portable unit.

Built in to the grille is a retractable shelf
that protects the iPod dock. It supports a
wide range of iPods up to the touch, though
it's not Apple-certified for the iPhone and
the speaker clicks during network activity,
so it's best to switch to airplane mode.

One lithium-ion battery is supplied
and there's an empty compartment for
another to boost playing time. You'll need
a screwdriver to remove the covers, and
a pair of tweezers is essential to attach the

tiny plug from the battery. This
fiddliness discourages users
from carrying spares, which are
available from Gear4.

Music continues to play when the
speaker is lifted out. There was a
small click, but we got 3 hours and
15 minutes of continuous music
from one battery – enough to spend
a relaxing afternoon in the garden.

The metal stand on the speaker is
integrated into the case and locks
firmly into position. We liked the fact
that the power connector and line-in port
are replicated on the bass unit and the
speaker. It uses a small power brick that's
reasonably portable.

Gear4 describes the speaker as
a satellite, but it works independently
of the bass unit – there's no cable to
run between them when detached,
and the bass only kicks in when they're
docked together.

The bundled remote control has all
the essential buttons for navigating and
controlling an iPod. The position of the menu
and enter buttons are counter-intuitive
though. Too many times, we pressed the
menu button on the right to select a track
and went back up a level in the menu.

▲ The Duo's clean-cut looks complement
the iPod touch and black iPods particularly
well. Volume and power buttons on the
separate speaker reduce the need to carry
the remote away from home.

Scrolling through a list of tracks, we came
to a grinding halt after advancing two items
on our iPod touch, and we quickly ditched
the remote in favour of hands-on control.

Quality is adequate for casual listening,
but lacks drama. It left Radiohead's
Paranoid Android feeling anti-climactic,
while Goldfrapp's *Road to Somewhere*
sounded as imprecise as the song title.

It's disappointing that the Duo's poor
separation led to a muffled sound that's only
really suitable for the most casual listener. At
the asking price, it's a shame that the Duo
falls down on such a pivotal feature.

iPOD SPEAKER DOCK
Griffin Amplifi

★★★☆☆

Price £88.49 (£75.31 ex VAT) from *amazon.co.uk*
Contact AM Micro 01392 426473 + *griffintechnology.co.uk*
Needs Third-generation iPod or later
Pros Well constructed + Integral sub-woofer + Well-priced
Cons Disappointing sound quality

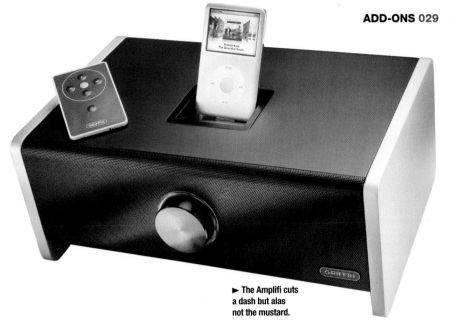

▶ **The Amplifi cuts a dash but alas not the mustard.**

Despite its pedigree in producing iPod accessories, Griffin is a relative newcomer to the world of speaker docks, so it is keen to make an impression with the Amplifi.

It certainly achieves that: this large wooden box looks unlike any other iPod speaker dock we've seen and has a reassuringly robust and weighty feel to it.

The iPod dock sits on top of the box and supports every iPod from third-generation to iPod touch with the exception of the shuffle. There's also a 3.5mm line-in port on the back, to which you can attach anything with a line-out or headphone jack. On the front a large volume knob has an electric blue LED around it and doubles as an on/off switch.

Inside the box are two front-firing 2¾in neodymium drivers and a 5in downward firing sub-woofer. Griffin says that the enclosure has been acoustically tuned and that this, together with the bass reflex port on the underside of the Amplifi, is supposed to give it warm, rich tones and 'amazing frequency response'.

Sadly our tests failed to back up this claim. To our ears the sound quality was no more than satisfactory, even for a unit as well-priced as this one. There was a reasonable level of bass and we're thankful Griffin didn't fall into the trap of punching up the bass excessively to mask other failings. There's decent treble too.

However, there is a noticeable gap in the mid-range that leaves the impression that the audio is rather thin and empty – anything but the warm, rich tones that Griffin lays claim to.

The credit card-sized remote control is fine but like all of these systems, if you want to do more than change volume or skip tracks, you'll have to use the iPod controls.

All in all, could do better.

iPOD RADIO ALARM CLOCK
Macally TunePro

★★★☆☆

Price £79.95 (£68.04 ex VAT)
Contact AM Micro 01392 426473 + *macally-europe.com*
Needs Any iPod with Dock connector
Pros Stylish + Small + Large snooze button
Cons Flimsy + Audio quality not as good as competitors + Position of snooze button

▶ **The TunePro looks okay but feels flimsy. Also the tone lacks warmth.**

Macally's TunePro looks very different from other iPod radio alarm clocks we've seen. In fact at first glance you wouldn't guess it was a clock radio at all.

The clock LED is displayed from behind the mirrored fascia, actually an NXT flat panel speaker that plays audio from a docked iPod, the radio, or any device with a 3.5mm input jack.

Along the front of the unit beneath the speaker are buttons for setting the two alarms and the clock, sleep, radio preset and volume, and selecting the audio source. There's also a large snooze button, which doubles as the on/off and mute switch. We're glad to see the snooze button in such a prominent position but its proximity to the dock itself could cause an iPod to be knocked over during early morning fumbling. And that could be disastrous.

On the back are an FM antenna, sockets for line in and included AM antenna, a DC connector, and buttons that dim the display and add more bass or treble.

The TunePro is easy enough to set up and operate and looks reasonably good, although the mirrored speaker does smudge easily. The whole unit and especially the speaker feel a little flimsy though.

Audio quality is reasonable. The NXT speaker packs a fair punch and picks out detail well. However, there's a lack of warmth in the tone but other than that, it's pretty good.

At £79.95, the TunePro is a bit expensive and unless you're bowled over by its handsome looks or space is at a premium, it may pay you to consider alternatives from iHome, Gear 4, and XtremeMac.

GRIFFIN

Now Shipping!
iTrip AutoPilot with SmartScan

87.9
Function
− +
iTrip

iTrip® Auto with SmartScan™

Charge and play your iPod or iPhone in your car.

Available from these fine dealers, or for your nearest dealer

Call authorized UK distributor AM Micro Distribution LTD

01392-823366 • www.ammicro.co.uk • info@ammicro.co.uk

Online applications

When Apple launched the iPhone, it made it very clear that it would not permit developers to write software that would work natively on the device. Instead they would have to write web applications that could be accessed through the Safari browser. Despite a few grumbles, it didn't take long at all for developers to start doing just that, and as the iPhone and iPod touch share much of the same Internet technology, they can be used on both devices. Here's a run-down of the best iPod touch-compatible apps to far posted online.

TypePad (*i.typepad.com*) lets you blog on the move with a portable, iPod touch-specific edition of its online diary-keeping software. It's not free to use, unfortunately, costing between $4.95 a month / $49.50 a year for the basic edition, and $29.95 a month / $299.50 a year for the Premium edition, which includes control over archive types and layout, multiple authors, unlimited blogs and extra bandwidth and storage. It's a quick and easy way of getting your blog online, but with the Safari browser rendering pretty much any web page without a flaw we find it hard to recommend this paid-for service over free alternatives such as Blogger, or the domain-hosted WordPress.

 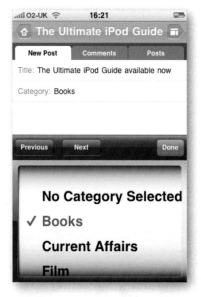

Digg (*davidcann.com/digg*) comes to the iPod touch with a slick sideways-scrolling app that takes you through the most recent postings in a range of top-level tech-related Digg directories, starting with Apple and progressing through Microsoft, Gadgets, Hardware and Linux.

It's a smart way to keep tabs on what the web is talking about when you're away from your RSS reader, and an easy way to stumble across stories you may never have otherwise found.

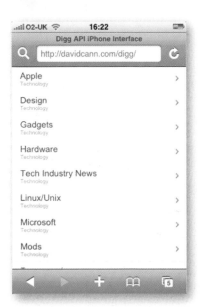 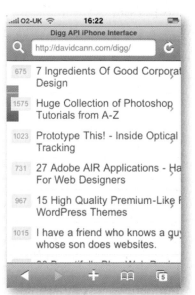

Use your iPod touch as a glorified shopping list with OneTrip (*onetrip.org*), which splits an average supermarket in common sections, such as food, fruit, frozen, drinks and household items. Tapping each one opens up a list of common items (lemons and bananas in fruit, for example, and cheese and bread in deli). Going on to tap these adds them to a shopping list stored on your iPod touch, that you can either email or text to yourself for use in the store. If you have unusual needs that aren't covered in the standard list you can of course add your own by typing them in. It's brilliant in its simplicity, and perhaps the best iPod touch application we have seen to date.

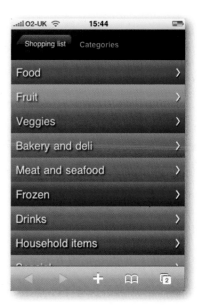

For a more generalised and freeform list-keeping service Ta-da List (*iphone.tadalist. com*) will neatly meet most users needs. Once you have set up a free account with the service, you can create multiple lists to suit any need, whether that be tasks, upcoming meetings, birthdays, shopping requirements or anything else.

Once an item has been completed or is no longer needed, you simply tap to edit it and then press done. The best thing, though, is that while this version of Ta-da List is optimised for the iPod touch's portrait-oriented screen, there is a desktop equivalent at *tadalist.com*, which lets you manage the very same lists on any regular computer, and subscribe to changes in the list using RSS.

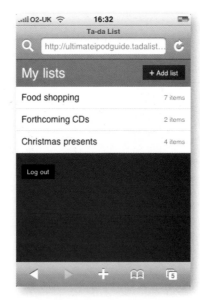
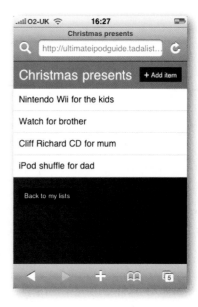

iPhlickr (*chandlerkent.com/iphlickr*) uses some clever interface design to really look like an iPod touch application, complete with iPod touch-style buttons and interface backgrounds. It's a simple idea that lets you search and browse your own and other members' Flickr photo galleries. Frankly, with Flickr being a Yahoo property, and with Yahoo providing push email services for the iPod touch, it's a surprise that Apple didn't provide this kind of functionality as a top-line application, just like it did with YouTube and (Google) Maps. Fortunately this implementation more than plugs the gap, and it's one we'd highly recommend you assign to a bookmark.

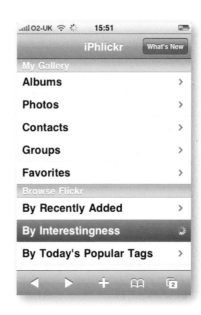

Apple loses some points for not including any games on the iPod touch, so iChess (*ichess.morfik.com*) will come as a welcome addition for many a bored commuter. As the name would suggest, it's chess, played against the iPod touch in a very clever manner where tapping in any piece shows you graphically which squares you can move it to. There is a choice of board designs and settings and it's not the most intelligent chess player around (we were able to wipe out some of the iPod touch's key pieces in just a couple of moves) but it's a welcome distraction on the journey to and from work each day.

If you have contacts in America with mobile phones, you can use your iPod touch to send them text messages for free.

TxtDrop (*txtdrop.com*) will send messages to any valid US mobile phone, and drop the responses into your email inbox. Of course, you will need to give a valid email address to use the service, but this is a small price to pay when you consider the alternative cost of sending text messages back and forth across the Atlantic.

For a spot of daily devotion, the iPod touch Bible (*ibiblespace.org*) includes a range of translations of the bible in an easy to navigate format. The breadth of the work is impressive, with extensive cross-referencing linking you to commentaries and allowing you to mark highlighted passages for easy future reference.

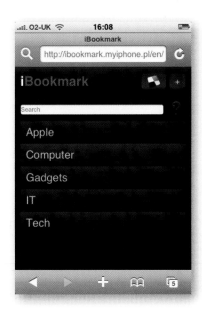

The iPod touch has a fully-fledged bookmark management system, and can synchronise bookmarks with a Mac or PC using iTunes, but unless you want to synchronise your iPod touch with every computer you own, you can only ever have them in two places at once. Unless, of course, you use an online bookmarking service like Delicious (*del.icio.us*). Using iBookmark (*ibookmark.myiphone.pl*), you can save bookmarks on your iPod touch and then either export them to Delicious, or import bookmarks you have already saved there.

It was still in development as we wrote this, but the developer promised to keep working on it as long as the very reasonable requested donation of $5 a head kept coming in.

audio-technica
always listening

Music to our ears

"Audio Technica's ATH-ANC7 is the best-sounding set we've heard, and includes active noise cancelling to reduce background noise."
Computer Shopper – July 2007

"Their isolation is excellent, and there's great timing and dynamic, detailed delivery... decent cans with excellent noise cancelling ability."
What HiFi? – June 2007

"Which of these models should you choose? ... when you throw price into the mix with comfort, noise reduction, and sound quality, my pick is Audio-Technica's ATH-ANC7"
Playlistmag.com – August 2007

"Not only do these little wonders provide superior sound quality but they also kicked some Bose butt in the noise cancellation category."
Gadling.com - September 2007

"...another winner... comfy, solidly built, absolutely great-sounding headphones. The circuitry cuts out a huge swath of engine, road or train noise, and the music is crystal clear..."
The Ledger – June 2007

"...the Audio-Technica ATH-ANC7 is a serious piece of work at a seriously good price."
Sound & Vision Magazine – May 2007

"Amazing sound, balanced and sweet, from Segovia to Snoop Dogg. Lightweight and comfortable."
Wired Magazine – May 2007

ANC7

Available on the Apple Store online at **www.apple.com/ukstore** and priced at just £129.95

Beginner

036 iTunes for beginners

037 Welcome to iTunes

041 Ripping

044 Playlists

046 Enter the iTunes Store

048 Regular vs iTunes Plus tracks

050 iTunes Store alternatives

054 Podcasts

056 Connect your iPod to a hi-fi

058 Watching a video on an iPod or a TV

059 Creating a compilation CD

062 App Store

063 Application highlights

iTunes for beginners

If you haven't used iTunes before, then chances are your music, if you have any, is collected together in several folders on your hard drive. This can make it difficult to sort, find and play. By switching to iTunes you will have the benefit of a powerful, easy-to-use piece of software that will catalogue, track, copy, organise and play your music. And best of all, it's free.

Ripping and organising

In its default state, iTunes will recognise a CD as soon as you put it into your drive and copy the tracks to your hard drive. It uses a format called AAC, which results in almost CD-quality results that can later be played back on an iPod.

As well as copying the music, though, iTunes also gathers together the names of the tracks, artists and albums for each track by comparing the contents of the CD with records in a massive online database. This ever-growing resource contains information on almost every CD in mass circulation.

Once your tracks have been added to your library, you can start to organise them into playlists. The simplest way to do this is by typing a search term into the search box at the top of the software interface and adding the results to a list in the left-hand column of the software. These playlists can then be burned to CD as a compilation.

Buying music

Once you have copied all of your CDs to your hard drive, you'll move on to buying music from the Store integrated in the iTunes interface. Although owned by Apple, this store has done deals with the major music labels so that it can carry almost as wide a range of music as a high street shop.

One noteable exception is the work of The Beatles. Most commentators attribute this to a long-running disagreement between Apple Inc, creator of the iPod and iTunes, and Apple Corps, the recording label set up by The Beatles. This has since been settled, but they remain conspicious by their absence.

Tracks cost 79p each, and as they don't need to be copied from a CD you get instant gratification by being able to play them as soon as they have been downloaded. Needless to say this works best with a fast broadband connection.

Videos

Since autumn 2005, it's also been possible to download videos through the iTunes interface. In the UK, the iTunes Store carries programmes from a wide selection of US and UK studios and broadcasters, including Channel 4, ITV and the BBC. As with the music side of the business, there is usually a free show on offer every week to encourage you to sample its output.

BBC shows appear on the Store seven days after broadcast, giving UK-based viewers time to watch them for free in the interim on the iPlayer.

Programmes cost £1.89 per episode, but there are opportunities to buy complete series in the same way that you would buy a box-set.

The whole of Series 2 of *Life on Mars,* for example, costs £13.99, which is a slim saving of just over £1 compared to buying each episode individually.

Welcome to iTunes

From downloading movies, listening to podcasts and tuning into worldwide web feeds, iTunes proves it is more than just a digital jukebox.

The sidebar lets you navigate all of your music and video sources, as well as playlists you have created, smart playlists that iTunes has created on your behalf, and connected devices.

The iTunes Store icon gives you access to Apple's online music and video shop. Tracks downloaded from here are automatically added to your library.

Any iPods connected to your Mac or PC are also organised in the sidebar. Clicking on them lets you inspect their contents and change the way they work.

The large central window displays your music, movies and TV shows in whichever way you choose to organise them. Here, we are sorting them by album name.

The search box at the top of the interface lets you quickly find tracks you want to listen to. Using it in the Store helps you identify tracks, artists, podcasts, videos, TV shows and applications you want to buy.

The Genius panel links your currently-selected track or album to other tracks in the iTunes Store that you may also like.

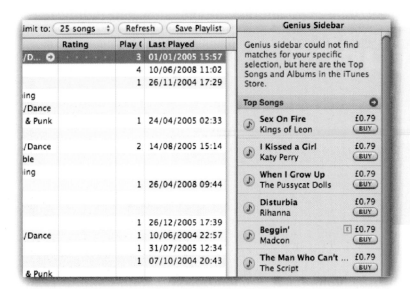

THE GENIUS PLAYLIST

The Genius playlist is automatically generated by finding common characteristics between the currently-selected song and other tracks in your library. Here iTunes has generated a playlist of 25 tracks that it believe will 'go with' *The Riddle* by Nik Kershaw.

The column headings at the top of the playlist let us sort the tracks it contains. Clicking on each one will use it as the sorting criteria. Unless set to shuffle, iTunes will always play the tracks in sequence from the top down, so sorting in this way will change the order in which the tracks are played.

THE iTUNES STORE

The iTunes Store is Apple's online downloads shop for music, movies and TV shows.

Every week it offers one track for free. The free selection is updated on Tuesdays.

iTunes U is a selection of free educational downloads from the world's leading universities, including the UK's Open University.

The Search box now only searches the contents of the iTunes Store, not your own music collection.

Downloaded material is stored in the Purchased playlist in the sidebar, as well as your regular library, allowing you to quickly find what you have bought.

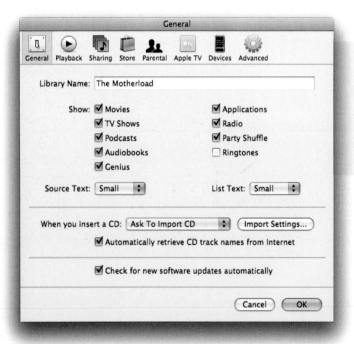

PREFERENCES

With iTunes' Preferences settings you can control how the application works and how it interacts with your iPod.

The various tabs across the top of the interface lets you access different parts of the settings. Some, such as the Apple TV entry, may be irrelevant, depending on what extra kit you own.

iPOD

Connecting your iPod and clicking its entry in the sidebar lets you examine and tweak its settings.

If you have a low-capacity iPod such as the shuffle you can specify here that iTunes should reduce the compression quality of drive-hungry songs when transferring them to preserve space on your player.

The Limit Maximum Volume slider tells your iPod not to play songs above a certain volume. This is particularly useful for parents who want to protect their children's hearing.

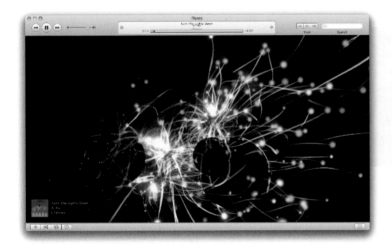

VISUALISER

iTunes has always featured a visualiser to keep your eyes entertained while your ears are enjoying the music. With the arrival of iTunes 8, Apple added a new visualiser to the pack. If you want to use your Mac or PC to provide background music for a party, you can set the visualiser to run in full screen mode, in which case you'll have no distracting iTunes interface running in the background.

PODCASTS

iTunes is an excellent podcast management application. Apple maintains a lengthy list of available podcasts through the iTunes Store, and you can add your own manually if they are not listed there. Once you have subscribed, iTunes retrieves any associated artwork and uses this as a placeholder to manage the feed inside its interface. Hovering over the graphic calls up a play icon, while double-clicking it opens a list of all episodes in the podcast, allowing you to choose the one you want. The number badge in the upper-left corner shows how many unplayed episodes there are in each podcast.

RADIO

iTunes doesn't just play back your own music – it's also a first-class radio tuner, allowing you to listen in to web feeds from all around the world. Helpfully, they are organised into logical categories, based on content or genre. Here we're looking at music from past decades, but the tuner also catalogues news and talk channels.

TV

iTunes was once an excellent name for this application, but over the years its abilities have become more extensive and varied, and just as the iTunes Store no longer sells only tunes, so the application has moved beyond simply playing them. It is also a fully-fledged movie and TV playback and organising application. Here we're playing back a TV show downloaded from the web, with full control over direction and speed, the ability to scrub to a particular point, and the option to watch it in full screen mode.

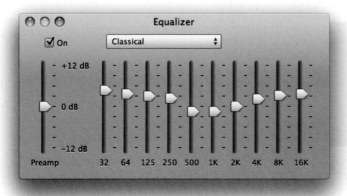

EQUALIZER

The equaliser lets you improve the sound of iTunes output. It ships with a number of pre-set defaults (we're using the 'Classical' preset here) to which you can add your own by dragging the faders into the appropriate position and then saving them. It is particularly helpful when it comes to tweaking your sound for particular sets of speakers or headphones.

Ripping

Saving your CD collection to your library will also save you the expense of buying your favourite tunes all over again.

If you already have a large collection of CDs, you don't want to have to buy all of your music again. That would be expensive and unnecessary.

Copying your existing collection into your library – a process called ripping – not only saves you money it also gives you great control over the way your music is encoded and stored. iTunes' flexible settings let you choose between better quality tracks and conserving space on your hard drive, while giving you the ability to specify precisely what data should be stored alongside them, including artist and album names, the year of publication and digital copies of the album art.

MASTERING MUSIC FILING

The first step in encoding your music is, obviously, to fire up iTunes and insert a CD into your drive. iTunes will interrogate an online music database, comparing the length and order of the tracks on the CD with the records found there to call up the most likely track names. Sometimes it will find several possible albums, and ask you to pick which one is correct. When you do, it will swap out the default names of Track 1, Track 2 and so on, for the actual names of the tracks on the CD.

Sometimes it will be unable to find any match at all, in which case you'll have to enter your own details, which you can then upload back to the database. This brings us to the system's first potential problem. Because the database is user-contributed, like pages in Wikipedia, it can sometimes contain inaccuracies, where track and artist names have been spelt incorrectly, the year of publication is wrong, or it has been assigned a genre that doesn't match the system you are using in your library.

That is why you should always think of the data drawn down from the database as a starting point. When you want to start building up Smart Playlists (see p72), the accuracy of this information is paramount, and so before you go any further you should examine the data iTunes has gathered and check that it is up to scratch.

To make corrections en masse, select all of the tracks on the CD and right-click on them (hold down control while clicking if using a Mac with only one mouse button) and select Get Info. iTunes will ask if you are sure that you want to edit the information for multiple items; say that you are.

The dialogue that appears is broken down into boxes, allowing you to enter common data such as artist name, composer and album. When entering information here, always beware of the fact that whatever you input will be applied to every track selected. So, if you are editing the information for a compilation album you should avoid entering anything in the Artist field, as it will not apply to each track in the collection. Likewise, a 'best of' album will have a copyright date for the collection itself, but each of the tracks within it was probably recorded and released in a different year, so in this instance you should avoid typing anything into the 'Year' box.

Genre, set using an input close to the bottom of the dialogue, is a powerful, but often-overlooked element. It allows you to group your tracks according to type. There is an industry-recognised series of genres that appear in most encoding applications and are already entered here, allowing you to choose one by clicking on the double-ended arrow button and picking one from the list.

On the off-chance that your chosen genre isn't included on the list, click within the box and enter your own. You will see that below this are the settings for Volume Adjustment and Equaliser Preset. You can safely leave these alone as it is better to make changes when you are playing back the tracks through iTunes, but if you know that a particular artist's albums are usually quieter than others in your collection, or you want to ensure your classical tracks have their own specific equaliser preset applied, you can specify that here.

There are probably a few tracks on every album that you don't like all that much; choosing the option to 'Skip when shuffling' will filter them out. You can also have iTunes play tracks without a break when they have been mixed together on the original disc by choosing the appropriate option under 'Gapless Album'.

Finally, the option to 'Remember position' lets you instruct iTunes or an iPod to remember where you most recently left off listening to a track.

For regular music tracks this isn't all that important, but if you are ripping an audio book, where you don't want to have to go back to the beginning of a chapter each time you come back to it, it can be a real time and frustration saver.

OK out of this dialogue and, if you want to make changes to any individual tracks, deselect the album's contents and then right-click on them one by one and pick Get Info. This way you can correct any errors in individual track names.

CHOOSING YOUR QUALITY SETTING

Now that you have ensured the data attached to your tracks is accurate, you can set about importing them.

However, before you do we would advise you to spend a little time thinking about how you would like them to be imported. Do this once and you can forget about it for all future imports unless you want to tailor them on each import. You could, but that would probably be overkill.

Open iTunes' preferences and click the import settings button on the general tab that appears.

This is where you specify what iTunes should do when you insert a CD. By default it will ask for permission to import the contents, but if you are planning on digitising a large collection, you should change this to Import CD and Eject. This way, just inserting a disc will add it to your library and, when it's done, it will be slid back out, ready for the next one.

The quality of your imports is controlled by the drop-down menu immediately below this, beside Import Using, and Setting. The Import Using entry controls the type of file created. By default, iTunes prefers AAC, which is a good choice as it produces comparatively small files with little in the way of degraded quality.

However, you can also choose Apple Lossless Encoder for the absolute best quality possible, AIFF, MP3 or Wav. If you plan on encoding your music just once and

then playing it on both an iPod and other non-AAC friendly devices, such as a mobile phone, we would recommend changing this setting to MP3 Encoder. All music players can handle MP3, making it a very safe choice with good future-proofing.

The Setting option below this is where you tell iTunes what sample rate to use. The sample rate defines the number of times per second iTunes will take a sample of the music from the disc and save it into the library. The higher the rate, the better the quality of the results, thanks to a smoother sound wave. The lower the rate, the less information it will sample, and the less disk space it will consume, although the pay-off will be a lower-quality result.

iTunes comes with three quality settings already entered. High Quality (128 kbps) matches regular tracks downloaded from the iTunes Store. It is good enough for most, and unless you have very good headphones you shouldn't notice much difference between this and the CD original. The other two options are Higher Quality (256 kbps), which matches the quality of iTunes Plus tracks, and Spoken Podcast, which is a lower-quality setting.

However, you can also set a custom quality level. The precise settings you can control here will vary depending on the encoder you have chosen to use, but it will offer a sample rate setting and the option of stereo or mono encoding. Obviously if you are ripping spoken word CDs, mono will

often be fine, and it will certainly save space on your destination drive, as it will have to store only half the quantity of data.

The option to 'Use Variable Bit Rate Encoding' lets you give iTunes responsibility for making its own assessment of the complexity of a track and choosing a quality setting of its own. Less complex pieces, such as spoken word or classical music with long, sustained notes, will be encoded with a lower bit rate. More complex pieces, such as pop music, will be encoded using a higher bit rate.

However, Variable Bit Rate encoding is intelligent enough to recognise that the complexity of a track can change over the course of its duration, and that a slow beginning can build into a fast-paced climax. As this happens, iTunes will automatically increase the sample rate to maintain the best possible results. The results should be – in theory at least – the perfect compromise between quality results and drive space conservation.

For more on choosing the most appropriate quality settings for your imported music, check out 'Better audio encoding' (see page 97).

IMPORTING YOUR MUSIC

Finally you are ready to import your music. OK out of the quality setting dialogues and the preferences panes, and click the Import CD button at the bottom of the interface. iTunes will show you how it is progressing in

the screen at the top of its interface, with a bar filling up as each track is copied to your library. You will also see them appear in the listing below.

When your CD has finished importing, it can be returned to its case and safely filed away. You now need to transfer the tracks to your iPod.

This can be done in two ways: either automatically or manually. When you connect your iPod, it will appear as a device in the left-hand column of iTunes. Clicking on its entry will let you change how it works, with the various options open to you varying depending on which model you have bought.

If you have a nano, touch or classic, you have the option of manually managing your music. If you have a shuffle, iTunes will manage it for you. To manage your own, click the option to 'Manually manage music a videos' and then click the Music tab at the top of the interface.

Here you can check a box to have iTunes sync the music between your iPod and your computer, so that whenever you play a track on the iPod, that fact will be reflected in the play count in iTunes. You can then go on to specify that the whole library, or just selected playlists should be synchronised.

However, by manually controlling your music and videos you can also drag them directly from the library to the iPod within the iTunes interface, and for many, this is by far the simplest option.

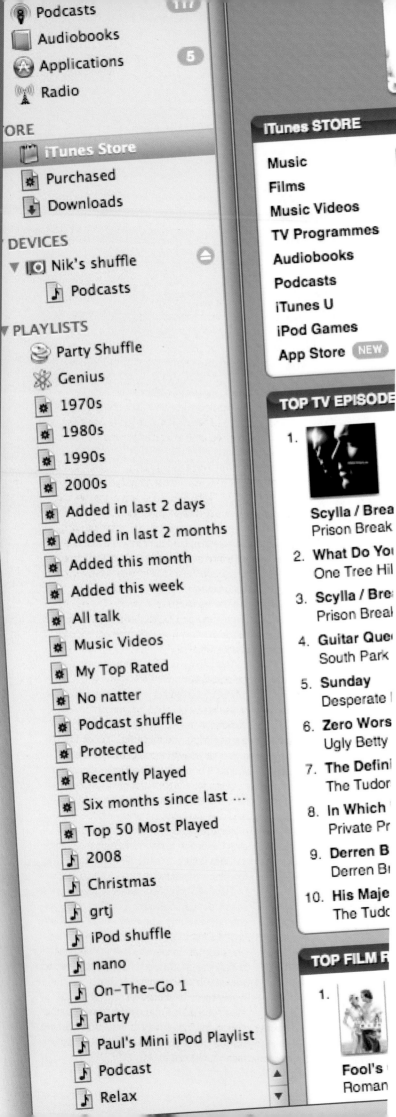

Playlists

Playlists are literally lists of songs in the order in which they should play. They are a great way to pick out a selection of your favourite tracks so you can play through them – in order or shuffled – without having to navigate the rest of your iTunes library.

They are organised in the iTunes sidebar so that you can click between them to pick different track selections and, when it comes to syncing your iPod with iTunes, you can use these defined ranges to slim down the number of tracks that are transferred to your portable player. This is great if you have two iPods: one for general use and a shuffle for taking to the gym. By setting up a playlist containing just motivational workout music, you can set your shuffle to only ever sync with this to ensure that your treadmill warm-up is never interrupted by your iPod slipping into a podcast or audiobook of French lessons.

There are four principle types: regular playlists, smart playlists, genius playlists and on-the-go playlists. We'll cover each in detail here.

REGULAR PLAYLISTS

Regular playlists are the best place to start when you want to get to grips with the way this kind of sorting tool works. Regular playlists are entirely manually sorted, and rely on you telling iTunes specifically which tracks you want it to include.

To create a new playlist, click the '+' button at the bottom left of the iTunes interface and you'll see a new entry – called untitled playlist – appear in the sidebar. Give it a name and hit return and you've completed the first step in creating your playlist.

You now need to work your way through your library, dragging the tracks you want to include over onto the playlist's entry in the sidebar. There is no limit to the number of tracks you can include in the playlist, but it is best to always keep in mind what the playlist is there for. It's not supposed to be a duplicate of your entire library, so create specific uses in mind, such as workout music, Spanish lessons, chill-out music and the kind of music you might like to have in the background when you have friends around to dinner, always remembering that you can create as many playlists as you want if a particular track won't fit into any particular one.

Tracks added to a playlist are not moved out of your library, so they can appear in more than one playlist at a time, and deleting the playlist when you have finished with it won't actually remove the tracks from your computer. Dragging them from one playlist to another also duplicates them in the new location, rather than moving them, so if you want to use one playlist as the basis of another, this is a quick and easy shortcut.

Regular playlists will play back in the order in which you have built them up, so if you have created one by dragging tracks in a random order and want them to play in a specific sequence you should now drag them into the correct order by holding down the mouse button on them and sliding them up and down the list to their new location.

You can also click on the headings at the top of each column to sort them in order. Clicking twice reverses the order, just as it does when you do the same thing in the regular library view.

The most obvious use for a regular playlist, of course, is to define a list of tracks that you want to burn to CD. Drag your chosen tracks into the playlist and the status bar at the bottom of the interface will keep you updated on their total length. So long as you keep this number less than 74 minutes, you know that the selection will fit happily on a regular CD.

SMART PLAYLISTS

Smart playlists are sorted and organised by iTunes itself on the basis of criteria you specify at the time they are created. Your starting point is very similar to that for regular playlists, in that you click the '+' button in the lower-left corner of the interface.

In this instance, however, you do so while holding down the alt key, which swaps its icon from a + to a cog. This is the smart playlist indicator, and it will appear on the icon beside the playlist's entry in your iTunes sidebar.

Once you have clicked it, though, you are no longer given an empty, untitled playlist as you are with a regular playlist, but instead presented with a dialogue box, waiting for you to enter the criteria that tracks must meet for inclusion in the playlist. iTunes will use the details you supply here to judge tracks in your library and add any that match to your new smart playlist.

Start by picking a criteria from the extensive list contained within the first dropdown menu, and then use the second one to refine it. As the second dropdown changes depending on what you have chosen in the first, it is important that you build your playlists in this order.

So, for example, you might want to build a playlist showing tracks you like but have not played in the last three months, to help you rediscover your favourite, forgotten music. As iTunes keeps track of the number

of times you have played a track on your iPod as well as within the application itself a playlist of this kind will track your music, no matter where it was last played.

Start by picking 'Last played' from the first dropdown and then 'is not in the last' from the second dropdown. At this point, the final part of the dialogue will switch from a regular date box to two entries: a box in which you can enter a number and a dropdown letting you choose between days, weeks and months. We'll enter 3 in the box, and pick 'months' from the drop-down menu.

That's the first half of the playlist done. Now we just need to narrow the results to the best possible tracks, so we'll click the '+' button at the end of the dialogue to add a new line and specify that the list should only include tracks with more than three stars by picking the appropriate entries from the dropdown list and clicking on the third star in the rating box that appears.

Leaving live updating checked means that as you rate more tracks over time the smart playlist will be updated, and as you play entries on that list they will slowly disappear, to be replaced by those that have not been played within the specified period, making this a living, self-perpetuating playlist.

GENIUS PLAYLISTS

Genius playlists are generated by iTunes (version 8 and above) and the latest breed of iPods (except the shuffle) by looking at the music in your collection and suggesting other tracks you might like. It does this by comparing your tastes with those of everyone else who uses iTunes 8 or a compatible iPod and making logical deductions from the results.

To create a Genius playlist in iTunes, start playing any track and click the button sporting the Genius icon in the lower-right corner of the interface. It's the one that has a curvy star with neutrons flying around it imprinted on its surface.

If you don't like the results, click again; if you do like them, you can save the playlist by clicking 'Save Playlist' at the top of the interface.

ON THE GO PLAYLISTS

On the Go playlists are created on an iPod while you're out and about. They let you make a note of tracks you want to store as you listen to them, by holding down the clickwheel's centre button as each track is playing and then selecting Add to On-the-Go playlist from the menu that pops up. These playlists are synchronised back to your iTunes installation the next time you swap data between your iPod and Mac or PC.

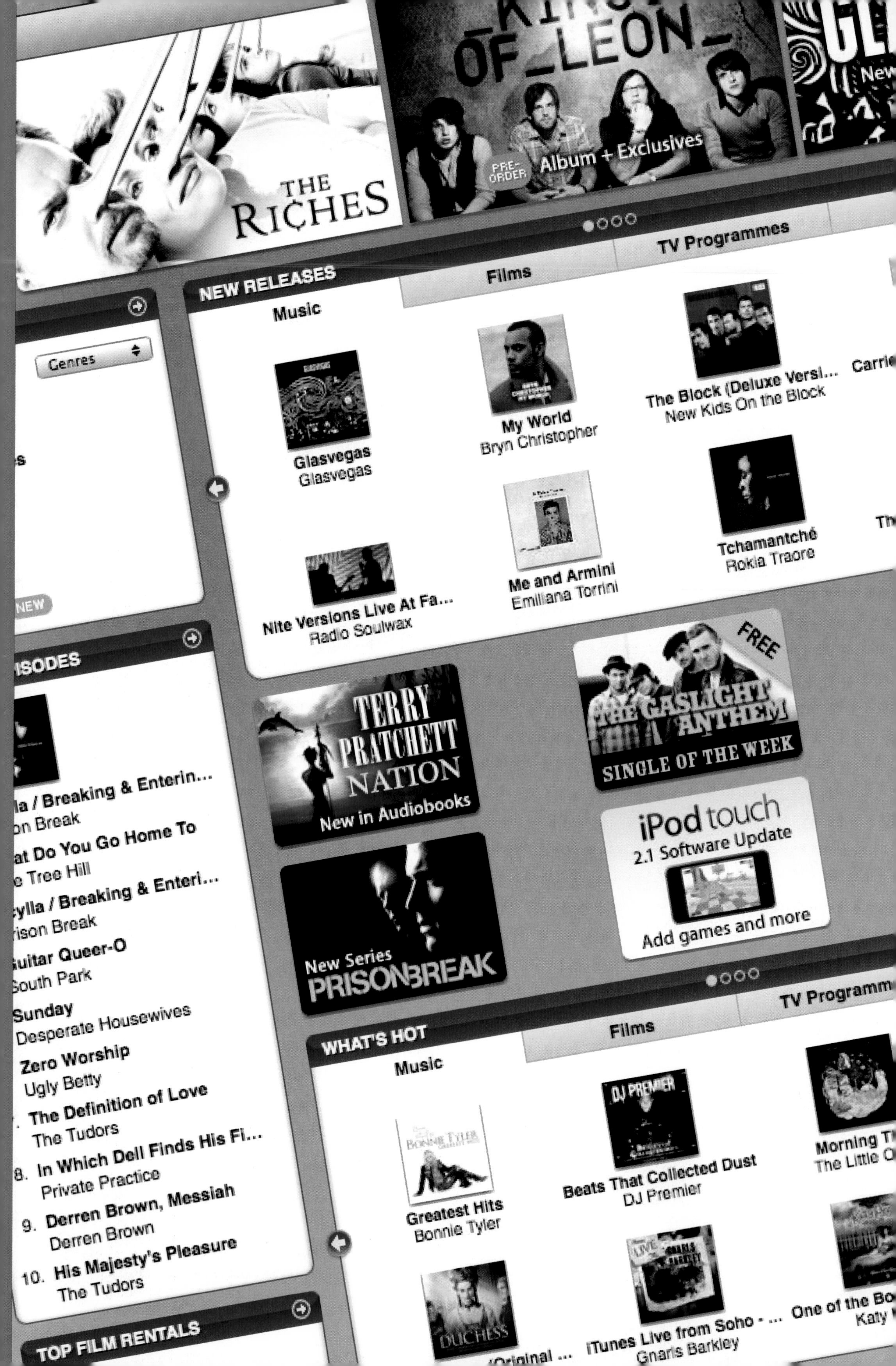

THE RICHES

KINGS OF LEON

PRE-ORDER Album + Exclusives

New

○●○○

NEW RELEASES

Music

Glasvegas
Glasvegas

My World
Bryn Christopher

The Block (Deluxe Versi... Carrie
New Kids On the Block

Tchamantché
Rokia Traore

Th

Nite Versions Live At Fa...
Radio Soulwax

Me and Armini
Emiliana Torrini

FREE

TERRY PRATCHETT NATION
New in Audiobooks

THE GASLIGHT ANTHEM
SINGLE OF THE WEEK

iPod touch
2.1 Software Update
Add games and more

New Series
PRISONBREAK

○●○○

...ISODES

...la / Breaking & Enterin...
...on Break

...at Do You Go Home To
...e Tree Hill

...cylla / Breaking & Enteri...
...rison Break

...uitar Queer-O
South Park

Sunday
Desperate Housewives

Zero Worship
Ugly Betty

The Definition of Love
The Tudors

8. In Which Dell Finds His Fi...
Private Practice

9. Derren Brown, Messiah
Derren Brown

10. His Majesty's Pleasure
The Tudors

WHAT'S HOT

Music

BONNIE TYLER

DJ PREMIER

Beats That Collected Dust
DJ Premier

Morning Ti
The Little O

Greatest Hits
Bonnie Tyler

One of the Bo
Katy

...Original ... iTunes Live from Soho - ...
Gnarls Barkley

DUCHESS

TOP FILM RENTALS

Enter the iTunes Store

The iTunes Store is the world's most successful outlet for legal downloads. Built right inside the iTunes interface, it makes short work of finding the artists and tracks you're after, downloading them and putting them onto your iPod. No wonder it sells more than 2 billion songs a year.

1. Flexibility and Price The secret to its success may be its proximity to the iPod, but it has some pretty smart features, too. Our favourite has to be the fact that you can buy single tracks, even if they were never sold as a single. This is because the vast majority of albums have been split up, allowing you to buy 10 tracks from 10 different artists for £7.90, rather than being restricted to buying a complete CD.

Although there is some variation in the pricing, and audio books in particular are often more expensive, the second great thing about the iTunes Store is the unified pricing structure, which means you'll almost always be paying 79p for a single track, or a penny shy of £8 for an album, which undercuts most shops.

2. Audio books Before the iTunes Store, the best place to look for audio books was Audible. Fortunately, much of the Audible library is available through iTunes, allowing you to download tracks in a format that beats even the AAC encoding used on iTunes Store tracks. The Audible format allows the iPod to keep track of where you left off the last time you were listening to a book, so the next time you press play you pick up from the same spot. This is a major advantage over CD-based talking books, which don't allow you to bookmark your position.

3. Staying legal The world of online music is a legal minefield. Plenty of sites offer free or cut-price downloads, but pay little attention to the kind of trouble they could get you into. Other options, called peer-to-peer services, let you download music direct from other users' computers, and almost always operate entirely outside of the law.

By sticking to an outlet like the iTunes Store you'll be buying safe in the knowledge that whatever you download will have been cleared by the studios and artist and be free from copyright infringement. At the same time, because of the way that Apple's FairPlay digital rights management system keeps an eye on how you use your music, you'll have clear guidelines that you can follow when you want to copy a CD or transfer tracks.

4. You keep your downloads How annoyed would you be if one day you found a truck outside waiting to take away all of your CDs? Well, that's what can happen with a music rental service, which is how some iTunes Store rivals work. Although they open their music catalogues for a low price, you never actually own your downloads. Instead, you must continue paying a fee. Once you stop, the music stops playing. By buying your music outright, you needn't worry about this.

5. Celebrity playlists Apple has done a good job of evangelising the iTunes Store to artists. Even Madonna has publicly endorsed it in a web conference with Steve Jobs, Apple's CEO. It's no surprise, then, that so many of them are willing to submit recommended playlists. They include playlists, from artists as varied as The Prodigy, Brian Wilson, Robbie Williams, Charlotte Church, *War of the Worlds* composer Jeff Wayne and Russell Crowe.

Not only do these give you a unique insight into the musical tastes of your favourite artists, but they give you the ideal means of expanding your collection by buying all the tracks at once, or just individual examples. Who would have guessed Robbie Williams would name *The Wichita Lineman* as his favourite song?

6. iMix We can't all be celebrities, but we can have our moment of fame by submitting our own playlists. Of course, it's a money-making scheme for Apple, but it means you can share your favourite tracks.

Producing your own iMix is easy. Once you've created a playlist, click the arrow icon to the right of its name in the iTunes sidebar. iTunes will analyse the tracks that are available, gather together the ones that it sells and bundle them in one place. You'll be given the chance to name your tracks and give them a description and, once they're published, see them featured on the store.

7. Suggestions Amazon hit the nail on the head when it started to suggest other books you might like on the basis of your past purchases, so naturally it was only a matter of time before Apple started to do the same. When it launched iTunes 6, the suggestions box was rolled out as a beta feature that was still in development, but available to all users from day one, on the understanding that it might not be entirely perfect.

At the time of writing this it really should be taken as a curiosity, as we have found that while a lot of the suggestions are appropriate, others are not quite so. This should improve over time, though.

8. Exclusives and pre-released tracks When you're the biggest outlet for online music, you can negotiate some pretty special deals, which is why the iTunes Store carries exclusive tracks from the likes of U2's Bono, Mariah Carey and McFly.

Even when it hasn't managed to negotiate a deal, though, its ability to publish music without requiring it to first be burnt to CD and then distributed worldwide means that it often has tracks ready for purchase long before they make it to regular high street stores. Sign up for the weekly iTunes new music email and you'll be informed of these deals before everyone else, as well as the weekly free download, which is always worth trying; you may not like it, but at least it didn't cost you anything to find out.

9. Bundles As operator of the iTunes Store and creator of the iPod, Apple is able to offer branded bundles not available in regular shops. In the past, these have proved highly popular, with black and red iPods signed by U2 available through the store, and special engraved Harry Potter players sold with every Potter audio book already loaded. They make a highly unusual, and highly appreciated gift.

10. Multiple downloads With an iPod you can take your music wherever you want, but sometimes you might want to have your tracks on more than one computer. With the iTunes Store this is easy, as Apple's FairPlay digital rights management system allows you to 'authorise' up to five computers to play your music. So you can download your tracks to each one of them.

Upgrade My Library

Your iTunes Plus music is currently up-to-date.

There's nothing for you to upgrade. Check back often as iTunes Plus music is continually being added.

WHAT'S HOT ●○○○

REGULAR VS ITUNES PLUS TRACKS

When Apple first announced the iTunes Store (back then called the iTunes Music Store, as music was all it sold) at the same time as iTunes 4, its brilliance was its simplicity. Many rivals had already opened their own stores, with mixed success, and most music purchases were still made in the real world. However, in the same way that it came late to the MP3 party with the iPod and then swept the floor, Apple bided its time until iTunes 4 and then produced a Store that beat every competitor hands down. Only now, several years later, are we seeing serious competition emerge once more.

The secret of its success? Simple pricing. Where other stores bowed to the whims of the music industry and sold their music at all manner of prices, Apple put its foot down and demanded a flat fee of 79p for single tracks (99 cents in both Europe and the US), and £7.99 for albums ($9.99 in Europe and the US respectively). Whatever you wanted to buy, you knew what it would cost before you stepped into the store.

Well, that was the theory, but of course there were some exceptions. For starters, it gave away one free song every week to try and stimulate sales of further material from the same artist or band. Eventually, it also started having occasional sales, which in a store with no actual inventory, sounds a little strange. It's not like it needs to make space in the iTunes store room, after all.

But then things started to change. First Apple CEO Steve Jobs wrote an open letter on the Apple website explaining that he, like the company's many customers, would like to see music sold online without any digital rights management features in place. And a few

weeks later, that's exactly what happened. British publisher EMI teamed up with Apple to offer tracks free of digital rights measures, meaning they could be played back on an unlimited number of iTunes-running PCs and Macs, and installed on as many of your iPods and iPhones as required.

Sold under the banner iTunes Plus and given their own section in the Store, these tracks were also encoded at higher quality, and you could set iTunes to always download Plus versions of any track by default if one was available. This was an important distinction in the early days as iTunes Plus broke Apple's simple pricing structure by costing more than the standard 79p a pop. Now everything has been standardised again – the prices dropped in October 2007 – so there's really no reason not to opt for the higher quality track.

However, just because the tracks don't have any digital rights management measures applied that doesn't mean that you are free to do whatever you like to them. You don't own the copyright in the tracks, and you are still not at liberty to pass them on to other people. The easiest way to think of it is to liken them to tracks that you have copied to your library from a regular CD. These recordings don't have digital rights measures in place, either, but you're not at liberty to pass them around.

To discourage you from passing on tracks you have bought through this part of the Store, the email address you used to register for your account is embedded in each one, making it easy for Apple or the publishers to track you down, should your purchases then appear online for others to download.

Feel the need for speed?

elgato **turbo**.264

Turbo-charged exports for your iPod, Apple TV and iPhone.

Turbo.264 converts videos to superior quality H.264 (MP4) files at amazing speed, and is the best way to put your own video content on an iPod®, Apple TV™, iPhone™ or Sony PSP®.

Compare Performance

11:17 with Turbo.264

59:30 without Turbo.264

Encoding time in minutes. Test conducted on a MacBook 2GHz Core 2 Duo with QuickTime Player Pro 7.1.5. Test file: 10 minute DV 16:9 clip. Export setting: Movie to Apple TV.

www.elgato.com/turbo

 Apple Store  CANCOM   KRCS

iTUNES STORE ALTERNATIVES

Some wouldn't believe it, but there are alternative digital music stores outside of iTunes. Apple's online media store has revolutionised the way we buy and download not only music, but now also movies, TV shows, audio books and podcasts. Yet it is not the only place to find great-value (or just great) digital music and media content. Here's the low-down on other places that are worth a look.

DIGITAL MUSIC STORES

PlayDigital *play.com*

PlayDigital is the download service offered by play.com, the popular Channel Islands-based online music, game, book, and gadget retailer. Highly competitive, with millions of tracks available from major artists, there should be something for everyone here. Available as 192kbps or 320kbps files, the retailer boasts that even the lower quality files deliver close to CD sound quality. Although there are no movie, TV, or audio book files available, all music downloads from PlayDigital are in the popular MP3 format.

Selections can be sampled before purchasing, and tracks or albums can be pre-ordered before a future release date. Prices are very competitive, with most single tracks typically costing 70p. If you buy an EP or album, this can drop further, with some tracks starting from as little as 65p. Downloading is fast and easy with multiple files bundled together in a Zip file, and songs can even be purchased and then downloaded at a later time. Files can be transferred to an iPod in the usual ways, and artwork should be picked up through iTunes – so long as you have an iTunes Store account.

All downloads from Play's digital store are fully licensed by the copyright holders, and so are perfectly legal, and have no Digital Rights Management coding to restrict playability or transferring. Purchased tracks are yours to keep, and even if the files are accidentally deleted, you can simply log back on to play.com and re-download the track or tracks from the 'My Downloads' section of your account where they will be listed, although there is a re-download limit.

Format MP3

Cost from 65p per track, 70p per track (typical)

Where *play.com*

HMV Digital *hmv.com*

HMV, one of the UK's biggest and most-trusted high street and online music retailers, has sold downloads through its digital store on hmv.com for some time. Single track or album MP3s have long been available, with individual songs starting at an iTunes Store-rivalling 79p. A typical album price also matches iTunes penny for penny at £7.99, and like other online digital music retailers, all files on HMV Digital are authorised by the owners, meaning that they are DRM-free and legal.

Downloads are delivered as high-quality 320kbps and super-quality 510kbps MP3s through a Download Manager application, and can be played through your machine on or offline, transferred to your iPod, or burnt to CD. A few words of warning, though. The site recommends backing up tracks after downloading, as they may be withdrawn and then not offered for cost-free re-download, and although content can be transferred to an iPod, downloading has to be done using a Windows-based machine.

DRM-free tracks are soon to be added to the HMV Jukebox subscription-based streaming service, too. Costing £5.99 a month, there are more than 4 million tracks to choose from which can be listened to an unlimited number of times, while members can create their own playlists. But, as the HMV Jukebox service is not compatible with Macs at all, Mac users will have no option but to stick to the regular HMV Digital MP3 downloading service.

Format MP3

Cost from 79p per track, £7.99 per album (typical)

Where *hmv.com*

7digital *7digital.com*

This UK-based service has seen much expansion in recent years, and it now offers music, video, and audio book files for download in a variety of formats. With a catalogue of titles from major record labels in every major genre, as well as a separate indie store offering new music from smaller bands and artists, 7digital is now very much a part of the UK's digital music download landscape.

As with more major online music stores, both singles and albums are available to buy, with prices starting at 99p per individual track, with a 13-track album typically costing £7.99, saving £4.88 if all the tracks are bought together. There are also some good deals to be had on new releases. Selected albums are often available at £5.00 in 320kbps MP3 download for around 12 tracks, making each track only 42p, and of a higher quality than those found in the iTunes Store. Other media such as audio books can cost as little as £1.59 a title, and are available in parts, costing 79p each, while video content is generally priced from £1.50 per file. But, again, proceed with caution.

DRM-free AAC and MP3 (with 192kbps and 320kbps encoding) music and audio book downloads are offered for the iPod, but potential purchases need to be checked to see if they are available in your desired file type. It's the same for videos; if you don't check that the file is a Portable Mpeg-4 download (higher quality Mpeg-4 files are also available), then you could end up with a WMV file, not compatible with an iPod. It's an easy enough process, though; just check the 'available formats' badge next to the album artwork.

Selections are downloaded in a Zip file through 7's Download Manager and can then be copied to your computer, burnt to a CD, and then transferred to your iPod. Purchases can then be re-downloaded from the 7digital Locker, a secure backup of your downloads from the 7digital store.

Format 192kbps and 320kbps AAC and MP3

Cost from 42p per track, 99p per track (typical)/79p per audio book part/£1.50 per video

Where *7digital.com*

eMusic *emusic.com*

Around since the early part of the decade, eMusic bills itself as 'a digital entertainment retailer focused on serving customers aged 25 and older'. It claims to be both the world's largest seller of independent music and the second-largest digital music retailer, and offers more than 4 million music tracks from over 27,000 independent labels, and more than 2,000 audio book titles. And with an excellent value cost-free 50-download, 14-day, yours-to-keep trial membership, eMusic is worth a look.

A subscription-based service dealing only in MP3s, eMusic users have a fixed amount of downloads each month depending on their subscription, which is reset every 30 days. Downloads are again in 192kbps MP3 format for music tracks, but audio book buyers suffer, having to make do with 64kbps files. As with other services, purchases are delivered easily and quickly via eMusic's Download Manager, and once again they can be transferred to an iPod, an unlimited number of computers, and recorded to CD. Pricing plans allow you to pay as little as 30p per track or £7.99 per audio book (with free re-downloads), and tools such as the eMusic toolbar offer members a free daily MP3 music download. But by offering just titles by independent labels, eMusic arguably dents its appeal to the broader audience. Championing the independent cause is to be admired, and indie kids will no doubt find something to tickle their musical taste buds, but many listeners may be left wanting. eMusic claims that 'independent music is simply about great music', and that might well be true, but potential members may be put off by the non-mainstream choices available.

Format MP3

Cost from 30p per track; pricing plans of £10.99, £11.99, and £14.99 per month

Where *emusic.com*

AmazonMP3 *amazon.com*

One of the most-recognised worldwide names in online retailing, amazon.com offers digital downloads to US customers only, under the amazonmp3 banner. Currently limited to music files, they are DRM-free, 256kbps in size, and range between 89¢ and 99¢ for individual tracks, with albums available between $5.99 (about £3.45) and $9.99 (about £5.76). Delivered quickly through the Amazon MP3 Downloader, there is a wide choice available, spanning all musical genres. As with other digital stores, tracks can be sampled before buying, a process which can be simplified using the site's 1-Click payment system. One neat and time-saving touch is that the Amazon MP3 Downloader can deliver files with cover art into the chosen media library of your choice; saving them directly into iTunes is just one option. Once purchased, the tracks are restriction-free, meaning that they can be transferred to any computer, iPod, or CD as many times as you like.

Format 256kbps MP3

Cost from 89¢ per track (about 50p), $5.99 to $9.99 per album (about £3.45 to £5.76)

Where *amazon.com*

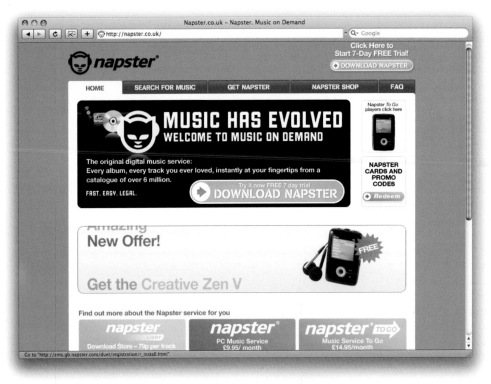

SUBSCRIPTION SERVICES

Napster *napster.co.uk*

The Napster name will be well-known to digital store early-adopters. The company claims that it is the world's most-recognised brand in online music, and has 'extensive content agreements with the four major record labels'. That may or may not be true, but how does it sell that content?

The answer is largely by subscription, and almost exclusively to owners of Windows and other MP3-compatible portable music players. But don't despair. There are ways to get content onto your iPod from the former peer-to-peer service.

There are catches, though. iPod owners can listen to more than 6 million tracks from 540,000 albums, from 450,000 artists on a non-Mac PC or home stereo system, and a subscriber account can be used to purchase tracks which can then be downloaded and burnt to a CD. These can then be imported into iTunes and the files transferred onto an iPod. The company claims this is a waste of time, though, and

recommends buying a non-Apple, WMA-compatible portable player instead.

Napster Light meanwhile, goes down the more traditional iTunes Store route, offering individual tracks in the ubiquitous MP3 format for 79p, while albums start at £7.99. Download is by a Windows-based system only, though, and while your individually-bought MP3 tracks can be transferred onto your iPod through iTunes, we suspect that as this provider offers predominantly WMA-encoded content, most iPod users probably won't bother.

Format MP3

Cost from 79p per track, £7.99 per album (typical)

Where *napster.co.uk*

Rhapsody *rhapsody.com*

Another membership-only service, the US-based Rhapsody offers a service similar to Napster. Music can be streamed to your home entertainment system or computer, or can be downloaded by way of DRM-free MP3 files. There are two levels of

membership; the $12.99 (about £7.48) per month Rhapsody Unlimited only permits streaming and is compatible with both Macs and PCs, while members of the $14.99 (about £8.63) per month plan, Rhapsody To Go, can download and transfer MP3s to iPods, but only if they are using a Windows-based computer.

Not interested in a subscription service? Rhapsody's catalogue of 4 million-plus MP3s can be purchased separately, from the site's MP3 store, which will be the best option for most iPod users.

Delivered by the company's Download Manager in Zip files, purchased tracks can be transferred and burned to other media just as with other digital stores. An important point to note, though, is that you can only download tracks once – there are no re-downloads available.

Format MP3

Cost $12.99 per month (about £7.48) for Rhapsody Unlimited, $14.99 per month (about £8.63) for Rhapsody To Go

Where *rhapsody.com*

FREE AND SPECIAL INTEREST DOWNLOADS

Artist homepages

The first stop to find cost-free tracks by your favourite artist or group, should logically be their official website. And it's not a bad place to start. With many artists and bands now embracing the digital age, you can often find unreleased tracks, videos, and interviews on their homepage. Some files may be of a lower quality than those of digital music stores, and stream rather than download, but for those sometimes rare and exclusive remixes and new single previews, an artist's or band's website can be hard to beat.

MySpace *myspace.com*

Social-networking and online community site MySpace has a surprisingly good music section with a searchable artist facility, enabling you to find favourite artists quickly. A built-in music player can be found on most artist's pages, playing a selection of their tracks. A download button lets you save your favourite no-cost tracks from the site to your computer, although not all artists have enabled this function. But with millions of pages and more than 30 genres to choose from, there should quite literally be something for you.

We7 *we7.com*

This UK-based site offers cost-free 192kbps MP3s, ready to download, play, and transfer to your iPod, but with a catch. As they are both cost- and DRM-free, a 6 to 12 second advertisement appears at the start of each song. However, the site which can count Peter Gabriel as one of its founders, also offers 320kbps tracks free of ads which can bought and downloaded, too. We7 also operates a credit system which can convert tracks to advertisement-free versions once they have been in your library for at least 28 days.

Special interest sites

There are many websites now offering free downloads, with lots of them targeting the non-mainstream music market. MacIDOL (*macidol.com*) claims to have tracks by some of the 'hottest musicians on the planet'. Aiming to spread the word about these artists' work, the site offers 'music made for the iPod', with thousands of tracks in all genres by independent singers. Similarly, Epitonic (*epitonic.com*), GarageBand (*garageband.com*), Matador Records (*matadorrecords. com*), and Subpop (*subpop.com*) all serve up tracks by indie and emerging artists.

Classical music fans haven't been left in the dark, either. The recently-launched Passionato (*passionato.com*) offers DRM-free downloads, with more than 18,000 recordings available. Single tracks or albums can be delivered in high-quality 320kbps files, and can be transferred to iPods and computers or burned to CD in all of the usual ways. Catalogues from major and independent labels are available, with albums typically starting at £7.99, although the service is currently only available to UK buyers. If that's not enough, Swedish site eclassical (*eclassical. com*) offers 192kbps and 320kbps classical DRM-free MP3s starting at US 49c, and puts a no-cost download on its homepage almost every day.

iTunes Store

And finally, don't forget the iTunes Store itself as another resource for downloading free tracks. Apple's omnipresent digital store offers no-cost files as part of album promotions, and a free 'Single of the Week' is offered up every seven days. There's also a 'Free on iTunes' page with more no-cost content. Independent website (*itsfreedownloads.com*) also offers links to no-cost content on international iTunes Stores, which can include tracks which have long since disappeared from the iTunes Store's own current free pages.

PODCASTS

Although podcasts seem to take their name
from the word 'iPod', they are not exclusive to Apple's
range of media players. They are pre-recorded audio
or video programmes that are posted up by their
creators and delivered to subscribers whenever a new
episode becomes available.

Audio podcasts are usually recorded as MP3 files,
and distributed in the same way as news items in an
RSS feed. You can subscribe to them using links on
their publishers' web pages, but the easiest way to
find and manage podcast streams is to use the
directory built in to iTunes.

The range of podcasts available is almost
unlimited, and they come from all manner of sources,
ranging from personal bloggers who want to tell us all
about their day-to-day lives, to national newspapers
like *The Guardian* and broadcasters like the BBC.
Often the major broadcasters use them to replay
episodes of regular programmes, such as the BBC's
The Archers podcast, which replicates each day's
edition of Radio 4's long-running farming soap.
Sometimes they act as 'best of' compilations, such as
those put out by many programmes on Radio 2. And
sometimes they are bespoke programmes recorded
solely for distribution as a podcast, such as those
from *The Guardian*, or the technology programmes
from *PC Pro* and *Custom PC* magazines.

SUBSCRIBING TO PODCASTS

To subscribe to a podcast, fire up iTunes and click on
iTunes Store. Podcasts are the exception in the Store,
for while most of the material you will download from
there carries a fee, the podcasts are free. Use the
search box at the top of the interface to type in either
the name of a podcast you know you want to
subscribe to, or use a keyword that might be found in
its description.

Cookery, technology, photography and politics are
all examples of clearly defined keywords that will yield
extensive lists of podcast results. iTunes will present a
list of results split into various categories, such as
Music, Videos, Spoken Word, Applications and
Podcasts. Each section will contain a couple of
examples of the genre, but clicking on the word
Podcasts at the top of that section will expose a far
more diverse list. You can then click on each item in
turn to read a short description and see a list of
previous episodes. A large Subscribe button lets you
sign up to receive each update when posted.

You will notice that most entries on a list of
episodes are accompanied by an information lozenge,
which is a small 'i' inside a grey circle. Clicking this will
give you a short written summary of the contents of
that episode, as entered by the producer.

KEEPING UP TO DATE

Now, whenever you start iTunes, it will check for
updates to your subscribed feeds. Whenever it finds
one it will download it and store it in the Podcasts

section in the left-hand column. You will see a numeric badge appear beside this indicating the cumulative number of downloaded episodes across all your subscriptions you have yet to hear.

iTunes monitors your listening habits and checks that you are actually playing each episode of a podcast stream to which you have subscribed, either through iTunes itself, or on your iPod. If it sees that you have not listened to several episodes recently, it will stop downloading updates so that it doesn't clog up your drive space with media that clearly doesn't interest you any more. To re-subscribe to a feed, click the grey exclamation point icon in the left-hand column and use the option to resume the downloads.

LISTENING ON THE MOVE

Half the fun of podcasts is the fact that you can listen to them any time, anywhere; even when you don't have access to a radio. To do this, you obviously need to transfer them to an iPod. Fortunately iTunes can help here, through synching.

Connect your iPod to your PC or Mac and it will appear in the left-hand column, as usual. Click this entry to view its settings. Ensure that the option to sync automatically is checked, and then click onto the Podcasts tab. Here you have the option of synchronising all podcasts or just those that you select. The results of synching them all are obvious, but if you want to listen to just a few on the move – perhaps because you have an iPod shuffle and so there's no point in even trying to copy the video podcasts to it – pick the option to synchronise only selected podcasts and then place a check in the box beside each one you want to synchronise. Initiate a manual synchronisation by clicking the Sync Now button, and from then on all transfers will be done automatically.

iTunes is clever enough to recognise that if you are doing most of your podcast listening on the move it needs to take this into account when assessing whether or not you are keeping up to date with the programmes it is downloading. Fortunately this isn't something you need to worry about yourself, as by its very nature synchronisation is a two-way process. Any episodes you listen to on your Mac or PC will be marked as listened to on your iPod, and any that you listen to on your iPod will also be marked as listened to on your Mac or PC the next time you synchronise.

UNSUBSCRIBING FROM PODCASTS

Unsubscribing from a podcast is just as easy as deleting a file on your computer. Click the Podcasts entry in iTunes left-hand column and pick the podcast you want to delete from the pane on the right. Each podcast source is presented as a distinct folder, with all of the episodes held inside it. Deleting the folder will ask you if you are sure you want to unsubscribe from the feed, and then what you want to do with any downloaded episodes.

Opening the folder and then clicking on the episodes inside lets you delete them individually, allowing you to free up space on your hard drive without unsubscribing from your feeds entirely.

MASTERCLASS
Connect your iPod to a hi-fi

Although the iPod was made for listening to music on the move, there are times, such as parties, when you want to share a playlist without sharing headphones. We look at the best ways of connecting your iPod to a hi-fi to make the most of your party tracks.

SUMMARY
Kit iPod
Time 20 minutes or more
Goal To improve sound output by connecting your iPod to a hi-fi

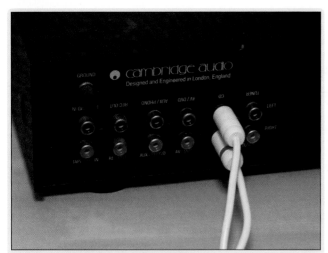

▲ STEP 01 **USING BASIC AUDIO LEADS** First, we'll assume you're using a simple headphone-to-phono lead rather than a dedicated hi-fi dock connector. Start by finding a spare input on your hi-fi. This is likely to be the Aux input, or perhaps a spare CD or Tape input. It is generally best not to use the Phono input, because this might have been designed for a different level of input than that provided by the iPod. Plug in the lead, but don't connect the iPod just yet.

▲ STEP 02 **SETTING THE VOLUME** Because the other end of the lead will plug into the iPod's headphone socket rather than its dock connector make sure its volume is set very low. Otherwise you may accidentally play something rather louder than you mean to, possibly damaging your speakers in the process. Turn the hi-fi's volume down too, for the same reasons, but note where the volume level normally is on the dial.

▲ STEP 03 **CONNECTING THE iPOD** Now go ahead and plug the lead into the iPod's headphone socket. There's likely to be a bit of a buzz as you do this, but as the hi-fi's volume is low it won't be excessive. Play a song, but adjust the hi-fi's volume dial to its normal level before you touch the iPod's volume control. This ensures that you'll end up with sound levels that remain roughly the same when you switch over to other hi-fi inputs and back again.

▲ STEP 04 **PLAYING MUSIC** Finally, adjust the iPod's volume level so that it sounds normal and not overloaded. This is likely to be around the two-thirds mark. Any higher and you'll probably be pushing too strong a signal. The inputs on the back of hi-fi amplifiers are designed for 'line-level' inputs, meaning, in simple terms, audio signals at a relatively modest level. If you provide a much stronger signal by pushing the volume right up on the iPod you'll simply get overdriven, distorted results coming through your speakers.

When you want to share your iPod's music with others then you need to do more than pass them your headphones. You can go with one of the many dedicated powered iPod speakers that are on the market, but if you already have a decent hi-fi and speakers then why not use that setup?

You may have a decent hi-fi 'separates' system at home already, and you can use this to crank out your iPod's party playlists until the windows shake and the neighbors either join the party or call the police.

To do this, you'll need to connect the iPod to the hi-fi, of course, so make sure you have either a mini-jack-to-phono lead (or something else if phono isn't what your equipment uses) or a dedicated iPod hi-fi Dock connector device with the appropriate (probably phono) connectors. This will use the iPod's Dock connector port rather than the

headphone socket, and it avoids problems caused by having the iPod's volume turned down too low or damagingly high.

A dock isn't strictly necessary, but it is a slight safeguard against damaging your iPod and the audio quality is better than through the headphone jack.

When all else fails, if there's a cassette deck available, you can resort to a cassette adaptor. These look like regular cassettes, however, they include a headphone lead that can be connected to the iPod. The iPod then 'plays' the audio signal directly to the cassette deck's read head.

Whichever connection method you use for your iPod, you can easily carry the necessary parts around in a pocket or a small bag, so when the opportunity strikes you can easily connect your iPod to any available hi-fi to share your favourite playlist.

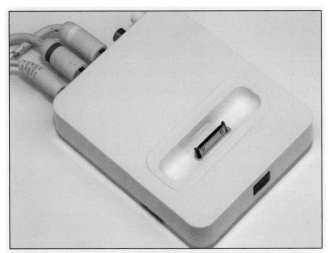

▲ STEP 05 **iPOD DOCK CONNECTORS** If you plan to use an iPod Dock connector device or lead you'll bypass the potential problems that can arise when using a simple mini-jack audio cable. The signal that's passed through the iPod's dock connector is line-level audio and isn't affected by the iPod's volume control at all. Connect the hi-fi end of the cable to the appropriate input in your amplifier, again avoiding the Phono input unless there's no other option available.

▲ STEP 06 **PLAYING MUSIC** Set the hi-fi amplifier's volume to something low, just to be on the safe side, although you shouldn't have any unpleasant audio surprises here. Now connect the iPod to the Dock connector and play a track. Because the signal that the amplifier is given is a line-level one then the results should already be roughly in line with the output volume of your other hi-fi equipment.

▲ STEP 07 **USING CASSETTE ADAPTORS** Cassette adaptors have been around for years. These are normally most useful when in a car with a cassette player rather than a CD drive fitted, but they can help you to play your iPod through someone's all-in-one midi hi-fi system when no inputs for external devices are available. Plug the lead into the iPod's headphone socket, pop the cassette part into the player, turn the iPod's volume down, hit Play on the cassette deck and the iPod. Adjust the volume as described in Step 04.

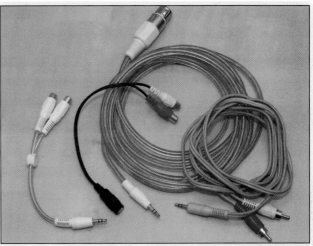

▲ STEP 08 **OTHER LEADS** Every hi-fi amplifier you'll see that uses 'separates' will use stereo phono sockets for the various inputs. But sometimes, for example, with some car stereos, you'll see a mini-jack socket for connecting external players. Get a lead with a stereo mini-jack plug at either end to make the connection. Guitar amps will need a quarter-inch jack plug lead with a mini-jack at the other end for the iPod. Those amps aren't really meant for this kind of use, but needs must when the devil's music drives.

Watching video on an iPod or a TV

With every iPod except the shuffle now sporting a colour screen, playing video and viewing photos are now key features for the classis, nano and touch.

Older video capable iPods used the iPod AV Cable for TV output using the composite (yellow, red and white phono jacks, *below left*) found on the front of many televisions. Anyone wanting higher quality output needed the iPod Universal Dock and its S-Video port.

The iPod classic, third- and fourth-generation iPod nano can only be used with this old cable in conjunction with the iPod Universal Dock (*below right*). Apple doesn't state whether this older cable works with the new Apple Universal Dock that was introduced alongside these models.

Now that TV programmes are available for download from the iTunes Store in the UK, it makes more sense to output video from iPod to a TV. So much modern content is presented in widescreen, and with some programmes running to about 40 minutes per episode, prolonged viewing can be uncomfortable on the small screen.

Alongside the 2007 iPod range a new dock and two new AV cables was introduced. The new dock has a subtly different name – it's called the Apple Universal Dock – and it has lost the S-Video output that was arguably the original dock's biggest benefit.

Neither the older nor the latest iPods require the new dock to output to a TV, so the best reason to buy it is the bundled Apple Remote, which lets you control the iPod from nearby.

The two new cables provide composite and component output and connect to your iPod's dock connector. The former is effectively an updated version of the old iPod AV Cable. Older iPods can't output component video signals, so that cable is reserved for the current models. The cable has three connectors to carry the component (Y, Pb and Pr) video and two (red and white) phono connectors for the audio (*above right*).

These cables are pricier than the original iPod AV Cable, but they come with a built-in USB connector and a mains adapter. This lets you charge from a computer, which you can do with your existing cable anyway. More usefully, it lets you keep the iPod charged while watching video or showing off holiday snaps on a television.

The component cable provides inherently better picture quality, but there's a difference in results when it's used with the iPod classic or nano compared to the iPod touch. The iPod touch is only capable of providing interlaced output (480i and 576i), but the cheaper iPods provide better, progressive scan output (480p and 576p) for a steadier picture. Combined with higher disk capacity, this makes the iPod classic the more viable option for anyone wanting high-quality video.

WATCHING VIDEOS ON THE iPOD

There are two video settings that affect video on the iPod itself. The Captions setting turns on subtitles for movies that have them, while the Fullscreen option scales video to remove the black bars. Though this crops some of the picture, it makes viewing long programmes a bit more comfortable.

These settings can be found under Videos > Settings on the iPod classic and nano, and under Settings > Video on the iPod touch.

WATCHING VIDEOS ON A TV

Connect your AV cable to the iPod or a dock, and to the corresponding inputs on a TV set. To keep the iPod powered, plug the cable's USB connector into the power adaptor and plug that into the mains supply. Set your TV to the channel for the inputs to which the iPod is connected.

Enabling widescreen output will send a letterboxed 4:3 signal to the TV. To fill a 16:9 display, use the TV's zoom function to enlarge the picture. Turning the widescreen setting off behaves the same as on the iPod's own screen; the picture is cropped but fills a 4:3 display. There's also an option to switch between Pal and NTSC signals, so you can watch videos in countries that use either TV system.

Through the Looking Glass, Pt. 2

MASTERCLASS
Creating a compilation CD

Creating a compilation CD is a simple task in iTunes, so if you fancy listening to your music while on the road and don't have an iPod adapter in your car, get burning now.

SUMMARY
Kit Blank CD and iTunes
Time 40 minutes
Goal To create a compilation CD from your songs in iTunes

STEP 01 CREATE A NEW PLAYLIST The first stage in creating our compilation CD is to make a Playlist. This allows us to group together all the tracks we want on our CD and arrange them in the order we want. Go to the File menu and select New Playlist. When it appears in the Source list on the left-hand side of the iTunes window, click on it and give it a new name. This will be the name of our CD.

STEP 02 ADD TRACKS FROM THE LIBRARY The first tracks we'll add to our Playlist are those that already exist in our iTunes Library, either ripped from CD or downloaded from an online music store. There are two ways to do this. The quickest is to search using iTunes' Search box. Type the name of the track, or the artist, into the box. When the track you want appears in the main window drag it and drop it onto your newly created playlist.

STEP 03 ADD MORE TRACKS If you're not sure which tracks you want on your compilation CD, you could browse your entire iTunes Library by scrolling through it. A better way is to narrow your search, again using the Search box. If you type the name of an artist or an album, iTunes will display the relevant songs in its Library. Similarly you can type a genre or year, or you can search by ratings, if you've done that to your tracks. Drag and drop selected tracks to your Playlist.

STEP 04 SOURCE TRACKS FROM CD There may be tracks you want to add to your compilation that you own on CD, but aren't in your iTunes Library. Connect to the Internet and put the CD in your CD-ROM drive and wait for it to appear in iTunes. The track names and artist will appear in the Library. If they don't, make sure you're connected to the Internet and go to the Advanced menu and select Get CD Track Names.

One of iTunes' most overlooked features is its ability to burn CDs directly from any playlist. You simply select the tracks you want included on the CD, click the burn button, and iTunes does the rest. Specifically, it converts your selected tracks to AIFF (the format used by CD audio discs) and burns them as an audio CD that can be played on any CD player.

These tracks can come from any source (subject to copyright considerations). They can be tracks that you already have in your iTunes library, tracks that you have on a CD or on an analogue source such as record or cassette, or they can be tracks that are available for purchase on the iTunes Music Store or any other legal music download site in a format that is compatible with iTunes.

In this workshop we'll show you how to acquire tracks from CD and the iTunes Store and combine them with the tracks already in your library. We'll also show you how to create a playlist and adjust iTunes settings to produce the best sounding CD. And we'll give you tips on how to arrange the order of tracks in your playlist in order to make the CD as enjoyable to listen to as possible. Finally we'll show you how to design and print your own CD case inlays and CDs. While this step won't always be strictly necessary, if your planning on giving your compilation CD to someone as a gift it makes a great and very personal finishing touch.

We'll assume that you already have iTunes installed on your PC or Mac and have populated its library with a few of your favourite songs.

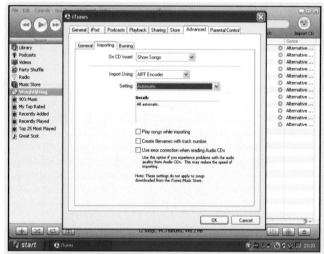

STEP 05 RIP CD TRACKS As we are going to burn the tracks from this CD onto another CD and we want to maintain the highest possible quality, there's no point in compressing them. Go to Edit/Preferences and select the Importing tab. From the Import Using menu choose AIFF Encoder and leave Setting at Automatic. Leave the three checkboxes unchecked unless you want to listen to the tracks while they're importing. Drag the ripped tracks to your new Playlist.

STEP 06 GET TRACKS ONLINE Click Music Store in iTunes' Source box to buy tracks from Apple's store. To search the Store for the track you want, use the iTunes Search box in the top right of its interface. Alternatively browse the Store using the various options Apple provides such as genre and recommendations. If your compilation CD has a theme, try using that to search or see if there is an Essentials list based on the same theme.

STEP 07 BUY THE TRACKS YOU WANT Once you have identified a track you want, click Buy Song. If you have bought songs from iTunes before and have 1-Click buying set up, you'll be asked if you really want to buy this song. Click Yes and the track will download. If you don't have 1-Click set-up, you'll be asked for payment details. Fill these in and the track will download to your iTunes Library. Once it's downloaded, add it to your Playlist.

STEP 08 ADD TRACKS FROM YOUR HARD DRIVE If you have music stored on your hard drive, key fob, or anywhere else, you need to add it to iTunes' Library. iTunes can play any MP3 or AIFF file, but it converts WMA files to MP3 after importing them. It can't import protected WMA files. Locate the songs you want and then drag them onto the Library icon in iTunes Source window. From there you can add them to your playlist as in step 2.

Legal considerations

Making a compilation CD in iTunes is a great way of making it possible to listen to your favourite tracks wherever you have access to a CD player. For example, if you have a CD player in the car but no way to connect your iPod, a compilation CD allows you to listen to your tracks while driving.

There are a number of things you should be aware of, though. The first is the legal position on burning CDs. iTunes digital rights management allows you to burn unlimited CDs of the tracks you buy from the iTunes Music Store – they should be for your use only. Technically, if you buy a track to listen to on your iPod, burn it onto a CD and give it to someone else, you're breaching copyright. This is also true of tracks you rip

from a CD. To stay within the law all tracks you rip must be from a CD you own, and any CD you burn subsequently which includes those tracks must be for your use only. You mustn't use tracks illegally downloaded from peer-to-peer file sharing programs, if you want your compilation CD to be completely legal.

Compilation CDs can make great personalised gifts but again, any tracks you include on the CD should, strictly speaking, be tracks the recipient already owns.

Similarly, album artwork is also controlled by copyright laws and while you will probably not run into any trouble if you print a montage of album covers on the CD's inlay cover or on the disc itself, you should at least be aware of the legal position.

STEP 09 ARRANGE TRACKS IN ORDER It's important that you make sure you're happy with the order of the tracks in your playlist before you commit to disc. You could place similarly paced tracks together – starting slowly and building to upbeat tracks at the end, or the other way round. Or you could put tracks that are linked in some way, perhaps the title, subject matter or band personnel, together. Drag tracks to the place you want them and drop them in.

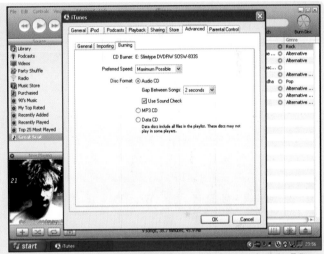

STEP 10 SET BURNING PREFERENCES Select Preferences from the Edit menu and click Advanced. Now select the Burning tab. If you have more than one CD burner connected to your computer you can specify the one you want, and the speed at which you want to burn. Set the speed to maximum and click the Audio CD button. Now set the gap you want between tracks. If you want iTunes to force all the tracks to play at the same volume, tick Sound Check.

STEP 11 BURN THE DISC Check that all the tracks are in the order you want them and that the total time shown at the bottom of iTunes' main window doesn't exceed 72 minutes. If there is more than 72 minutes of music, it won't fit on one CD so you'll have to get rid of a track or substitute a long track with something shorter. When you're ready, insert a blank CD in your drive and click Burn Disc.

STEP 12 CREATE A JEWEL CASE INSERT It's easy to create an insert for your CD case, complete with track listing. Go to the File menu and click Print. Select Jewel Case Insert and pick a theme. If you have album artwork in iTunes you can use it to create a cover. We've chosen the White Mosaic option. Click Page set-up and check everything is correct for the paper type in your printer then click Print. You now have a compilation CD complete with case insert.

The App Store

Downloading new applications to your iPod touch or iPhone is simple.

The App Store is a sub-section of the iTunes Store dedicated to downloadable software that runs on the iPhone and any iPod touch updated with the iPhone 2.x software. If your touch is an old model, bought before the iPhone 2.x software was available, you'll not be able to download anything from the App Store until you upgrade. You can do this by purchasing a copy from Apple's online store by clicking the link at apple.com/uk/ipodtouch/whatsnew.html. It costs £5.99 (for American users it's at apple.com/ipodtouch/whatsnew. html and costs $9.95).

Not all of the applications on the Store are compatible with the iPod touch, and so it is important to check the system requirements on each one.

The App Store can be accessed either by clicking the App Store link in the left-hand column of the iTunes Store homepage, or by using iTunes' search function to search for an application name. Any applications found as a result of the search will be displayed in the results pane at the top of the Store interface, dropped into their own lozenge and organised with matching terms from the music, video and podcast sections.

Some applications are free, while others are charged-for, with the developer of each one taking 70% of the proceeds, and Apple taking the rest to cover the costs of distribution and processing the payment. Each price is indicated on the product summary, and in the full description that you will see when clicking on the application name or icon.

As with books on Amazon and albums elsewhere on the iTunes Store, applications can be reviewed and rated by users, allowing you to take guidance from their judgement before you splash out on an application. Apple also vets all of the applications that it sells, ensuring that they reach a minimum quality threshold, and that they will not be harmful to your device. However, in the past, Apple has withdrawn some applications after they have been posted on the Store, and is even able to stop them working after they have been installed, so just because they appear here is no guarantee that they are free from problems or errors.

Small applications, measuring less than 10MB in size, can be downloaded direct to the iPod touch and iPhone, but others must be downloaded using iTunes and then transferred to the device the next time you perform a sync.

Applications downloaded using iTunes are stored in an Applications entry in the main application sidebar. iTunes will offer to copy back those that you downloaded direct to the iPod touch to your Mac or PC when you next synchronise so that if you should lose your iPod, or suffer a hardware failure, you won't be forced to buy them all over again.

Both iTunes and the iPod touch (and iPhone) will track when new versions of your applications have been released. In iTunes this is indicated by a number badge that appears beside the sidebar's Applications entry; on the iPod touch and iPhone, it is indicated using a similar badge on the App Store icon on the device.

Software updates can be delivered for free and, like the original applications, downloaded either through iTunes, or direct to the device itself, depending on size.

Software can be uninstalled by holding down your finger on the application's icon on the iPod home screen until you see the icons start to shake. Once they do, each one will have a small white X overlaid on the corner. Tapping this will remove the application from the device.

TASK MANAGEMENT
OmniFocus

★★★★☆

Price £11.99 (£10.20 ex VAT) from the App Store
Direct link *tinyurl.com/6e4mdv*

MacUser magazine awarded the desktop version of OmniFocus an impressive four out of five when it reviewed it in February 2008, praising its excellent task management features despite one noticeable omission. Due to the lack of support for MobileMe (then .Mac), information was largely constrained to the

Mac on which it was originally entered. Clumsy workarounds included copying the data files to flash drives to transport between machines, but the lack of seamless synchronisation in the background was stifling for freelancers, whose work takes them to different places.

This will change with OmniFocus 1.1, a free update that adds exactly that – it will synchronise over MobileMe and other WebDav servers. Omni Group has posted a preview version on its website, but it has exceeded expectations with an iPhone version that takes task management on the road. Information is always to hand, helping you to get things done wherever you are.

Synchronisation between multiple Macs is a big improvement, but breaking free of the Mac desktop, so that information is

▲ OmniFocus presents information in the clean, nested menu-style already established by the iPod.

always at your fingertips, ought to be lapped up by existing converts to the Getting Things Done methodology. There's a small cost involved, but at roughly a quarter of the cost of the desktop version, it's a small price to pay for the freedom that it brings.

GEOGRAPHIC SEARCH
Locly

★★★☆☆

Price Free from the App Store
Direct link *tinyurl.com/5fzfzj*

Locly is an iPhone application that taps into the device's location services to help you discover what's around you, such as ATMs, taxi firms and other local amenities. It's a great example of how GPS can serve all iPhone owners, not just in-car navigation to which it is traditionally linked. Its accuracy can be tailored by flipping the application

over to reveal the settings page, where it can be adjusted from a best setting, or through a range of values from 10m up to 3km.

The software is comprised of two parts – a native application that uses the iPhone's location services to determine where you are, and once it has pinned you down, the application passes the information on to its website component, which opens in Safari. The website lists several categories of useful information, including Wikipedia articles on local points of interest, pubs and restaurants.

Other areas, notably the often pages-long streams of Flickr photos, could do with sprucing up or being searchable by tags. It's the information-driven listings that prove most useful, especially when trying to find a venue or a cash machine. They link directly

▲ You have control over the accuracy of your location and how far away results in the various categories can be.

to the Maps application, which presently sets the target as your current location. It could do with a tweak to automatically switch to this, but Locly is still invaluable when you find yourself wandering off the beaten track.

INTERNET TELEPHONY
Truphone

★★★★☆

Price Free (requires payment for call credit) from the App Store
Direct link *tinyurl.com/6d7jev*

Truphone is the first Voice over IP application to hit the App Store and only works on the iPhone. It ignores superfluous features, such as instant messaging, and instead concentrates on the core feature – making affordable international calls for as little as 1p per minute to landlines, provided you're connected to a wifi network.

The application's interface scores highly since it replicates the layout of the built-in phone application. The tab bar at the screen's bottom is identical to the built-in application, except for the right-hand icon, which links to a web page where you can top up your credit. The amount remaining is displayed on the keypad screen, but sadly it's omitted from the others. We'd like to see it listed on the Favourites page, in particular, since we'd be more likely to dial an international number that's already stored in the phone.

Truphone uses your existing address book, so you can continue to maintain one list in multiple locations, whether on your Mac or iPhone, using MobileMe. The Favourites list, however, is a different one, because you'll add international

▲ Once you get used to the liberal sprinkling of garish colours, Truphone's layout is anything but alienating.

contacts to it. Cheap international calls are a convincing argument for checking out VoIP providers anyway, and the instant familiarity of Truphone only helps to make the temptation to install it all the harder to resist.

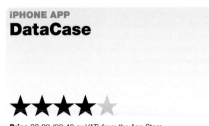

iPHONE APP
DataCase

★★★★☆

Price £3.99 (£3.40 ex VAT) from the App Store
Direct link tinyurl.com/5svdpw

With up to 32GB on your person, it's annoying that neither the iPhone nor the iPod touch can be used as portable storage. For a few pounds, DataCase adds this capability, so you don't have to carry a USB flash drive around with you. It allows up to 16 volumes to be created, each with their own read and write permissions, and a setting to request confirmation before allowing a connection to be established.

Access to volumes is seamless on Leopard, where the device appears in the Shared list of the Finder's sidebar, while other systems can fall back on manually-established AFP, FTP and HTTP connections. However, the web-based interface doesn't sport the drag-and-drop functionality that's seen in some Web 2.0 applications.

Individual protocols can be disabled in the Settings application, but we'd like the option that prevents the iPhone from going to sleep to be relocated to this application, since it's easy to forget to enable it for long transfers, which amounts to anything that takes over five minutes.

The opening screen gives a graphical and colour-coded breakdown of the space used by different file types and transfers are shown with an arrow to indicate their direction, what's being transferred and how much has been copied. Volumes can be configured and browsed by tapping the large folder in the middle of the screen, and PDFs, Office documents and any other documents that the iPhone can read. The viewer is rudimentary, offering no way to jump to a specific page or bookmark a PDF.

When browsing, files can be filtered by type, but there's no search bar like the one in Contacts to filter by file name, so you have to be well organised. There's no way to share files with other applications either, and that's why we'd rather Apple had implemented file storage on the iPhone.

For volumes that are set to request permission before allowing a connection, a

▲ DataCase's summary screen gives a clear breakdown of files, but it's filters could do with improvements for searching a large quantity of files.

pop-up on the device shows the connecting computer's IP address. This can be turned off, but we'd prefer the ability to pair MAC addresses to DataCase to add an extra layer of privilege to remove pop-ups.

While Veiosoft isn't the only developer to tackle the issue, its wireless approach and avoidance of dedicated uploader applications is an elegant solution. There's room for some small improvements here, but this first version lays a solid foundation for further development. So long as you have access to a wifi network or can create a temporary one on your Mac, DataCase is a great addition to the iPhone.

iPHONE APP
eBay Mobile

★★★☆☆

Price Free from the App Store
URL tinyurl.com/4yf3zg

eBay's iPod touch application is of practical benefit to anyone that bids or sells on the auction site. Say you're bidding on a rare CD or some other item, but you forgot that the auction is ending before leaving the house. The most keen bidders will be online and keeping an eye on the price as time ticks away, ready to place a bid in the closing minutes and snap up a bargain. You can do the same even if you're miles from home and meeting your friends in a few minutes - just find a wifi hotspot and place a last-minute bid of your own.

As soon as you open eBay Mobile it gives you a clear summary of your current activity. There are counters for how many items you're watching, winning or losing and how many you've already won. Sellers can also keep

track of the number of auctions that are scheduled to go live in the future, and how many Immediately you see whether you've been outbid on any auctions, and sellers can keep track of how their auctions are doing with counts of how many auctions are currently running or scheduled, how many items have been sold or failed to attract bids.

The application also lets you search listings with a reasonable amount of precision. You can search all types of auctions (regular, Buy It Now and stores) and categories and choose the sort order, so you can see best matches and results by highest or lowest price first and distance.

In essence, though you're browsing eBay on a portable device, there are still plenty of options to find the items that you actually want. In that regard, it's a great application to have if you're out shopping for rare records, furniture or whatever else you might find on eBay. Just find a coffee shop with a wifi connection and you can might find big savings in a Buy It Now auction.

You can also search auctions direct from your iPod touch, so if you're browsing through rare but pricey items in a shop, it's very little work to find out if similar items are available online and how much they're going for. A photo browser is also integrated so you can

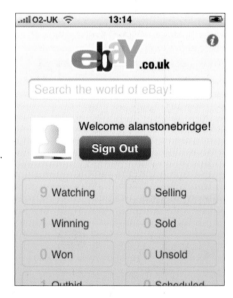

flick through all of the images that a seller has listed.

The drawback to the mobile application is that it doesn't handle special formatting in item descriptions very well; the text isn't well formatted for display on the iPod's screen, so reading many or long descriptions is slowed down by having to pinch and drag around the screen. Otherwise, eBay Mobile is free and it's something that all account holders should have installed on their iPod touch.

iPHONE IM SOFTWARE
Palringo Instant Messenger

★★★★☆

Price Free from the App Store
URL tinyurl.com/6dk34w

Palringo enables instant messaging (IM) fans to chat over several IM services, including iChat/AOL, Yahoo, Google Talk and Windows Live. It also lets you chat over the phone network.

You must sign up for a Palringo account, after which photos and audio clips recorded on an iPhone can also be uploaded to

Palringo's servers and a link given to your contact, who has 10 days to download the content.

Three tabs at the top of the screen switch between accounts, contacts and Palringo's chatrooms. New ones can be added, but extended account management is thin on the ground – you can't block contacts or assign your own nicknames, say.

A useful search box limits needless scrolling through a long contact list, while the Palringo button displays a yellow envelope on incoming messages; tapping it lets you switch between conversations.

A thing or two could be learnt from Adium, which uses colour to indicate contacts that are signing in or out rather than the abrupt amendments shown here.

▲ It takes a few minutes to get used to Palringo's interface, but it quickly proves its worth.

A more significant rough edge is the lack of recorded conversation histories when leaving the application.

Once you're up and running, you'll find Palringo to be an able messenger that's bound to get even better with future releases.

iPHONE VNC CLIENT
Jaadu VNC

★★★★☆

Price £14.99 from the App Store
URL tinyurl.com/6csfju

Jaadu VNC lets you keep an eye on your Mac from elsewhere in the world via your iPhone, whether you're checking on a lengthy video conversion, recording a TV or radio programme or emailing that important file that you left sitting on the Desktop.

After a little groundwork to configure our router and Mac for VNC, we ran into some trouble connecting to a Mac with a 1920 x 1200 monitor due to 'low

resources'. Holding the Home button, as Jaadu advises, to quit Mail and Safari reliably cleared this hurdle.

Jaadu excels with its use of gestures for navigation. One finger moves the mouse cursor, while taps and double-taps simulate the left mouse button. Dragging two fingers controls scrollbars, while three-fingered taps zoom in and out of the Desktop to avoid hunting around for small dialog boxes. The cursor carries momentum so it can be thrown over short distances without coming to an abrupt halt.

The iPhone's virtual keyboard is used to enter text, which is superimposed above the keyboard for verification. Since it's missing modifier and function keys, they're replicated in a separate keyboard that shows good consideration for the differences in using a full-size keyboard,

▲ You can use VNC to check that you set your Mac to record your favourite TV or radio programme.

as tapping a key twice keeps it held down. We'd like to see these modifications adopted by Apple.

Jaadu's £10 more expensive than Mocha VNC, but its responsive screen redraw and excellent interface will have existing converts nippily navigating around their Mac desktop from anywhere in the world.

iPHONE APP
Tetris

★★★★☆

Price £4.99 from the App Store
Direct link tinyurl.com/4efpyu

Tetris has appeared on so many computers and games consoles since its debut in 1985 that its appearance on the iPod touch was near certain. But how does it measure up to the challenge of preserving the gameplay alongside touch-based controls? Even the Nintendo DS version took a purist approach to the classic mode, reserving touch for alternative modes.

Thankfully the graft has taken well, allowing this version of Tetris to stand proud alongside

versions with traditional controls. You simply drag your finger left and ride to position a tetromino, and there's a feint grid and a ghost piece shown below to help guide you. Thankfully the game can be paused with an on-screen button and you can continue where you left off even if you jump out to another application.

It only takes a short while to get the hang of slowly dragging down on the screen to accelerate a tetromino's descent, and quickly swiping to perform a hard drop. Timing is critical, especially on faster levels, so there are no clever gestures to rotate pieces and the game is better for it. Instead the screen is invisibly split down the middle so that tapping in one half rotates a piece in that direction. You can even get up to old tricks to slide and rotate a piece into position to fill awkward empty spaces and clear lines.

There's another gameplay mode that sets a specific number of lines to be cleared in each of 15 levels. Magic mode adds items that have special effects such as turning all of the blocks into bubble wrap that can be popped until a timer runs out. The game also records statistics about your performance in both modes, so there's always the temptation to give it another go and set a new record.

The only downside for die-hard fans is that the tune most of us associate with the game – there were several pieces, in fact – is replaced in-game by a chilled and indistinct dance tune.

Ultimately It's Marathon mode that will keep you coming back for more. It's just as addictive after more than two decades, and you should definitely keep this application on your iPod touch at all times.

Intermediate

068 Applying parental controls to an iPod

070 iTunes Equaliser

072 Smart playlists

075 Digitise your vinyl

082 Simple steps to synchronising

086 Plug-ins for iTunes

MASTERCLASS
Applying parental controls to an iPod

If you have children, it's best to have a strategy that enables you to prevent them from downloading content meant for more mature eyes and ears. iTunes offers several options that allow you to rest easy.

SUMMARY
Kit Any up-to-date version of iTunes
Time 15 minutes
Goal To control what your children can listen to or watch on their iPod and in iTunes

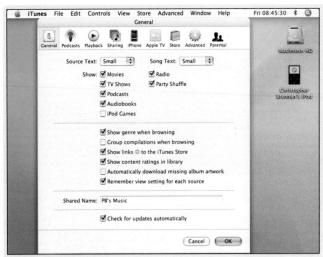

STEP 01 PARENTAL CONTROLS Open the Preferences pane by going to the iTunes menu. From here you can edit all the functions of your iTunes experience. We're interested in the Parental Controls, which is the icon with Parental below it. Click on the icon to show the options for controlling your content. If you are using Windows, click on the Edit menu to get to the Preferences window. Again the parental controls are located to the far right of the window.

STEP 02 SELECT RESTRICTIONS Once the window is open, all you have to do is select what content you want to restrict. There are four main options that allow you to disable Podcasts, Radio, the iTunes Store and Shared Libraries. If the iTunes Store is disabled, the Mini Store at the bottom of the iTunes window will also be disabled. This restricts all those types of content regardless of whether there's an explicit tag or not.

STEP 03 ACCESS TO iTUNES STORE AND PODCASTS Now if you want to allow access to the iTunes Store and Podcasts but restrict the type of content that's available to youngsters then you'll need to leave the Disable iTunes Store and Disable Podcasts options unchecked. In the iTunes Store section, click on the Restrict explicit content checkbox and now anything deemed explicit will be left out of any searches. In the case of a single song on an album being explicit, it will restrict the entire album but it is a good way of managing content.

STEP 04 SWITCH TO UK RATINGS There are only a few movies on the iTunes Store at the moment, but Apple is due to start adding more content very soon. It's best to be prepared for this and the controls are there for you to be ahead of the game. By default the video settings are for the US. To change these to use British classifications, click on the drop-down menu and choose UK. You'll notice that the ratings change to reflect the certificates used in the UK. Choose the rating you think appropriate in the corresponding menu.

Podcasts, music and videos can all contain words, lyrics and images we'd rather little ones aren't exposed to until they get to the playground and there's an easy way to make sure this happens.

This is all managed through the iTunes software so if your children have their own iTunes account you can restrict what they download or purchase as well as managing their iPod. Some fairly simple steps can ensure that you and you alone can make sure that no explicit content makes it to the iPod.

The video part of this Masterclass is specific to video playing iPods but the rest also applies to the audio-only iPods such as the shuffle. This isn't a foolproof system because it only applies to music and video downloaded from the iTunes Store and even

then the audio has to be encoded in AAC format. There's no way to add the explicit tag to music from your own CDs but we'll show you a good, if not foolproof, way to manage any content you may deem inappropriate for your children without actually using the explicit tag.

There's no substitute, however, to keeping an eye on what content you and your children have access to. Only you can decide what is and isn't appropriate for your family. Some of the explicit content on the iTunes Store refers simply to one track with a solitary swear word, so don't just assume that the tags apply to everything. Parental controls can't be universal, so use the tools in iTunes but remember that it's you who should have final say.

STEP 05 PADLOCK SETTINGS Before you exit the Parental Controls, click on the padlock symbol and type in your administrator password. This ensures that the parental controls can't be opened to undo the settings. Once you've done this all the options should be greyed out. If you want to change them, click on the padlock and enter your password, and you can edit the restrictions. Remember to click on the padlock to keep your settings safe once you've finished.

STEP 06 CHECK THE INTERFACE Click on OK to go back to the iTunes interface to check that everything is fine. You'll notice that the iTunes sidebar contains fewer options and that the iTunes Store has disappeared. If you click on the Podcasts icon in the Preferences pane, those options can't be edited either. This doesn't protect your kids from material that you might have ripped from DVD or CD already, so now we'll show you how to manage that content.

STEP 07 TAGGING CONTENT The Explicit tag is part of the AAC framework so can't be added to any music encoded in another format. It's not that easy to add it to AAC files really, but there is a way to keep your files organised so that the songs not meant for children are kept separate. The first step is to add an item to the ID3 data. Click on a track you think isn't suitable, go to File and click on Get Info. Then click on the Info tab. In the Grouping text box type 'explicit'.

STEP 08 CREATE SMART PLAYLIST Once you've added the explicit tag to all the songs you want then you're ready to go. Now create a new smart playlist. Choose Grouping in the first drop-down menu and then 'does not contain' in the second. Type in explicit in the text window and you're ready to go. The playlist won't contain anything you deem inappropriate.

Equaliser

If your music is sounding muffled or tinny, don't just blame your ears – the lack of precision could simply mean that your settings need adjusting.

The tracks in your library have been mixed by a professional producer with a particular sound in mind, but some speakers and headphones can leave music sounding lifeless, muffled and even distorted. Parts of music that are heavy in bass can break up, or treble can sound painfully tinny.

This is where the Equaliser steps in, helping you to overcome such problems by adjusting the level of particular frequencies to compensate for these deficiencies. Used incorrectly, though, it will drastically change the sound of your music. iTunes uses a 10-band equaliser that works on the same principles as the bass and treble controls on a regular hi-fi, but it gives more precision due to the number of divisions in the range.

It's easy to miss the Equaliser in the latest version as it has been tucked away in a menu. Choose Window > Equalizer on a Mac or View > Show Equalizer on Windows and it will appear in a separate window that's small enough to move to the edge of the desktop.

The series of sliders with numbers underneath roughly cover the range of human hearing, measured in hertz (Hz). The first time the window is opened, all of the

sliders should be set to 0 decibels (dB) in a flat line across the window. This means that no changes are being applied to any of the frequencies and tracks are played back as intended by the producer, not accounting for any flaws in your particular speakers.

Immediately above the sliders is a list of presets that serve as a good starting point for experimentation. Most of them are named after a musical genre, based on the frequencies typically found in that type of music. A few are more practically named after their specific results, so start by selecting the ones that specifically target bass or treble. Visualise a smooth line running through all of the sliders and you'll see a gradual curve that begins in the centre, where the mid-tones lie, becoming more pronounced towards the corresponding end of the range; bass lies to the left and treble to the right.

Distinctions between the other presets are often much more subtle. Choose the classical and jazz ones and you'll see only a slight difference in their effect on bass and treble, while the midrange is reduced. Choose pop and the curve shifts to very much the opposite, with strong emphasis placed in the midrange, having a prominent

effect on vocals that tend to fall around this area. To the left is one more slider, the preamp, which acts as a secondary volume control that applies to all frequencies. You might notice distortion as you ramp up the bass as the audio is pushed too far and begins to break up. Then you should reach for the preamp to lower all frequencies uniformly.

Selecting presets and dragging sliders in this window applies the changes live to whatever tracks are playing, but they can be applied more permanently by selecting one or more tracks and pressing Command + I (Mac) or Ctrl + I (Windows) to edit their settings.

On the Options tab you can select an equaliser preset that will always be used when playing that track, though the Equaliser still needs to be turned on in its window for this to take effect.

Mixing and matching the two approaches doesn't work well, and when iTunes reaches a track with a preset attached it will correctly switch the Equaliser to that setting. However, it continues to use it even when it returns to playing tracks that have no permanent preset, and it won't automatically switch the Equaliser back to

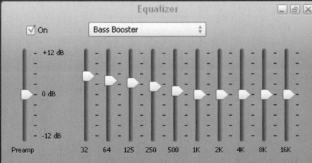

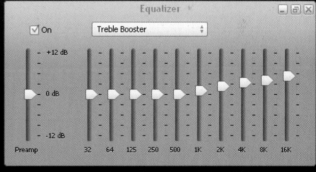

its previous setting. Also, it will only switch next time it comes across another such track.

This means either keeping an eye on the Equaliser window or committing yourself to setting presets – even if that means the flat preset – on every track. Otherwise you'll find the feature is especially problematic in Party Shuffle mode, where one track's assigned preset will throw the mood off kilter for all those that follow. The other option is to build up experience of which settings work and choose appropriate settings as you play a particular song or album. This is easier for albums that have a consistent sound throughout, except one track can still contain excessive bass that

doesn't work with your speakers, and it'll take a long time to develop instinct to work with compilations, for instance.

iPods also have a built in equaliser, though it's far simpler than the one in iTunes. There's no way to set up custom presets by dragging sliders, but you do get a pretty comprehensive list of presets that match the ones in iTunes. The exception is the Loudness preset, which isn't present on all models though does exist on the iPod touch and iPhone.

When you transfer tracks to an iPod, any Equaliser settings are copied across. The corresponding preset kicks in whenever that track plays, while tracks without one set will use whatever you've set as the

default in the iPod's playback settings. Custom presets, of course, aren't transferred. Don't approach the Equaliser expecting to set the sliders once and leave them there. You'll eventually come across a track that doesn't sound quite right because each one has its own qualities that depend on the instruments and vocals and how everything has been produced.

We're not convinced that a perfect Equaliser setting can be applied uniformly; such claims are subjective and don't take into account the variation in speakers and their position, nor the shape and other physical qualities of the room in which they're placed and – most importantly – it ignores that everyone's ears are different.

MASTERCLASS
Smart playlists

Creating smart playlists in iTunes will save you time, plus you'll always be able to find the exact tune you want whenever you want.

SUMMARY
Kit iTunes + Any flavour of iPod
Time From 15 minutes to an hour depending on the size of your music collection
Goal To sort your library dynamically

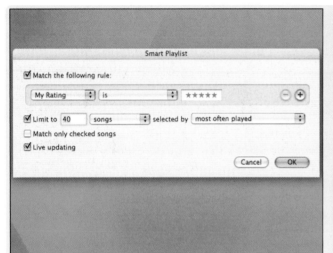

AUTOMATIC TOP 40 The simplest way to begin managing your tracks is to rate them. This can be done easily from the iTunes icon in the Dock or System Tray while you're listening to a track, or by right-clicking on an item or selection in the iTunes browser. iTunes comes configured with a 'My top rated' playlist, but ours is more fun. By limiting it to only 40 five-star tracks, selected on the basis of what you listen to most often, you're guaranteed it will contain only your favourites.

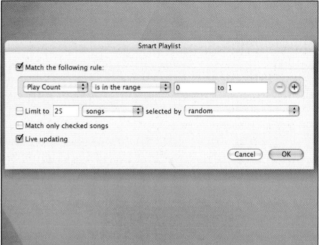

DARK RECESSES One of the disadvantages of owning a 60GB iPod (and admittedly these are few) is that it is all too easy to forget about some of the more obscure corners of your music collection. Each track in your collection automatically 'knows' how often it has been played, and you can use this information to build a 'Dark recesses' playlist. Use these settings to create a list of tracks you have only listened to once (or not at all) – a great antidote to the previous Smart Playlist.

BAROQUE Tracks can only be allocated one genre, so if you want to be more specific, you have to get creative. In our example, we have decided to focus on Baroque music rather than the more general 'Classical' genre these tracks will have, but this technique will work equally well with any style of music. By choosing 'contains' rather than 'is' after Composer, we're making sure that no matter if we have entered Bach as 'J.S. Bach', 'JS Bach', or 'Johann Sebastian Bach', his music will be included.

FRESH POP Because iTunes keeps track of when you add items to its library, you can create playlists that exploit this. Our 'Fresh pop' playlist will automatically contain the pop tracks you added to your library in the last two weeks. Note that we have switched to 'Match all', as otherwise any track marked Pop would be added. You could create a similar playlist that is not limited by genre and simply displays the most recent additions to your iTunes library.

For years now we have been promised computers that will do all our work for us. This has not quite happened – yet – but the most common Apple software titles are bursting with features that help automate your computing life.

We're not talking fundamental changes to the way you work, but with the smart list features of iTunes a little good housekeeping will be the start of a richer and easier Mac life.

Using Smart Playlists in iTunes can require some initial care – for example, you must ensure your tracks are fully and accurately 'tagged' with data such as year of production and genre, and you

should avoid implicitly trusting the data you get from iTunes' Get CD Track Names menu command. Once it is all in place, though, a whole new way of managing your music and photos opens up.

What follows are key examples of what you can do using smart lists, all of them designed to fire your imagination. These examples aren't set in stone, and each can be tweaked to suit your needs.

To create a Smart Playlist, pick the command from the File menu or hold down the Alt key (Mac) or Shift key (Windows) while clicking the plus button at the bottom left of the iTunes window.

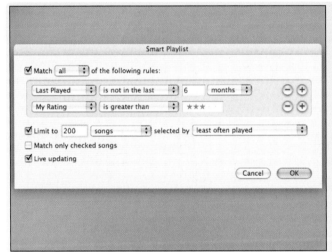

FORGOTTEN FAVOURITES If 'Dark recesses' sounds too esoteric, try this one, it's designed to highlight tracks you enjoy but haven't listened to in a while. We want to make sure only tracks matching both conditions are included. By asking iTunes to select those that have been played less often, you'll guarantee some nice surprises.

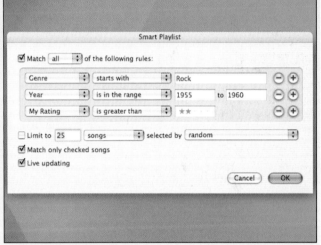

GOOD OL' ROCK 'N' ROLL Assuming all your songs are tagged well, the more specific you can make your Smart Playlists, the more you'll enjoy them. We've asked iTunes to build a list containing rock tracks – by selecting 'starts with' rather than 'is', we're including our own custom Rock 'n' Roll-tagged tracks as well as Rock.

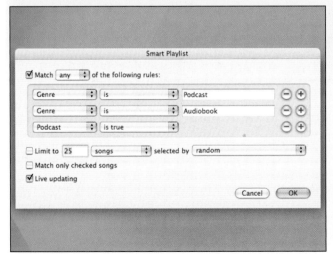

SPOKEN WORD On its own, this Smart Playlist is of limited use, bringing together, as it does, audiobooks and podcasts into a single list. But it comes in handy when building other playlists. If you create a playlist based solely on high ratings, good spoken word content can creep in. But if you create this playlist (and optionally store it away in a sub-folder in iTunes' Source pane to keep it out of the way) you can use the 'Playlist' 'is not' 'Spoken' word filter to exclude speech from other Smart Playlists.

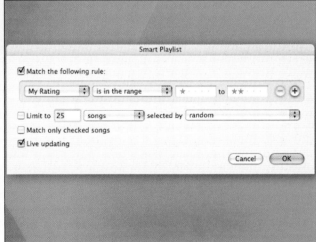

AVERAGES This is just for fun. Create a folder in iTunes' Source pane called Averages, and in it create three Smart Playlists: 'Above Average', 'Average' and 'Below Average'. For 'Above Average', set the rating to be higher than three stars, and the Average playlist should include only three-star tracks. 'Below Average' isn't simply set to 'is less than' three stars, as this would include unrated tracks. Together, these three playlists give you an interesting overview of your musical taste.

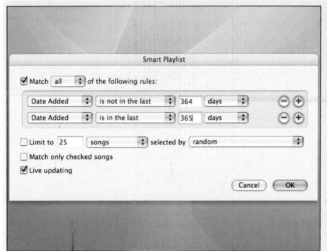

THIS DAY IN HISTORY Historical pages show you what happened on a particular day one, two or three years ago, so why not do the same thing with your iPod library? This smart playlist will filter out the songs added in the last 365 days, and then remove anything added in the last 364, leaving you with the tracks added on this day exactly one year ago. Unless, of course, it's a leap year.

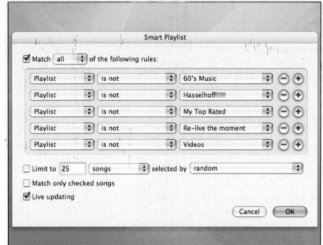

HOMELESS iTUNES By generating a new smart playlist that sorts out only those tunes not in any of your playlists you'll quickly discover the ones that still need categorising. Build a playlist like this one with an entry for each of your already existing named playlists, and exclude them all from the results.

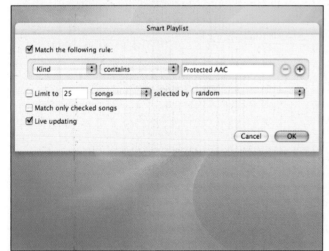

MUSIC STORE BACKUP Keep your iTunes Music Store purchases safe by backing them up to CD. The easiest way to pick them out from the rest of your library is to make a smart playlist containing only tracks of the 'Protected AAC'. The playlist it draws up can then be burnt to CD in order to protect your investment,

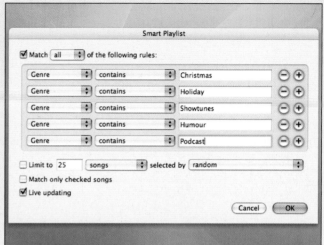

DOUBLE-SMART PLAYLISTS You can easily get tracks you don't like, or which are totally inappropriate, mixed up in your smart playlists, so setting up a playlist dedicated to tracks you don't want to hear on your daily commute will allow you to then exclude all of its members from future smart playlists. Saving this as 'unwanted' allows you to then select 'playlist' 'is not' 'unwanted' on a future smart playlist.

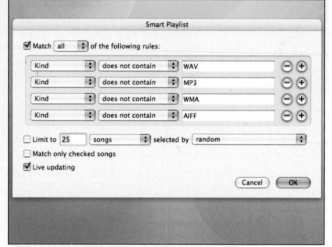

APPLE'S FAVOURITE FORMAT Although iTunes can read many different audio file types, the preferred format is AAC, which many claim offers the best sound quality. Sort out only your AAC tracks by filtering any other formats out of your library.

REVISE, REVISE, REVISE If you have bought audio revision aids, such as a language course or history series, you can build a smart playlist in iTunes to help you revise for exams by slimming down the results to just spoken word tracks containing the subject's keyword. Limiting the results to, say, 25 tracks and playing them on shuffle means you'll be learning by traditional recall methods, rather than simply by rote.

Digitise your vinyl

The rise of iPods has seen many of us stash our records away in boxes and attics. But it's easy to resurrect those vinyl tunes – simply transfer them into digital format.

The demise of analogue audio formats and the rise in popularity of firstly CD and CD-R, and now compressed digital formats like MP3 and AAC, has seen thousands of us convert vinyl LPs and albums bought on cassette into formats we can play on our Macs and PCs.

The next step is to transfer those tracks from your computer onto your iPod, but before you do that, you'll want to clean up pops and crackles and make sure you've labelled each track correctly and completely so you can identify it easily on your iPod. With so much vinyl and cassette tape sitting in the garages, attics and cupboards of the world and so many of us now listening to much of our music on an iPod, it's no surprise that there is a whole array of hardware and software designed for just these tasks. From one-stop solutions from the likes of Numark and Ion, which will transfer analogue music to your iPod at the touch of a button, to multi-device options that give you more control, there's something for every music fan.

CASSETTE

The steps for connecting a cassette deck and digitising the contents of cassettes are almost identical to those described here for vinyl. The main difference is that there is no RIAA curve applied to cassette recordings, so less need for a pre-amp or amplifier. You can either connect the phono outputs from your cassette deck to your Mac or PC using a phono to line in cable, or connect a mini jack to mini jack cable between the cassette player's headphone socket and your computer. If your cassette player has a large jack socket, you may need an adaptor.

If your player has a line out level control, set it close to its maximum and if it has Dolby noise reduction, make sure it is switched on.

ONE-STOP SHOP

There are a couple of devices on the market which allow you to convert audio from vinyl and transfer it to your iPod directly. Both devices have an iPod dock mounted on the same plinth as the turntable and allow you to put a record on the deck, press a button and have the songs from the record digitised and transferred to your iPod.

The Numark TTi turntable has a dock which allows you to record directly to a fifth generation iPod, also known as the iPod video, and second generation nano. If you have another model, you can use the Numark TTi to record to your computer and import the digitised music to iTunes then sync it with your iPod. Its belt drive runs at 33rpm and 45rpm and in addition to connecting to your Mac or PC using USB, it has line-level phono outputs so you can connect it to a mixer or amplifier and play music from your iPod or use the turntable as a regular record player. The TTi ships with EZ Vinyl Converter for PC, EZ Audio Converter for Mac, and Audacity for Mac and PC.

Ion's LP Dock has exactly the same functions as the Numark and looks almost identical. Ion also makes a Tape 2 PC product that consists of two cassette decks and a USB connector. It converts your cassettes to MP3 files and then sends the music to your Mac or PC.

THE MANUAL WAY

This one stop shop approach is very simple and without a doubt is the easiest way to transfer your vinyl to your iPod. However, it doesn't give you any control over how tracks are split, how silences at the start and end of each side are dealt with and doesn't allow you to eliminate noise or apply equalisation. And of course, you can't name tracks before they're added to your iPod.

The manual method, which involves either hooking up your turntable or stereo system to your Mac using its mic input or by way of a USB interface, is less

straightforward but gives you far greater control. Performing the task manually involves a number of steps; digitising the music by recording it in an application such as Garageband, Freeverse Sound Studio, or Audacity, removing pops and crackles, chopping up the tracks and removing the silences at the beginning and end of each side, importing the tracks to iTunes, and then numbering them and naming them.

If your turntable is part of an all-in-one hi-fi system which has phono outputs or is connected to an amplifier or pre-amp with those outputs, connecting it to your Mac is as simple as buying a phono to 3.5mm jack cable and plugging one end into your computer's mic socket and the phono plugs to your amp, pre-amp, or hi-fi. If it's just a record deck, you'll need to hook it up to a pre-amplifier or USB audio interface first.

There are a number of USB and FireWire audio interfaces on the market with prices ranging from around £30 to several hundred pounds. One of the most popular is Griffin's iMic. The iMic has a couple of 3.5mm jack sockets, one input and one output. The input socket can be used either as a mic jack or a line level input. The output jack allows you to monitor the recording using headphones. A switch on the device allows you to specify whether the input is line level, say from an amp or pre-amp, or microphone, from a mic or turntable without pre-amp.

The iMic ships with a software application called Final Vinyl which works in Mac OS X and Windows XP and allows you to split tracks, edit out silences, and remove pops and crackles. It also has an equalisation curve setting which removes the RIAA Curve (see box p78) from the recorded audio.

Other USB audio interfaces, such as Edirol's UA-1EX and Behringer's U-Control UCA202 perform a similar function but both these devices have two phono inputs and outputs compared to the iMic's single 3.5mm input and output. The Edirol also has S/PDIF input and output and a mic input

and headphone jack, while the Behringer has a S/DIF output and headphone jack.

GETTING READY WITH VINYL

The first stage in transferring vinyl to your Mac or PC is to connect your turntable to your computer using one of the methods outlined above. If you connect your turntable to an amp or pre-amp first using its red and white phono plugs, you don't need to worry about the RIAA Curve, the hardware will take care of it. If you use Griffin's iMic, the accompanying Final Vinyl software includes an equalisation preset which removes it. If you use an audio interface, you may have to apply an equalisation setting manually to remove it. You should also plug a pair of headphones into your computer or audio interface so you can monitor the recording.

The second stage in your preparation is to clean the records you want to digitise. You can remove crackles and pops in software, but it's much easier if you minimise potential noise before you start, and removing dust from the grooves of a record is an easy way to remove some of the unwanted noise. Use distilled water, not tap water, and a mild detergent applied with a lint free cloth or soft brush. Apply the solution in the direction of the grooves, in a circular motion, and rinse with water. Dry the vinyl using another lint free cloth, again working with the grooves.

Check the cartridge on your turntable. If the needle is dirty or clogged with residue, that will affect the playback and thus the digitised recording. If it looks dirty, clean it with a specialised brush made for the purpose. If it's damaged, you should seriously consider replacing it, particularly if you plan on digitising a substantial number of records. Remember that whatever the result of the recording, you'll be listening to it in that stale – software clean-up notwithstanding – for evermore. So investing in a new cartridge may be wise.

With your vinyl clean and your turntable connected to your computer, you're ready to start. First, make sure that your computer is set to take its audio input from the device your using to pass the music on the record to your computer. In Mac OS X, go to System Preferences and click Sound. Now click the Input tab and select the device. In Windows go to Control Panels, select Sound and Audio devices and select the input device.

Launch the software application you intend to use to record. We've used Audacity because it's free, very well specified and is available for Mac and PC. You could also use CD Spin Doctor, Griffin's Final Vinyl, or Garageband. In Audacity, click on Preferences. Click the Audio I/O tab and check that the input and output are set for the devices you want to use. To monitor a recording, click Software Playthrough in Audacity's Audio I/O preferences. And if you want to record in stereo, select 2 (stereo) from the Channels drop-down menu.

While you have the Preferences panel open, click the Quality (figure 1) tab. Set Default Sample Rate to 44.2KHz and the Default Sample Format to 16-bit. Next, click the File formats tab and AIFF (Apple/SGI 16 bit PCM). We're going to export in AIFF format as this will give us greater flexibility later on. Principally it will allow us to burn an audio CD without any loss of quality caused by compression. Also, Audacity doesn't export to AAC which tends to give higher quality audio at smaller file sizes than MP3 or Wav. We can compress the tracks when we import them to iTunes later. Also check the Make a Copy of the File Before Editing setting. This will mean that you always have a master, unedited copy of the recording should anything happen to your edited version.

Now you need to set the volume level for the recording. In Audacity's toolbar click on the downward arrow next to the microphone symbol under the VU meters and select Monitor recording. Then find a particularly loud point in the audio you want to record and play it. Next adjust the slider on the toolbar next to the other microphone icon so that the red level indicators are close to, but never touch, the right edge of the meter.

You're now ready to start recording. Press the red record button on Audacity's toolbar and start your record playing. Let it play all the way to the end of side one, then press pause, turn it over, and start recording it again. This way, the whole album will be stored in one file. When side two finishes, press the yellow Stop button and go to the File menu and select Save Project As.

The audio recording will be represented in the application you use for editing as a sound wave whose peaks and troughs represent the amplitude, or loudness, of the recording – the wider the symmetrical peaks, the louder the audio at that point in time. So, identifying the breaks between tracks is relatively simple – just look for long periods of silence, represented by a straight line.

Before you split tracks up, however, you might want to remove noise such as crackles and pops. In the next section, we'll show you how to edit your recording in the free cross-platform Audacity, so that you end up with numbered tracks, complete with track names and metadata, free from unwanted noise, and ready to be imported into iTunes.

EDITING

If you connected your turntable direct to your computer or your input device does not remove the RIAA Curve (see box) you can do it here. Click in the track window, press Command-A on a Mac or Ctrl-A on a PC to Select All, go to the Effect menu and select Equalization. Choose RIAA from the presets options and click OK.

There are two more things you will want to do here: remove pops and crackles, and split the recording into multiple tracks. Audacity has a built in Noise Removal (figure 2) function in the Effects menu. However, like all software noise removal systems, it degrades the recording as it moves noise, so you need to be careful how you use it. The first step is to click the Selection Tool – the one that looks like the letter 'I' in the toolbar and use it, by clicking and dragging, to select a portion of the recording which is particularly noisy. Now go to the Effects menu, select Noise removal, and Get Profile.

You can choose to remove noise from the whole recording or from selected portions. If you remove it only from areas where it is most noticeable, you'll avoid degrading the whole track but the difference between the sections where noise has been removed and where it hasn't may be noticeable. You may need to experiment with different approaches and levels of

RIAA CURVE

The RIAA Curve is a name given to an equalisation setting that is applied to analogue audio recordings before the first acetate or vinyl cut. The curve reduces the amplitude, or loudness of bass frequencies and boosts the amplitude of high frequencies. The pre-amplifier or amplifier to which a turntable is connected for playback reverses the curve, boosting bass frequencies and reducing the amplitude of the treble range. There a few reasons for applying the curve. The first is that higher amplitude bass frequencies require wider grooves to be cut in the vinyl. By reducing the amplitude of these frequencies, grooves are narrower and so more can be cut on each side of a record, meaning longer playing time. Wider grooves also place more stress on the stylus on a turntable and can damage it. The curve mitigates this. The RIAA Curve also has the beneficial effect of attenuating hisses and crackles from the surface of the vinyl. The drawback of the RIAA Curve is that reversing it in a pre-amplifier also amplifies the rumble from the turntable's drive mechanism and so turntable manufacturers have to take steps to minimise the noise from the drive mechanism. The RIAA Curve has been an international standard since 1954. Before that, each record company had its own setting and between 1940 and 1954, there were over 100 equalisation settings in use. This made it much more difficult for amplifier manufacturers to build in settings to reverse the equalisation.

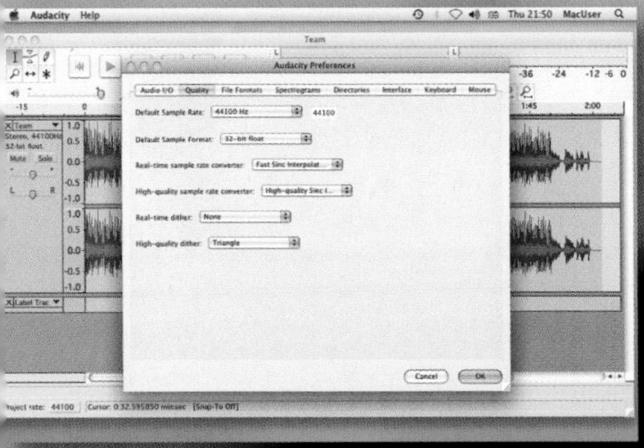

FIG 1.

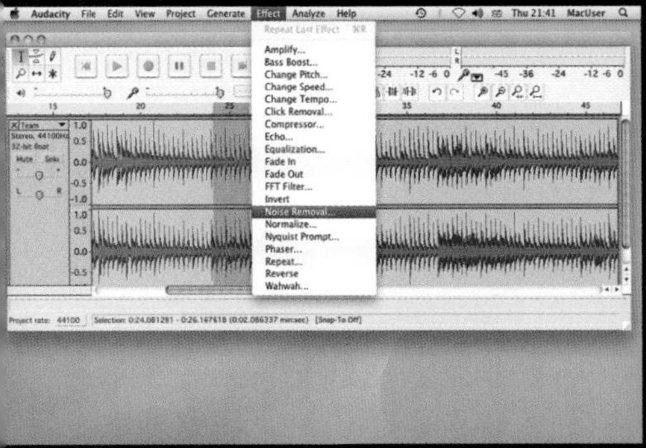

FIG 2.

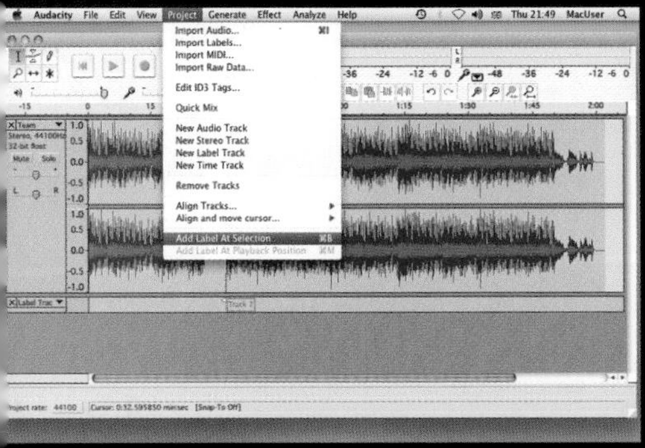

FIG 3.

noise reduction to get it right. To remove noise from a section, select it with the Selection Tool. To remove it from the whole track, click on the track and press Command-A on a Mac or Ctrl-A on a PC. Go back to the Effects menu, select Noise removal, and this time select Remove Noise.

This tool works reasonably well for hissing and crackling, but if there are clicks in your recorded audio, you'll need to use Remove Clicks, which is also in the Effects menu. This tool is used in the same way as Remove Noise and works by identifying spikes in the audio waveform and removing them, then joining the audio either side together.

Once you have removed the noise or reached a satisfactory compromise between getting rid of it and maintaining the highest possible audio quality, you're ready to remove the silence between side one and side two. Silence is represented by a flat line on the graph in the track windows in Audacity. Finding the silence between sides one and two should be easy as it will be around the middle of the recording. Once you've located it, click on the Selection Tool and drag it over the silence on the graph. You can expand or contract your selection by pressing Shift and clicking on the point you want to expand or contract to.

When you're happy with your selection, press Ctrl-X on the PC or Command-X on a Mac, to cut it. You can use the same technique if you want to cut silences between tracks. Now you're ready to split the recording into individual tracks and name those tracks. This is done using Audacity's Labels tool. We'll use the labels you give the tracks here as the filenames when we come to export tracks so make sure you use the track names exactly as they are listed on the record sleeve. Here's how you use it.

Click in the track window at the point where the first song begins, in other words, where the first waveform starts. Go to the Project menu and select Add Label at Selection (figure 3) or press Command-B on a Mac or Ctrl-B on a PC. Now type the name of the first track. When you're done, click on the track window just before the start of the second track and repeat, this time typing the name of track 2 as the label. If you want to add more distance between tracks, before you type the label name, go to the Generate menu and select Silence. Type the length of gap you want to add into the box. You can also use this method to replace the recorded gap, which may be noisy, with silence. Just select the whole gap and then generate the silence.

With all the tracks in the recording labelled, you're ready to export them. Choose Export Multiple (figure 4) from the File menu. This opens a dialogue box that presents you with a number of options. The dropdown menu at the top asks you to choose the export format, you should select AIFF. Next is the export location. Click the choose button and navigate to your desktop. Click the new folder and name it after the album. In the name files section, choose Using Label/ Track name and make sure the File Name Prefix box is empty. Now click Export. You'll end up with a folder on your desktop containing AIFF files, one for each track on the album, with filenames corresponding to the track names on the album. If

you wanted to, at this point you could burn an audio CD from the folder using your preferred CD burning application.

We're not going to burn a CD, however, we want to import them to iTunes so we can put them on an iPod. The standard way to import songs into iTunes is to go to the File menu and click 'Add to Library', however if we do that here, it will just add the AIFF tracks to the Library so we need to go a step further. Either use the Add to Library command and select all your tracks, or select them on the desktop and drag them onto the iTunes Library window. Now, go to iTunes Preferences and click the Import Options button in the General tab. We prefer 160-bit AAC as an encoder as it's an excellent combination of good quality and reasonable file size. However, if you prefer MP3, you can choose that from the dropdown menu. Close Preferences when your done and go back to the iTunes Library. Click on the first track in your newly added album, then Shift-Click on the last track to select the whole album. Go to the Advanced menu, and in the second section of that menu, choose Create AAC version – if you chose MP3 in Import Options, it will be Create MP3 version. New versions of each track will be created in the format you specified. Now you have two versions of each song taking up space on your hard drive so go through the list and delete the AIFF versions. They should be the first version of each track, but if you want to make sure, right-click on the track and choose Get Info. Hit backspace to delete the track, and choose remove, then Move to Trash.

The last thing we need to do before syncing your iPod and transferring the songs is to edit the meta data. Select all the tracks again and Get Info, either by right-clicking and choosing the first item in the contextual menu or pressing Ctrl-I on a PC and Command-I on a Mac. Press return to dismiss the dialog box. Enter the name of the artist, the album, and anything else you want to into the box that opens. This only adds information that relates to the whole album. So you need to select each track individually, Get Info and add the track name and its number to the Info tab in the box that opens. Adding the track number is important, because iTunes and your iPod use it to determine the order in which tracks on an album should be played.

Finally, you'll want to add album artwork. Select all the tracks again, right click on them and choose Get Album Artwork. If this works, the album artwork will be added to the tags of each track on the album and be displayed when they play. If not, you'll have to source an album cover manually. You could scan the cover of the album you digitised and save it as a Jpeg at around 300 pixels x 300 pixels. You can then Get Info and in the box that opens, you'll see a box on the right hand side labelled Album Artwork. Just drag your scanned image into that box and it will be added to each track.

If you have your iPod set to copy all the music from iTunes, your newly digitised LP will be added next time you sync. If not, create a playlist for the album and when you next sync your iPod add the playlist to the list of synchronised playlists. You can now either burn a CD from the folder of AIFF files on your desktop, if you haven't already, archive it on an external disk, or trash it.

ICY DOCK

Protect your hard drive with a coat of armor...

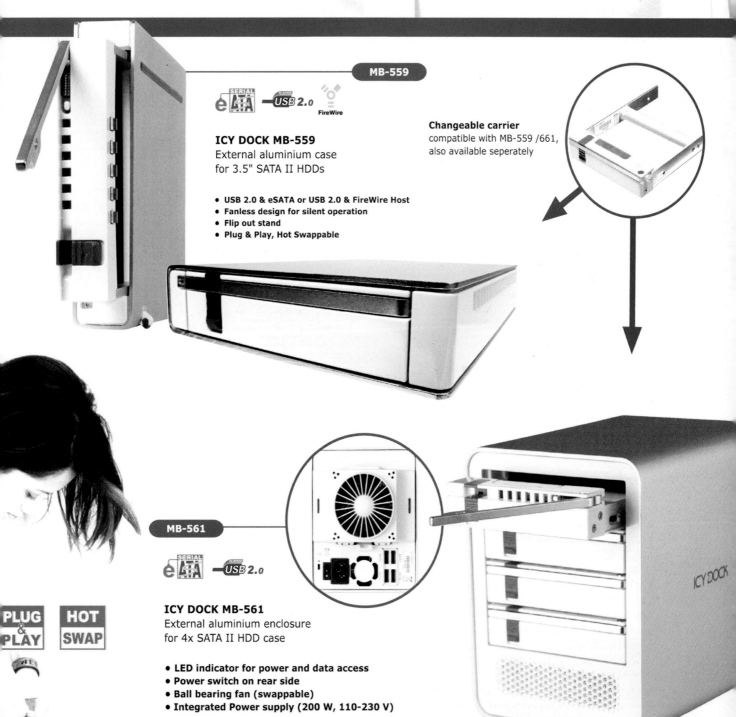

MB-559

SERIAL eATA — USB 2.0 FireWire

ICY DOCK MB-559
External aluminium case
for 3.5" SATA II HDDs

- USB 2.0 & eSATA or USB 2.0 & FireWire Host
- Fanless design for silent operation
- Flip out stand
- Plug & Play, Hot Swappable

Changeable carrier
compatible with MB-559 /661,
also available seperately

MB-561

SERIAL eATA — USB 2.0

ICY DOCK MB-561
External aluminium enclosure
for 4x SATA II HDD case

- LED indicator for power and data access
- Power switch on rear side
- Ball bearing fan (swappable)
- Integrated Power supply (200 W, 110-230 V)

PLUG & PLAY   HOT SWAP

Simple steps to synchronising

Adding contacts and appointments stored on your Mac or PC to your iPod needn't take too much time. We show you how with our straightforward, no-nonsense how-to guide.

Recent versions of iTunes for Mac and PC can synchronise contacts and appointments between your computer and your iPod, allowing you to have your events always to hand. The method for doing it, however, depends on whether you're using a Mac or a PC, which version of the operating system you're running and what application you use to manage your contacts and appointments on your computer.

You can only synchronise your contacts and appointments with one computer. However, if you use Microsoft Exchange or MobileMe to keep your data synchronised on all your computers, this doesn't matter. Before synchronising your contacts, it might be worth carrying out an audit to see which contacts in your address book are relevant and up to date and which aren't. You can also remove duplicates at this stage. While it's no problem having hundreds of out of date contacts that you'll never use again on a computer, on an iPod

where space is limited and navigating lists and finding contacts more difficult, it's more of an issue. It's also worth making sure at this stage that contacts are complete. If you think you'll only need access to a relatively small number of contacts from your iPod, it's worth creating a Group in Address Book, calling it iPod Contacts and adding those contacts to it. You can then specify that iTunes synchronises only this Group.

If you're using Mac OS X 10.3.9 or earlier, synchronising contacts with Address Book and calendar entries with iCal is handled by iSync, not iTunes. Just connect your iPod, launch iSync, add your iPod as a device and press Sync Devices. If you're running Mac OS X 10.4 or later, synchronising contacts and calendars is done through iTunes.

However, it will only synchronise contacts with Apple's Address Book and calendars with iCal. Plug your iPod in and when it appears in the Devices list in the Sources pane, click on it. Click on the Contacts tab, click Sync Address Book Contacts and select whether you want to select all your Contacts or only specific groups, like the iPod Contacts group discussed above.

Do the same for calendars. Here you can either sync all your calendars or specify which of your iCal calendars to synchronise. Your contacts and calendars will now be synchronised with your Mac every time you sync your iPod.

If you're running Windows XP, you can synchronise calendar and contacts with Outlook, Outlook Express and Microsoft Address Book. The process for syncing data is exactly the same as described above for the Mac, except that you have to specify which of the three applications you want to synchronise with. If you choose Outlook, you'll be asked to allow iTunes access to your Outlook data and specify a time limit.

In Windows Vista, you can synchronise data with Outlook, Windows Calendar, and Windows Contacts. The process for synchronising contacts is the same as for XP. It's worth noting that Windows Contact Groups won't be synced and that iTunes can sync from either Outlook or Contacts, but not both.

If you're synchronising with Outlook, you can synchronise calendars in the same way as contacts, but if you're running Windows Calendar you must export calendars as .ics files and import them into Outlook and then synchronise them. That's all well and good if you use one of the Apple or Microsoft

supported applications to manage your contacts and calendars, but what if you don't? The good news is that you can still transfer data to your iPod, the bad news is that unless you import everything into one of the supported applications, you can't keep the data in sync with your iPod automatically.

To transfer contacts and calendars manually, you have to enable hard disk mode. This mode allows you to use your iPod as a storage disk and works on all iPods except the iPod touch. To enable this, connect your iPod to your computer, click on it in the Sources pane, and click on the Summary tab. At the bottom of the tab, in the Options section, is a button labelled Enable Disk Use. Click it. If you have a shuffle, you'll have to specify how much of the disk you want to keep for music and how much you want to use for data. Your iPod will now be visible in the Finder on a Mac and My Computer in Windows. If you open it, you'll see that inside are folders labelled Calendars and Contacts. Copying files to these folders makes them visible on your iPod. But they have to be in the right format. The Contacts folder supports .vcf or .contact files. So to copy contacts to the

folder, you first have to export them from your contacts application in one of those formats. When you've done that you can drag them to the folder to copy them to the iPod.

The Calendars folder only supports .ics files. This is an open standard and is supported by many calendaring applications. You should be able to export calendars in that format from your calendar application and then drag them to the Calendars folder on the iPod. The downside to this method is that you'll have to manually export a calendar or contact and copy it across every time you update it. And, of course, it's a one way process, you can't update contacts or calendars on your iPod and pass the updated versions back to your Mac or PC, regardless of which method you use.

You can store notes on your iPod in much the same way. You just need to export any text document as a plain text file from your word processor and drag it to the Notes folder on your iPod. Different word processors have different ways to save files as plain text. In Text Edit in Mac OS X, for example, you select Make Plain Text from the Format menu. In other programs, you

choose Save As from the File menu and specify Text or .txt as the format. To view notes on an iPod, select Extras from the main menu and then Notes. Use the Click Wheel to scroll through the note titles and then click on the one you want to read.

It's worth noting that while the iPod will store very long documents, it will only display up to 1000 files, and only show the first 4K, or 4096 characters from each file. The rest of the document is still there, the Pod just can't display it.

The Notes feature doesn't work on the iPod touch or iPhone because you can't enable disk use on those. However, there is a solution, if you have a Mac. FileMagnet, which costs £2.99 from the iTunes App Store works on both the iPod touch and the iPhone and allows you to transfer files between your Mac and iPhone or touch. The iPhone OS can display text documents, Microsoft Office (Word, Excel, and PowerPoint) documents, PDFs and iWork files, so by using FileMagnet to transfer files from your Mac, you'll be able to read them on your Phone or iPod touch. As with the Notes feature in other iPods, you can view files but can't edit them. There's no current equivalent for Windows.

Plug-ins for iTunes

Whether you want to add artwork to your digital albums or ratings to your tracks, downloading free and inexpensive plug-ins can make the process easier and less time consuming for you.

iConcertCal (Windows and Mac)
iconcertcal.com
Price Free

Do you ever hear about concerts retrospectively, perhaps when you're standing within earshot of a water cooler while colleagues or classmates talk feverishly about the amazing performance that the bass player put in? iConcertCal is a fantastic plug-in that live music fans should install right away. It uses the concert database from JamBase, a site based in America but which holds concert details for the UK, as well.

It cross-references the list of artists in your library against an online database to find matches in your area. You can also maintain two additional lists of artists. The first excludes artists from the results, so that you won't be prompted to see Barry Manilow just because you happen to own 'Copacabana'.

A second list monitors artists that aren't in your library but who you're interested in checking out.

The last step is to enter your city, UK as the state and the number of miles that you're willing to travel to a performance. Concerts that match the criteria are then shown in a chronological list to one side, and a much more pleasant calendar view that takes up most of the window. All of the results are clickable and lead to the JamBase site so you can find extra information including contact details and a map to the venue.

Register for an account on the JamBase website and you can make a contribution to help other music lovers. A link in the plug-in takes you to a webpage so you can add details of missing concerts. They're verified by the site's staff to maintain the quality of the service for everybody's benefit. iConcertCal also retrieves a schedule of CD releases, but you can ignore these as they're US dates, not UK ones, but that doesn't detract from the main purpose. Mac users also have the option of adding results to iCal, where they sit alongside your other calendars to make it easier to check for conflicts.

Last.fm (Windows and Mac)
last.fm
Price Free

Genius recommendations from iTunes are a great way to discover new music on your own, but their anonymity will leave more sociable music fans with a cold feeling. Last.fm goes a step further and doesn't just recommend music based on your library, but also puts you in touch with others with similar listening habits.

The plug-in sits in the background monitoring whatever is playing in iTunes – and what has been played on your iPod since it was last plugged in. So long as you listen to at least 50 per cent of a track, the artist and track name are recorded on your profile, and the site uses this information to compile data about you.

As soon as you've set up a profile on the website, you can add a list of your favourite artists to get immediate recommendations. They'll be obvious to start with, so if you enter Blur then chances are you'll be unimaginatively invited to check out side projects by band members, but the results will become more personalised as you play a wider variety of music.

Last.fm's software has an integrated media player that will stream full-length recommendations from outside your library, based on your listening habits or by entering an artist name. Leave its window open at the side of the desktop and you'll be able to glance at artist biographies and learn more about those you had never heard of before. It also gives a list of relevant tags, similar artists and the top listeners on the site as clickable links for further research.

The intention is that you'll take an active interest in other people's habits, and you can go deeper into the site to form friendships and join groups, where users gather around a common interest such as a particular label, artist or genre.

That's when the discoveries become particularly exciting as Last.fm takes the data recorded for each member and calculates group statistics, where you'll discover artists that have been on the fringe of your awareness – or even completely off the radar – for years.

Last.fm's strength over Genius is that it removes the shroud of anonymity and adds a more visible human touch to music recommendations.

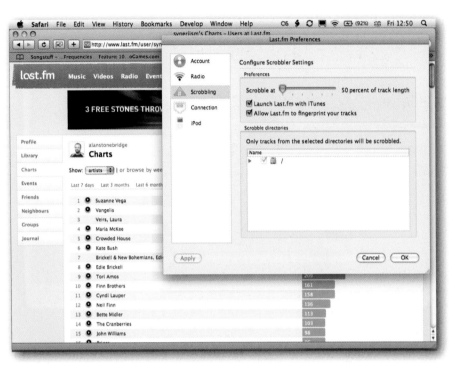

SizzlingKeys (Mac) and iTunesKeys (Windows)
yellowmug.com +
mattberube.com/software/iTunesKeys
Price Free ($5 for Pro version) + Free (Donationware)

Each of us spends time filling in track, album and artist names as they're essential for finding songs in the library. More keen iTunes users may even fill in genre and composer information, although things start to get a little time-consuming with pop music and the different composers throughout an album. However, a real difference can be made when ratings are applied to each individual track.

One of iTunes' most powerful features, Smart Playlists, only reaches it full potential when this very personalised metadata is present. Ratings can make an invaluable contribution to keeping the mood right in Party Shuffle, and they're also a great way to ensure low capacity iPods, such as the shuffle, are only filled with your favourite tracks.

The trouble is that they're a real chore to set when your attention is firmly focused upon a website or work in another application.

You can't impulsively press a keyboard shortcut to set the rating as you would to skip, pause or mute playback on keyboards with media keys. The sheer disruption caused by jumping back to iTunes every few minutes is a very good reason why many of us ignore ratings altogether.

SizzlingKeys and iTunesKeys are the perfect remedy as they allow you to set up global shortcuts to various features regardless of wherever else your attention may lie.

At the press of a key combination, you can set the rating of the current track. It soon becomes like second nature, and it's so instinctive you will have quickly filled a large gap in your library's metadata.

SizzlingKeys installs as a pane in your Mac's System Preferences. Should your keyboard not have media keys, you can set up shortcuts to skip tracks and control the volume, for which there's a neat enhancement that all but mutes it during interruptions.

It has some other neat enhancements too, such as panels that appear above all other windows for you to search the library or select a playlist, then neatly fade away once you're finished with them.

iTunesKeys provides similar global shortcuts for Windows users. Both applications have the option of temporarily displaying information about a track as it begins to play, saving screen space beyond even iTunes' MiniPlayer mode, but it's the ratings shortcuts that make them essential if you're to get the most out of iTunes.

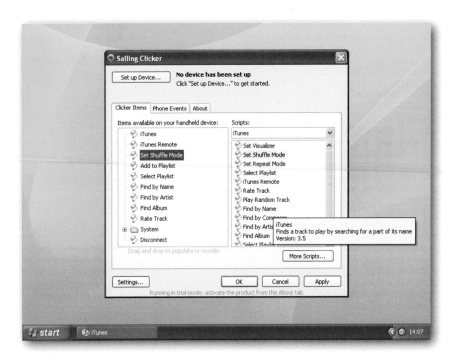

iArt 3 (Windows)
ipodsoft.com
Price $10 (about £5)

Cover art really brightens up your iPod and it's essential for iTunes' Cover Flow and Grid views on the desktop too.

However, not all album art can be added using the built-in search feature, which offers a tedious solution even if you're only missing a few dozen covers.

Interest is easily lost and promises to return to the task later are just as easily discarded.

iArt is a wizard-based application that steps through the albums with missing artwork and tries to fill it in. It uses the artist and album tags to search album art on Amazon. You get a choice of which of Amazon's international sites to use, making it more likely that you'll get the art for the correct edition.

The wizard can be run in automatic mode, which means it will run unattended and pick what it thinks is the best match based on the information in your library.

However, the wiser route for updating many albums is to step through one album at a time, confirming the correct artwork as you go rather than having to browse the library to verify many items.

Should you have too many covers to add in one sitting, iArt will ask whether you want to pick up where you left off.

iArt will cost you a few pounds but it's a great way to add a lot of missing artwork.

It's money well spent as it means not having to type artist and album names – the information is already in your library, so why not let a computer do the hardest part for you.

Salling Media Sync (Windows and Mac)
salling.com
Price Free with speed limitation, otherwise $22 (about £13)

Nobody likes to be bogged down carrying an iPod and a mobile phone when they're heading out to meet friends.

Your pockets are already full with a wallet or purse and your house and car keys. Do you really need to carry an iPod as well? It's likely to be the first thing that gets left behind, even if you could do with some music to get you in the mood before meeting friends.

With Salling Media it doesn't matter that you don't have an iPhone to sync with iTunes as this software copies unprotected tracks to other kinds of handset.

It supports a modest but popular range of recent handsets; you'll find list a list on the website. It also won't transfer copy-protected music to any old handset because such tracks won't play on any old handset. So long as you have unprotected tracks such as MP3s ripped from CD or iTunes Plus tracks from Apple's store, you can leave your iPod behind and still have some mood-setting party music to get you into the swing of things.

Salling Clicker (Windows and Mac)
salling.com
Price $23.95 including VAT (about £13.92)

Apple provides its Remote application so that you can control iTunes over a wifi connection from an iPhone or iPod touch, but by installing Salling Clicker more than 300 models of mobile device with wifi or Bluetooth can also be used as a remote.

After running through a short process that pairs your phone to the software running on your computer, the top of the window tells you how to reach it on your phone. Then it's just a case of choosing which actions appear there.

The list includes some really useful items including playlist selection and editing, and searching for an artist, song, composer or track by entering the text on your phone.

Best of all, you're not forced into having all actions available on the phone; you can keep it just to the ones that are essential for you.

Salling Clicker is a reasonably inexpensive way to remain in control of your music. For working in the kitchen, or even further afield such as the garage or garden with music streaming to remote speakers over AirPort Express, you can near effortlessly skip embarrassing blasts from the past. Think of the possibilities for house parties, too.

Among the more advanced options is a really useful one that pauses iTunes while you take a phone call.

Of course, iTunes is just one of the applications that can be controlled; it also works straight away with other media applications including DVD Player on a Mac and Windows Media Player on Windows, while others such as PowerDVD can be added with plug-ins.

Fetch Art (Mac)

fetchartblog.blogspot.com
Price Free

Fetch Art does much the same job as iArt for Mac owners, but it's more neatly integrated into iTunes' own interface. It installs as a script item in the menu bar that, when clicked, brings up a separate application that retrieves artwork for whatever is selected in iTunes.

The selection can be a single track, a whole album's worth, or even tracks from different albums. Fetch Art will retrieve artwork for them all at once. Applying artwork that's correct simply involves scrolling through the results in Fetch Art's window and selecting all of the correct ones by holding down the Command button.

Once that's done, just hit the Copy to iTunes button and the artwork for each track will be copied across.

The artwork is added to each individual file, and it'll remain attached when the tracks are copied to your iPod, making your display a whole lot prettier.

We strongly recommend that you assign a keyboard shortcut to Fetch Art in the Keyboard & Mouse preferences pane, otherwise it has to be activated through the Scripts menu.

A keyboard shortcut proves a lot less tiresome when working through a library in smaller chunks and assigning album art to a few albums at a time.

MixMeister BPM Analyzer (Windows) and Tangerine (Mac)

mixmeister.com + potionfactory.com
Price Free + $24.95 (about £14.82)

Almost certainly the beats per minute (BPM) field is the least used piece of metadata in iTunes. However, like ratings, it can really enhance the results of Smart Playlists by maintaining a strong rhythm for exercise or an up-tempo party feel in a better way than permitted by broad genre tags.

Adding such detailed information is not only difficult but time consuming – far more so than fixing missing album artwork. It could take you months to plug the gaps, but you can let your computer do the work for you by running some automated tools that analyse audio.

BPM Analyzer can handle MP3 files but it will ignore AAC, the format used by the iTunes Store and the default for iTunes. It simply displays any existing information and gives you the option of rescanning the file, but it automatically does so for tracks that don't have a value attached and adds its results.

Mac users will be glad to hear that Tangerine doesn't just add AAC support, but also scans protected tracks that you've bought from the Store. There's a price attached to the software and you'll have to pay to automatically transfer the data back to iTunes.

Before doing so, it'll warn you if there's already different information on tracks in iTunes and you can selectively pick which ones are overwritten.

MAKE THE WORLD YOUR PALETTE

TAKE YOUR COLOUR INSPIRATION FROM ANYTHING, ANYWHERE AT ANY TIME.

colormunki™ DESIGN

» Capture colour from any surface and find the perfect match

» Instant access to onboard PANTONE libraries

» Synchronise palettes with your favourite design application

» Easy, accurate monitor to print match

ColorMunki – Let your creativity run wild

Available from: Cancom | Cherlyn Electronics | Computer Warehouse
Dabs.com | Jigsaw Systems | London Graphic Centre |

 Distributed by Colour Confidence www.colourconfidence.com

Advanced

092 Transferring tunes

094 Encoding video for use on iPods

097 Make tracks

102 Servers

106 Create a speech autocue using QuickTime Pro

Transferring tunes

Ripping music from your iPod to your computer for personal use is a tricky business, especially as copyright laws are still under review. However we've found five applications which enable you to transfer tunes simply and safely.

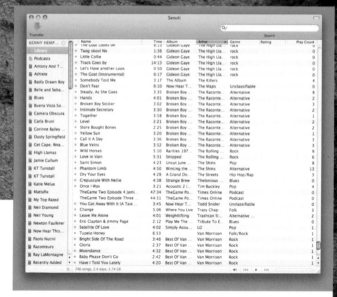

iTunes is a fantastic application for syncing your music on your computer with that on your iPod. But it's a one-way street. You can't copy music and playlists from your iPod to a computer. The one exception to this is music bought on the iTunes Store. The Transfer Purchases option in iTunes allows you to copy purchased music from iPod to computer. However, you'll only be able to play those tracks on the computer if it's one of the five computers authorised to play tracks downloaded through your iTunes Store account. iTunes does provide one way to copy music from your iPod, by enabling hard disk mode, setting iTunes to manually sync, and then copying your iTunes Library to your iPod by dragging and dropping the folder containing your music into the iPod in the Finder or My Computer. You then do the opposite on the computer to which you want to copy music.

That's fine if you want to transfer music from an old computer to a new one, but doesn't help at all if your hard drive dies suddenly leaving you with all your music locked inside your iPod.

Restrictions on the way you can upload music from an iPod is meant to block illegal music sharing, but that's no comfort if you have a corrupt hard drive and no access to your music collection. You could rip all your CDs again, but that takes a huge amount of time and effort. Far easier to add it directly to iTunes from your iPod.

SENUTI
Price Free

fadingred.com/senuti

Senuti is a Mac OS X only application that allows you to search your iPod for the music you want to copy to your Mac, select it and even listen to tracks from the application before copying them. It also identifies songs which are already in your iTunes Library and marks them with a blue dot. You can choose to allow it to add tracks to your iTunes Library, organise them in folders, and copy playlists from your iPod to iTunes. The current beta version supports the iPod touch and iPhone as well as the classic, nano and older iPods. It's backed up by comprehensive support pages and is one of the most popular applications for copying iPod applications onto a Mac. If you don't need support for the iPhone or touch, download the older, non-beta release as it is likely to be more mature and stable.

YAMIPOD
Price Free

yamipod.com

Yamipod is a Mac, Windows, and Linux application that runs directly from your iPod and therefore doesn't need to be installed on your computer. It supports older iPods, as well as the classic and nano, but not the iPhone or iPod touch. YamiPod allows you to search for music, play tracks, and remove duplicates. It also recognises your iPod's playlists, including On-the-Go. It's fairly basic, and its Mac interface isn't great, but it does the job. Transferring music to your hard disk isn't a drag and drop affair however, it necessitates highlighting the songs you want and either hitting the keyboard shortcut or a trip to the Song menu. You can, however, choose to organise the music you copy in folders by album or album and artist.

SONGBIRD
Price Free

getsongbird.com

Songbird comes from the same Mozilla developers who brought us Firefox and Thunderbird, so it has an excellent pedigree. And it's far more than just a method of copying music from your iPod to your Mac or PC. It's a fully-fledged, open source media player with support for a wide range of devices, including all iPods except the iPod touch and iPhone. To copy music from your iPod to your hard disk, just drag the music you want from the iPod track listing in Songbird onto a folder on your hard drive.

Songbird's developers freely admit that it has a long way to go: it can't rip CDs or play video, and support for metadata and album art is limited. But they're working on it and Songbird is shaping up to be the Firefox of media players.

IS IT LEGAL?

The issue of whether it's legal to rip music from your iPod to your Mac or PC is a thorny one. Technically, making a copy of any copyrighted work is illegal and can be a criminal offence. Many people believe that recording TV programmes or digitising your music collection is exempt from copyright law. It's not. Despite the fact that the technology is widely available, widely promoted, and widely used, it remains illegal in the UK to rip CDs. The position with regarding copying music in the other direction, from your iPod to your Mac or PC, is exactly the same.

The Gowers Report, published in December 2006 concluded that the UK's intellectual property regime was 'broadly satisfactory' but recommended changes with regard to the way the law regards copying media for personal use. Following that, the government published a consultation document in January 2008 and invited responses. That consultation ended in April 2008 and another one is due to open in late 2008. Until a bill is drafted and passed by Parliament, a process which could still take years, ripping CDs to your Mac or PC and copying them to or from your iPod remains illegal.

All of the above notwithstanding, no one has yet been prosecuted for digitising their music collection, nor are they ever likely to be. So there's no legal reason not to copy your own music from your own iPod to your own computer. Sharing your music freely is another matter however and won't be covered by future legislation. If you're caught doing that, you may well be prosecuted.

MUSIC RESCUE 4
Price £10

kennettnet.co.uk/musicrescue

Music rescue is a Mac and Windows application that can recover music from all current iPods, including the iPhone and iPod touch. It has a QuickRecover feature which allow you to recreate the iTunes Library from your iPod in its entirety on your computer. It also allows you to customise what music is copied across and how files are organised on your computer. Rules allow you to define which tracks are copied based on their metadata and there are a number of presets for common rules. Its media player allows you to play songs on your computer directly from your iPod.

Music Rescue is available in one of two formats: one allows you to use it with one iPod and multiple computers, the other with one computer and multiple iPods.

IPOD MUSIC LIBERATOR 5.1
Price $24.99 (about £14.82)

zeleksoftware.com/liberator.htm

iPod Music Liberator has a simple interface which enables access to some powerful features. In addition to recovering all the music from your iPod, complete with playlists, and even ratings, you can specify which music is copied. Liberator recognises which songs are already on your computer and allows you to copy only those which don't already exist on your hard drive. It has 'on the fly' searching and can automatically rename songs according to your preferred combination of track name, artist, and album. It can also organise files by album and artist on your hard drive. The most recent version, 5.1, supports the iPhone and iPod touch and there's a free demo version so you can try before you buy.

Encoding video for use on iPods

The last year has seen big growth in the amount of video available on the iTunes Store, in a format that's ready to watch on your computer in iTunes or to be transferred to an iPod or iPhone and watched wherever you choose. Yet they can both play video from other places too, including your home movies. This video just won't play while it's stored as an AVI, Mpeg or one of various other formats.

Instead your iPod needs video to be stored in any one of a small number of formats. It can play video that's formatted as Mpeg4 or H.264, with accompanying audio stored as AAC. These aren't the friendliest of terms and the exact specifications published on Apple's website only get more technical, but there's no need to stumble at the first hurdle as there's plenty of assistance on hand to help you get video onto your iPod.

iPods have been able to play video for quite some time now, so thankfully there's a selection of software to handle the technical conversion process to save you the hassle. All that you need to provide is the video. You also need to consider what you need to convert – a DVD, a TV recording or a file.

iTUNES AND QUICKTIME
iTunes includes a video converter but you'll quickly find that it's very limited. That's partly due to the types of video that can be added to the library; iTunes doesn't like Windows Media and AVI files, for example, and although multiplexed Mpeg movies (where the audio and video are interwoven) can be added, you'll run into a limitation of QuickTime (iTunes uses it to play back media) that strips the audio out, leaving just the video in the converted file.

QuickTime Pro has the ability to export movie files to the iPod, but it's not the friendliest of options. The best thing is to ignore Apple's cheapest options and look to one of the free or commercial applications that can do a better job.

CONVERTING FILES
There are plenty of applications to convert video files for the iPod, including some free ones. Mpeg Streamclip (*www.squared5.com*) is a versatile converter that's available for Windows and Macs and can handle AVIs, Mpegs and QuickTime files, and it doesn't suffer from QuickTime's lost audio issue when converting Mpegs. Even better, it can cue up several files for conversion, applying different settings to each one so that you don't have to worry if they don't all have the same aspect ratio or if you're content with some videos being encoded at lower quality.

Mpeg Streamclip is also a good option for grabbing a video from YouTube to stash on your iPod for later amusement. Just visit a YouTube video's page, copy its address to the clipboard, then choose File > Open URL and paste it into the dialog and choose the option to convert the video. By opening the batch list first, you can even cue up YouTube videos for conversion.

The downside for Windows users is that Mpeg Streamclip can't handle Windows Media Video, so you can rule it out for converting home movies or downloaded videos in this format. Both iPod Video Converter (*koyotesoft.com/indexEn.html*) and Videora iPod Converter (*videora.com*) can handle WMV though they are sponsored by advertising that loads directly into the application, but they are free to download and use.

CUSTOMISING PRESETS
You may need to change the presets supplied with applications such as Mpeg Streamclip and Handbrake, but always bear in mind the specifications quoted by Apple. It recommends that H.264 video is limited to 1500kbps for viewing on an iPod. Video purchased from the iTunes Store often comes close to this limit and that's why it looks so good, but that video has also been created from a high quality source.

The data rate simply sets a limit on how much bandwidth is allocated to the video and how much space it can take up on your iPod as a result. Apple also recommends a maximum of 160kbps for the accompanying audio.

Video quality depends heavily on the material you put into the encoder. If it's taken from a digital compact camera or from YouTube then it's already heavily compressed. Converting the video for your iPod means there is a risk of losing even more quality when the allocated data rate is too low, but recklessly increasing the data rate beyond Apple's recommendations may prevent the video playing on your iPod altogether.

The presets provided with the applications that we're talking are usually tuned to use a little bit less than the maximum, which proves unnecessary in many cases. This leaves you a little room for manoeuvre when video comes out blocky.

You don't really need to get into data rates unless you're keeping the converted files as part of a permanent archive, or if the original copy is already of noticeably low quality. That may be the case if you're taking old home movies back from DVD and, in particular, VHS or other analogue media, where the signal quality is already reduced.

Further degradation by compressing the video for iTunes and iPods generally exhibits itself as blockiness, especially when there's a lot of motion in the frame, such as when it pans across a scene or when it zooms in or out.

Footage shot with a video camera is also formatted for television. This means it's interlaced and televisions alternately draw all of the odd lines then all the even ones each time the screen updates. Watch on a non-interlaced display such as your computer or iPod and you'll often see an interlacing artefact called combing. It's often noticeable on fast motion, so keep an eye on family members that suddenly raise an arm or move quickly across the frame.

Many applications offer the option of deinterlacing your video, and sometimes there are different settings that affect the time spent analysing the source video. It also depends on the speed of your computer, and if it's particularly old then you'll want to steer clear of the more intensive settings, at least when working with long videos.

Although H.264 video can be very good quality, you'll find it takes a long time to encode on slow computers. This can be overcome by using Elgato's Turbo.264, a USB 2.0 stick for Macs that contains dedicated video-encoding hardware to speed up this process.

The speed boost will depend on your computer, and it's of less use to those with very fast, recent iMacs. Video files can be dropped into its companion software, and it can convert your home-made DVDs too. All you need to do is select a preset for each one. Mac owners can also use the hardware with Roxio's more versatile Popcorn 3 software.

CONVERTING FILES WITH MPEG STREAMCLIP

▲ **STEP 01** Choose File > Open Files. You can select several files but they'll appear joined together in the next window and the results of the conversion will be stitched together. Choose a single file and click Open, then play the file in the main window to ensure its video and audio can be seen and heard.

▲ **STEP 02** Choose File > Export to Mpeg-4 to show a window with an overwhelming number of settings. Ignore them and press the iTunes button at the top-right to reveal dedicated iPod and iPhone presets. All bar the 3GP setting encode high-quality H.264 video. We'll ignore the Apple TV and 3GP presets.

▲ **STEP 03** The presets are divided by width (320, 480 and 640 pixels) with two aspect ratios for each. The two smaller widths match the displays of the iPod classic and nano, and the iPhone and iPod touch, respectively. Use them for video that will only be watched on one of those players to conserve disk space.

▲ **STEP 04** Pods will scale down files produced by the 640-pixel-wide presets to fit. Their resolutions match TV shows sold on the iTunes Store and they're the best option if you may watch the video on your computer. They come at the expense of wasted disk space, though. Choose a preset and click OK.

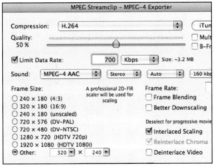

▲ **STEP 05** The presets are just starting points and can be tinkered with, so you can increase the video's data rate if the results are blocky. You can even go beyond Apple's quoted maximum values of 1500kbps, but there are no guarantees that your iPod will be able to play it.

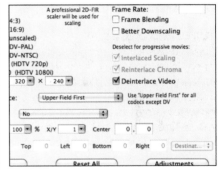

▲ **STEP 06** The Multipass option better analyses the original file to retain quality, while the Deinterlace Video option can reduce banding on video that was originally formatted for TV, such as DV camera footage. They'll increase the encoding time though. Any changes can be saved and retrieved using the Presets button at the bottom left.

▲ **STEP 07** When you're ready to convert your video, press the Make MP4 button at the bottom right of the dialog and choose a location and file name and you'll see two progress windows. Once finished, drag the file into the iTunes library, where it'll appear under Movies. Right-click it and choose Get Info to set appropriate metadata.

▲ **STEP 08** If you have many files to convert, choose List > Batch List and click the Add Files button. For files that require the same settings, choose them all now and click OK, then select Export to MPEG-4 and ensure the option to join the files is turned off to process them individually.

▲ **STEP 09** Choose the destination and the settings window from Step 2 will appear. Your choices will apply to each file selected in Step 8. Click To Batch to add the files to the list, where you can add more files that require different settings. When you're done, click Go to begin converting the whole list.

CONVERTING HOME-MADE DVDS

Now that you have a way to convert files, your edit of the next big family wedding or even just holiday footage can be put onto an iPod. What about all the ones you've produced in the past, for which you only have the final edit on DVD and perhaps the original, unedited version on tape? Don't worry as there's another free tool called Handbrake for Windows and Macs (*handbrake.fr*) that will step in to save the day.

Handbrake is just as detailed in settings as Mpeg Streamclip is for files, but they also have presets in common. They appear in a pane to the right of the window, where you'll find, among other things, an iPhone and iPod touch preset along with high and low resolution ones for other iPods that

correspond to the 320 and 640-pixel-wide presets in Mpeg Streamclip.

To convert a DVD, first copy its Video_TS folder to your hard drive. On windows, check beneath the Browse button that the Folder is selected, then click the button on Windows, or in the toolbar on a Mac, and point at the Video_TS folder. Handbrake will take a short

while to inspect it, after which you'll be able to choose which part to convert.

Now you can select the exact title, if your DVD is a compilation of several videos, and a range of chapters to be converted. Similar options for two-pass encoding and deinterlacing are available in Handbrake, too. Probably most important of all, since you'll likely use the presets, is the Chapters tab. Should your DVD contain such markers, they can be renamed from the dull numbered monikers to more descriptive titles that appear in iTunes and on your iPod.

Multiple titles can be queued for conversion before hitting the Start button on the toolbar to begin. Once you're ready, hit

the Add to Queue button and run through the process for any additional titles. Then press the Start button in Handbrake's toolbar to begin.

During conversion on Windows, a second window will appear that shows progress, whereas on the Mac the information appears in both the main window and the queue. Once the process is finished, its output can be dragged into your iTunes library and synchronised to your iPod.

POPCORN 3

Should you prefer an all-in-one solution that strips away all of the unnecessary detail of the Mpeg Streamclip and Handbrake windows then Roxio's Popcorn 3 (*roxio.co.uk*) fits the bill nicely and it's available for Macs and Windows. Its interface is very clean and uncluttered. Down the left you'll find two categories, but we only need the Player one at the bottom, which handles iPod conversions.

You can point at an unprotected physical DVD using the DVD Disc option or else point at a Video_TS folder located on your hard drive. After selecting a source, the button adjacent to it reveals title selection – Popcorn automatically selects the longest title on the disc, or you can select specific parts of the disc if you only want to convert video of a post-wedding reception, for example. Copying a DVD to the hard drive gives the added advantage that you'll be able to convert more than one DVD at a time.

Video files can be converted separately but also en masse just by dropping them into the main window. With everything lined up, hitting the red button asks you to select a device, video quality and where to save the output. Popcorn is a really easy solution to converting both DVDs and video files. It will also convert Windows Media Video even on a Mac, although there you'll have to purchase a Flip4Mac encoder (*flip4mac.com*) since the player will watermark your videos.

WHEN YOU'VE GOT VIDEOS INTO iTUNES

You can drag files directly to your iPod or iPhone from Windows Explorer (or the Finder on a Mac), but it must to be set to manually manage songs and videos. Enabling this option will erase the contents of your iPod, but adding the occasional video to your iPod is much easier as they can be dragged individually from the Movies and TV Shows sections of the library direct onto the iPod to transfer them, rather than having to use the Video tab and its awkward checkboxes.

MAKE TRACKS

THE DEFINITIVE GUIDE TO GETTING THE BEST OUT OF YOUR MP3 ENCODER FOR TOP NOTCH SOUND EVERY TIME.

Like us, you've probably spent some time ripping CDs into your MP3 collection. But have you been using the right settings, or are your precious tracks full of low-level distortions? And should you consider converting everything to the new AAC format that Apple's been championing? What about different playback conditions? Should you even care how iTunes is set up, or do you trust Apple to make all the right decisions for you? Over the following pages we'll explore the issues involved in turning out top-quality digital music files and look at what settings you need to get the best possible results.

To begin with, remember that converting music to MP3 or AAC formats is all about compression and compromise. Just as with photos that are saved using Jpeg image compression, the harder the source material is squeezed the lower the quality of the final result. One minute of CD-quality stereo sound takes just over 10MB of space, whereas a minute of the same audio turned to MP3 or AAC using standard settings will take little more than 1MB.

Budget MP3 players with solid-state memory typically have 512MB of storage, ready to take up to an hour of standard-quality music. It is just as frustrating having to constantly swap songs as it is boring listening to the same tracks all the time, so compressing songs to smaller sizes can be tempting. However, squeezing the life out of tracks can make them sound like seriously damaged goods. The result can be more annoying to listen to than a badly tuned radio station, so proceed with care and don't over-compress your tracks.

PUSH IT

At the other end of the scale, the iPod and other hard disk-based players offer many gigabytes of space; room for thousands of songs. Space isn't nearly as much of an issue if you have one of these and encoding to reduce file sizes as much as possible isn't an issue. This means you can go for quality, but how far should you try to push this?

The answer depends on a number of factors, from how much room you feel like

devoting to your music collection and how many CDs you're likely to encode, to what kind of equipment you'll use to play back your music and how carefully you listen to the sounds. The environment is also a key factor, particularly when it comes to pocket players such as the iPod. We listen to music in very different places, from the quiet of a library to the bustle of rush-hour buses and trains, while jogging, working out at the gym, and so on. Some people use their digital players as components in a hi-fi setup, playing the tracks through amplifiers and top-notch speakers. Of course, some do this with their Macs, playing music using iTunes, Audion or other player software. The more distractions of any kind the less you'll worry about minor imperfections, but you should work to the most demanding, revealing conditions.

The next question is how do you define good enough? We're a little sceptical when we read claims that these formats are CD-quality, particularly at standard settings. Lossy compression throws away sound data, so no matter how cleverly it does this there's always going to be some degradation. On the other hand, there are some that insist that any form of lossy audio compression is a sin, and that even regular CD-level audio (16-bit, 44.1kHz stereo) is barely good enough. This can be true when it comes to mastering audio and specialist archiving, but it just doesn't square up with real-world listening needs. It's important to balance perfectionism with realism, as with most tracks, you don't notice any difference, at least not through your average headphones.

You'll have to decide which format you'll use. AAC isn't MP3, and won't play back with software or hardware players that don't support AAC as well as MP3. The iPod handles AAC perfectly well, as does iTunes, of course. However, most other MP3 players don't, so if you think you'll stray away from the iPod/iTunes straight and narrow in the foreseeable future, you had better switch encoding to MP3.

The MP3 format has been around for many years. Like AAC, it provides efficient compression of sound. It can be read by just about every digital music player around, and the format name itself has been synonymous with digital music since the beginning of the millennium.

Apart from differences in player support, each format has its own foibles. Pre-echo (where a sharp sound is presaged by an echoing lead-in noise) is a common problem in MP3 encoding. AAC tends to lose the fine details of such sounds instead, and both suffer from various forms of audio artifacting where over-enthusiastic compression effectively damages the audio, adding

unwanted oddities to the sound. These differences are usually barely noticeable, but complex sounds, particularly with faster encoding and lower bit rates, will throw up more of these problems.

PLAYBACK

It isn't clear when AAC will be supported by other products. Playback in software is likely to happen without too much of a problem, as this is now a regular part of QuickTime. However, licensing AAC encoding technology for third-party software is a hugely expensive business; figures of more than $250,000 (about £144,000) per year for patent licensing have been mentioned, whereas the annual license for the Fraunhofer MP3 encoder is around $15,000 (about £8,600). You may think this isn't any of your concern, but it could affect the broader acceptance of the AAC format in the short term. Of course, if you're an iPod and iTunes junkie, you can use either format without worry. The choice then boils down to quality issues.

Picking an encoding setting isn't necessarily simple. The bit rate determines how many bits of data are used to store the sound and is measured in kilobits per second, or kbps for short. For many years 128kbps has been regarded as a happy medium: a good balance between quality and file size. The more critical listener will find this level less than perfect, though, and with today's low-cost multi-gigabyte hard disks and capacious iPods, it's wise to think about using higher-quality settings.

Before iTunes added the AAC format, it defaulted to MP3 at 160kbps. Our tests

TEAM JUDGEMENT

For our team judgement test we asked four music fans to listen to a sample from each key encoding type and bit rate. Each has their own opinions and preferences when it comes to music, from Aston Leach, who is a DJ in his spare time and brought his own headphones to the test, to Julian Torreggiani, a self-confessed X-Ray Spex fan. The samples they listened to were the ones that had been re-encoded 10 times to bring out the specific deficiencies far more clearly than standard encoding does.

Low-quality encoding (64kbps)	ASTON	CHRIS	JULIAN	NIK
AAC	Terrible. Similar to the LAME form of MP3 but even less inspiring.	Crude, but the best at this low bitrate; seems less muddy compared to higher-bitrate AAC.	Not as sharp as the MP3 tracks, but the whole thing is dogged by distortion.	This manages the best balance between the voice and instruments.
MP3 – FRAUNHOFER	This is the worst of all, it lacks clarity and is muffled and undefined.	A decent range, although definitely lacking higher sounds and notes as well as clarity.	Duller than the original, but less distortion; better than the LAME low-rate MP3.	Sounds like AM radio, with considerable distortion of loud brass sections.
MP3 – LAME	Strange noise accompanying this, like a cheap Dr Who sound effect.	Vocal and bass reasonably reproduced, but treble horribly messy with distortions.	Far too sharp, with lots of distortion and reverb, and echos in the background.	Quite unpleasant, with a lot of watery background noise.
Mid-quality encoding (128kbps)				
AAC	Lacks clarity and crisp high frequencies of the original. Dull, slight flange effects.	Soft and muddy, less offensive than the others. Listenable, but not obviously compressed.	Very dull, there's a complete loss of treble, echo on the voice and too bassy.	A narrow sound spectrum, it's heavy and lacks top end, but it's the best of the lot.
MP3 – FRAUNHOFER	Harsh and lacking the warmth of the original, amplified imperfections of the original.	A decent spectrum of sound, but some tinny popping echo in evidence.	This seemed practically identical to the LAME-encoded MP3 track.	Distorted voice, windy and noisy, with over-harsh trumpet sounds.
MP3 – LAME	Some harsh 'flanged' sounds, slightly more top sound equalised.	Horribly scratchy, squeaky sound in the background. Some loss of bass, but vocals OK.	A certain amount of hiss and warbling on the voice, and a loss of mellowness overall.	Lots of swishing background noise, like the sharpening of knives.
Best-quality encoding (192kbps)				
AAC	Still stripping the track of crispness at the top, slightly heavy mid and low tones.	This is still noticeably muddy compared to the original.	Some loss of clarity and all the treble seems to have been rounded off.	Better than the original recording; removed hiss at a cost of slight clipping of the voice.
MP3 – FRAUNHOFER	Good, but a bit dull in parts. Overall, the sound was pretty faithful to the original.	Pretty impressive. Very slight distortion apparent, mainly in vocals.	As with the other MP3 file, this sounded just like the original unencoded track.	This is still a little harsh; not a perfect reproduction of the song.
MP3 – LAME	The best of the bunch; kept the most detail throughout the song.	A slight loss in richness, with a noticeable tinny hissing in the treble end.	This version seemed to be identical to the original to my ears.	Brings the voice to the fore. Still not perfect when compared to the original.

WHY AAC?

So what is AAC and why has Apple decided to switch to this format? Technically, this is the audio compression format used in Mpeg-4 video, whereas MP3 was the format used in Mpeg-1 and Mpeg-2. Although it has been around for years, the MP3 format is the subject of copyright disputes. AAC, although pretty much the new kid on the block, is being established as the future-proof standard for audio compression. There's also the fact that QuickTime is part of the basis for the Mpeg-4 standard, so it makes perfect sense for Apple to support another aspect of the video standard. There's also the cynic's view: AAC provides the ability to copy-protect files while the MP3 format doesn't; a vital issue for the iTunes Music Store.

JARGON
Word up

MP3
Strictly speaking, Mpeg-1/2 Layer 3: the audio encoding format devised for Mpeg-1 and Mpeg-2 video.

AAC
Advanced Audio Coding: the audio encoding format used in Mpeg-4 video.

KBPS
The rate of information used per second to store audio data, in kilobits per second. Higher Kbps levels take more disk space than lower levels.

have shown this to be a fairly good option. By contrast, the 128kbps AAC format iTunes now starts with isn't quite as good in some areas. However, in our degradation tests it produced slightly more listenable results (as opposed to technically clearer results) than 128kbps MP3. Mid-tones felt closer to the original than with degraded MP3s, although high tones, particularly percussive elements, were muffled in standard AAC, as compared to the over-noisy results of MP3.

Variable bit rate (VBR) is an option in MP3 encoding, although not AAC. It means exactly what its name suggests: rather than using a specific throughput regardless of the sound being processed, the bit rate used to encode the audio varies. It does this according to the complexity of the music at any given point, so simpler passages will take fewer bits than more complex ones.

You still have some control over the final sound quality or file size. These are determined by a simple quality setting, which determines how much data is to be used on average, and equates, in a sense, to a fixed bit rate setting. Although pinning down precisely what bit rate a VBR setting will use on average is a futile exercise, it certainly is the case that higher-quality VBR levels will use more bits per second to encode a given portion of audio.

When VBR is selected in iTunes the bit rate selected determines the minimum rate that will be used in any circumstance; it determines the minimum quality rather than the maximum data throughput. The quality setting is related: as well as setting how hard the Mac works at making the right bit choices, it defines how far up the bit rate ladder the encoder will go when dealing with more complex sounds.

As we just mentioned, the quality setting for encoding also relates to the amount of computation taken to encode the audio, and it makes a significant difference to the end result. With quick-and-dirty encoding, your Mac has less work to do, but the results are more sloppy. If you force it to take longer working out the encoding, you'll get better-sounding music – eventually. Just how long a track takes to encode depends on a host of variables, but the difference between best and fastest encoding speed can be three times or more. Unless you're using a particularly slow Mac or PC and really can't hang about, pick the best quality every time.

SOUND CHECK

In order to find the best possible format for ripping CDs we created a series of test files using both MP3- and AAC-formatted tracks at different quality settings. We used Audion

INTERFACE OVERVIEW
iTUNES ENCODING

Most people will use iTunes for encoding and playback. The controls in iTunes' preferences offer a lot of customisation options, but they aren't all explained particularly well. In the Importing section of the preferences you have the option of choosing AAC or MP3. (You can ignore the AIFF and WAV encoders unless you have specific reasons for using them.) The Setting option for AAC is the basic 'High Quality (128kbps)' setting and Custom, which opens the detailed AAC Encoder dialog. Select MP3 and the Settings offer Good Quality, High Quality, and Higher Quality, at 128kbps, 160kbps and 192kbps, plus the Custom option, which opens the all-important MP3 Encoder dialog.

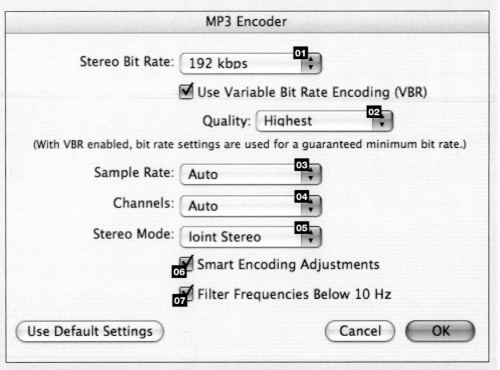

MP3 Encoder

Stereo Bit Rate: 192 kbps **01**

☑ Use Variable Bit Rate Encoding (VBR)

Quality: Highest **02**

(With VBR enabled, bit rate settings are used for a guaranteed minimum bit rate.)

Sample Rate: Auto **03**

Channels: Auto **04**

Stereo Mode: Joint Stereo **05**

06 ☑ Smart Encoding Adjustments

07 ☑ Filter Frequencies Below 10 Hz

Use Default Settings   Cancel   OK

TUNING IN iTunes' main encoding interface falls under the Advanced Importing section in its preferences. Select your format of choice from the Imports Using pop-up menu and then select Custom to bring up the detailed encoding dialogs shown here.

01 The Stereo Bit Rate setting determines how much data will be used per second of audio, in kilobits per second.

02 When the Variable Bit Rate option is selected the Quality options control the amount of extra data that's used for more complex portions of audio.

03 The Sample Rate option sets the sampling rate for the audio. This is almost always best left on Auto, as it will then always be set to match the sample rate of the music.

04 If you want to force encoded sounds to mono (saving roughly 50% of space) this is where to do it. Most users should leave it on Auto.

05 Joint Stereo handles stereo channel data differently to normal stereo, putting data that's the same on both into one channel, and storing the unique left and right data on the other. This saves some space at medium and lower bit rates.

06 With the Smart Encoding Adjustments setting checked, iTunes will adjust your settings

when necessary to improve the quality of the audio as you encode.

07 Filtering low frequencies will reduce file sizes to an extent without affecting the results to any appreciable extent, as those frequencies are below the hearing threshold.

JARGON
Word up

VBR
Variable bit rate: this uses more data per second for demanding sections of audio than for simpler sounds.

FRAUNHOFER
A copyright-protected MP3 encoder technology from Fraunhofer IIS (*iis.fraunhofer.de/amm*).

LAME
An open-source MP3 encoding technology. It stands for 'Lame Ain't an MP3 Encoder', see *lame.sourceforge.net* for details.

(*panic.com*), as it offers both Fraunhofer and LAME-based MP3 encoding, and iTunes 4.1 for MP3 (Fraunhofer) and AAC encoding. (LAME encoding can be added to iTunes using third-party software.)

It's not easy to judge the quality of formats designed to sound as good as possible, so we re-encoded each track again and again until it had gone through 10 generations. This compounded all of the slight failings of the different formats and settings until they became painfully obvious. Finally, a test panel listened to the results using a pair of high-quality headphones.

At low bit rates – 64kbps and 80kbps – the audio proved to be a long way off from what anyone would call comfortable music quality. The AAC file didn't have as much presence as either MP3 versions,

but as before it also lacked their level of pre-echo and over-sharpness. Both of them suffer from general warble-style artifacting that makes music sound terrible. However, this isn't as much of a problem for plain voice recordings, where the emphasis is on the meaning of the words rather than the precise timbre of the voice.

This is the kind of compression that's required for reasonable Web delivery. A 64kbps track takes less than 8K a second for streaming, and if it is encoded in mono it needs just 3.9K a second – that's less than 80K for a 20-second portion of sound. Of course, it doesn't sound great, but for background music or incidental sounds it can be better than no sound at all or painfully large files.

When we stepped up to a medium-level bit rate the differences were astonishing.

INTERFACE OVERVIEW

AUDION ENCODING

Panic's Audion offers three different MP3 encoding formats as standard. The first in Audion's list of MP3 encoders uses the Fraunhofer encoding method (labelled just MP3), while the second, as indicated by the name, MP3 – LAME, uses the open-source LAME encoder. The third, mp3PRO, hasn't taken off as yet and isn't covered here, as it doesn't perform well in non-Pro-aware players.
To bring up Audion's encoding options, select Encode from under the Console command in the Tools menu. Although, Audion provides more control over MP3 encoding and management than iTunes, it doesn't offer any form of AAC encoding.

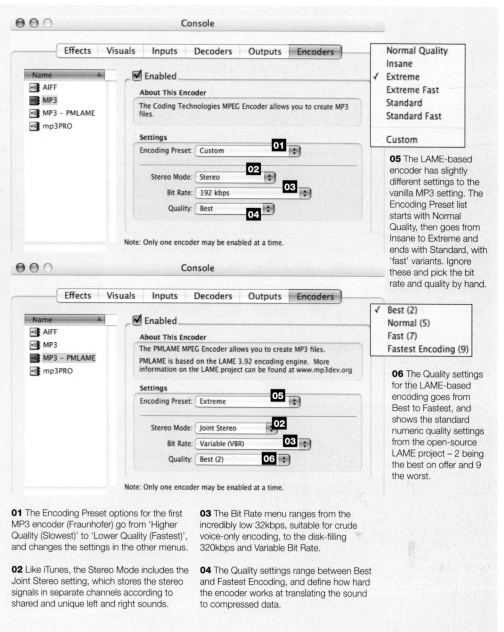

05 The LAME-based encoder has slightly different settings to the vanilla MP3 setting. The Encoding Preset list starts with Normal Quality, then goes from Insane to Extreme and ends with Standard, with 'fast' variants. Ignore these and pick the bit rate and quality by hand.

06 The Quality settings for the LAME-based encoding goes from Best to Fastest, and shows the standard numeric quality settings from the open-source LAME project – 2 being the best on offer and 9 the worst.

01 The Encoding Preset options for the first MP3 encoder (Fraunhofer) go from 'Higher Quality (Slowest)' to 'Lower Quality (Fastest)', and changes the settings in the other menus.

02 Like iTunes, the Stereo Mode includes the Joint Stereo setting, which stores the stereo signals in separate channels according to shared and unique left and right sounds.

03 The Bit Rate menu ranges from the incredibly low 32kbps, suitable for crude voice-only encoding, to the disk-filling 320kbps and Variable Bit Rate.

04 The Quality settings range between Best and Fastest Encoding, and define how hard the encoder works at translating the sound to compressed data.

At 128kbps settings both forms of MP3 encoding produced quite harsh, rough-edged results filled with exaggerated high-end attacks. This tended to dominate the sound in most recordings, despite the mid tones being not too far out from the originals. By contrast, the tenth-generation AAC encoding delivered sounds that lost much of the clarity of crisp high-end tones and felt muffled and oddly warbled overall. It felt as though the whole thing had been softened too much and then sharpened again, giving the sound a slightly unreal quality. However, it proved to be much easier to handle than the hissy fuzziness of the tenth-generation MP3.

At the higher end of 160kbps and above, the results were more pleasing, but not perfect. The tenth-generation 192kbps AAC file sounded slightly less accurate than

the MP3 files; there was a very slightly anaesthetised sense to the sound, whereas the MP3s held more detail but included clearer artifacting and traces of pre-echo. The AAC encoding did come across as being nicer on the ear. It must be said, though, that the AAC sounds were further from the original.

HIGH FIDELITY

For getting the best musical fidelity without filling up your Mac and iPod too quickly we recommend LAME-based MP3 at 192kbps or 224kbps, with VBR turned on and the highest quality option selected. These last two settings turned out to make a significant difference to the outcome, with VRB in particular preserving quality through successive encoding generations to an astonishing degree.

Our tests were performed using files that had been through their respective encoding processes 10 times over; the results we heard were greatly magnified compared with what you would normally experience. You should also remember that they point out the underlying damage that audio compression does, even at high-quality settings.

Should you care if you can't tell that there's a difference between the original sounds and the compressed version? Possibly not, but remember that the headphones or speakers you use tomorrow may be much better than the ones you use today. You should always try to encode to the best quality you might want without actually going back to your safely archived CD masters.

Servers

If you want to share your iTunes Library across several computers, check out these storage devices.

Hosting your iTunes music on your computer is fine if you are the only person in your house or office who wants to listen to it and if your music collection is small relative to your computer's hard drive. If, however, you have a large collection or want to allow access to other Macs and PCs at home or in the office, you might want to host your music on a server.

Network attached storage devices are ideal for this task, and not just those that list 'iTunes server' among their attributes. An 'iTunes server' is a storage device which shows up in the iTunes Shared list as if it were a Mac or PC on the network running iTunes with Sharing switched on. That allows you to play music stored on the server in iTunes on any computer in the network. However, it doesn't allow you to create playlists or otherwise organise your music.

The best way to use a network attached storage device with iTunes is to copy all your music onto it and then in iTunes Preferences, go to Advanced, click the General tab and uncheck 'Copy files to iTunes music folder when adding to Library.' Now go to iTunes' File menu and click 'Add to Library' and select the folder on your Nas which houses your music. The files will now be added to iTunes Library, while remaining stored on the Nas. You can also organise them into playlists as if they were stored on your hard drive. Do this on each computer on the network and each family member or office colleague can create their own playlists from the same music library.

There is one problem with this approach. If you buy songs from iTunes on one machine, or you rip a CD on that machine, the songs will be added to the appropriate folder on the Nas, but won't be propagated to the playlist of the other iTunes Libraries on the network. In order for the music to be added, you'll have to manually Add to Library on each machine. If you only buy tracks or rip CDs occasionally, this may not be too much of a problem but if you're in the process of ripping your entire CD collection and want it available on every machine on the network, it's more of an issue. You'd have to remember to manually add every CD you rip which probably means taking notes

and working your way around every Mac and PC on the network with it.

There are, however, ways to make this less of a problem, and in any case, in our view it's still preferable to having a list of songs on a shared drive that you can't organise into playlists. One solution is to create a new folder on each occasion you rip CDs or buy tracks. Give the folder a name that includes the date you rip the CDs or buy the tracks and store the music in that folder within the folder that houses your music on the Nas. That way, when you come to add tracks to the Library on a different machine, rather than trying to remember what CDs you've ripped recently or referring to notes, you can search for folders with dates after the last time you added tracks to that machine's Library — assuming you can remember roughly when that was. You still have to manually add the tracks on each machine on the network but you've made finding tracks that you haven't yet added much easier.

One alternative to hosting your music on a Nas box is to store it on one of the Macs or PCs on the network and share it from there, either on the computer's internal hard drive, or an external drive. The main problem with this approach is that in order to access the music library, its host computer will have to be running. If the host computer is permanently on or if it is on whenever the other machines on the network are in use, that's not an issue. However, booting a Mac or PC purely to serve music is less convenient than using a Nas. A Nas is more likely to be up and running and can be started more quickly than a computer, and is more environmentally friendly as the computer will usually use more power than the Nas box.

Another option is to store your music on an external portable hard drive or USB stick and build a library on each computer based on the music on that device. However, the disadvantages of this solution are that only one user can access the music library at a time (unless you have multiple copies on multiple devices), portable drives and USB sticks get lost or misplaced, and you still have the issue with adding music from different machines on the network.

All in all, if you want to share music between multiple machines over a network, a Nas is the best solution, although by no means perfect. With that in mind, you'll need to choose which Nas best suits your needs. Nas devices can be split into two categories, wireless and non-wireless. The former category usually has an Ethernet, probably gigabit, port and support for 802.11g or 802.1n wifi. The latter, just a Gigabit Ethernet port. Which you go for should be determined by whether or not you have a wireless network, obviously, and where your router is located in relation to where you want to position the Nas.

If the router and the Nas are likely to positioned close together, for example, there's no point paying extra for a wireless Nas, just get a wired model and hook it up to a spare Ethernet port on your router. You'll then be able to access it from any computer that has wired or wireless access to the router. If, on the other hand, you want to lock the Nas in a cupboard, away from your router then a wireless device may be essential. Don't discount wired-only Nas devices, though, as many have a USB port into which you can plug a wifi adaptor. That option may be significantly cheaper than buying a wireless Nas. And if you have a powerline element to your network, where data is shuttled around using the ring main in your house or office, you could buy a wired device and a powerline adaptor, assuming you have a spare power socket close to the Nas.

The other factor you should consider when choosing a Nas device is data security and transfer rates. Many Nas boxes have multiple drives or can be bought as bare bones boxes with multiple drive bays. These devices can be configured using a system known as Raid, which stands for redundant array of independent disks, which can be used either to maximise data transfer or provide an automatic back-up of your data by mirroring everything you copy to it on two or more disks. If you're planning on using a Nas to house your music and video collection, having a mirrored back-up which you can use immediately should one disk fail is a very good idea.

LACIE NETWORK SPACE

Price £165 (£140 ex VAT) for 1TB
Contact LaCie + *lacie.co.uk*

LaCie's network space doesn't have most of the software features of the Thecus or the Buffalo, instead it offers 500GB, 750GB or 1TB of storage on a stylish hard drive. The Network Space connects using gigabit Ethernet and has a media server and an iTunes server.

There's a USB port on the front which allows you to connect a USB hard drive or digital camera in order to transfer files to the Network Space. It's got one hard drive which is configured with one public share and one password-protected private share. The Network Space can be accessed remotely using FTP.

While the Network Space doesn't have the security of two mirrored drives, or allow you to use it as a print server, it's a stylish, reasonably priced Nas and one of the few that you won't be desperate to hide away in a cupboard.

THECUS N299

Price £250 (£213 ex VAT) for 1TB
Contact Origin Storage + *originstorage.com*

The N299 is a two-disk Nas which supports striping (Raid 0) where data is 'striped' across both drives to make transfer quicker, or mirroring (Raid 1) which copies everything to both disks, providing you with two identical copies of your data.

The two drive bays can hold up to 500GB, giving a maximum capacity of 1TB if you choose striping, or 500GB if you mirror your data. The N299 has an iTunes server and media server, but it also has a photo server for sharing digital photos and can be made wireless by plugging in a USB wifi adaptor. There's also a USB port on the front which allows you to plug in a USB memory stick and copy its contents to the N299 at the click of a button.

When we tested the N299 for MacUser, we found that setting it up was remarkably straightforward. There's a utility on the accompanying CD which when installed on your Mac or PC, allows you to perform a basic set-up and then access the Thecus's configuration pages in a web browser. There are dozens of menus and options here, but the PDF manual explains each one clearly. Unlike many Nas devices which require you to use Samba to connect to them, Mac users can specify Apple File Sharing Protocol (AFP) to use with the N299.

IOMEGA STORCENTER

Price £241 (£205 ex VAT)
Contact Iomega + *iomega-europe.com*

Where the Network Space and MyBook are stylish, the StorCenter is probably best kept under a desk or in a cupboard. It's available as a 1TB device and houses two Sata II 500GB hard drives which can be configured as Raid 0 or Raid 1. It connects to your network by gigabit Ethernet and has two USB ports which can be used to connect up to two printers, or four external hard drives (with a USB hub).

It supports the native network file formats in Windows, Mac and Linux, and can also be accessed remotely using FTP. It has a media server, but no iTunes server. As we noted earlier, however, you can still store your music in a folder on the StorCenter and tell iTunes to build its library from that on any computer on the network.

The StorCenter comes with a copy of EMC's Retrospect backup and recovery software.

BUFFALO LINKSTATION LIVE

Price £180 (£154 ex VAT) for 1TB
Contact Buffalo + *buffalo-technology.com*

Buffalo makes a range of Nas boxes under the LinkStation and TerraStation names. LinkStation Live is the name it gives to its range designed for the home media market because it has software for sharing music and video files and acting as an iTunes server. As we noted on the previous page, running an iTunes Server like this isn't necessarily the best way to share an iTunes Library over a network, but having media streaming capability could be useful. For example if you own, or plan to buy a DLNA (Digital Living Network Alliance) certified media adaptor from the likes of Pinnacle, Netgear, or Roku, the Linkstation Live will be able to share its media files with the adaptor. The Linkstation Live has a single 7200rpm hard drive, available in capacities from 250GB to 1TB. It also has two USB ports which can be used to connect a USB hard drive for additional storage or for connecting a digital camera and downloading pictures directly to the LinkStation.

You can also make scheduled back-ups to a USB hard drive. There's a built-in print server so you can share your printer over the network and the gigabit Ethernet port auto-senses whether its connected to a 10-Base-T, 100-Base-T, or gigabit network. There's no wireless support, however.

NETGEAR READYNAS DUO

Price £460 (£391 ex VAT) for 1TB
Contact Netgear + *netgear.co.uk*

Netgear's ReadyNas Duo ships with a hard drive installed in one of it's two Sata II drive bays, and the other bay empty. You can install your own hard drive, which must be at least the same capacity as the existing disk, to enable Netgear's propriety backup system to mirror the original drive and keep a perfect copy. If disaster strikes, the second drive will automatically take over.

The Netgear ReadyNas Duo supports native network file formats for Windows, Mac, and Linux, connects to your network over gigabit Ethernet and has media sharing support for iTunes, universal plug and play, Logitech's Squeezebox, and Sonos. It has 3 USB ports which can be used to connect hard drives or USB memory sticks to download files or add extra storage or a printer for printer sharing. The ReadyNas can be accessed through a web browser from anywhere on the Internet and a built-in BitTorrent client allows files to be downloaded to it without the need for a computer on the local network — it can be controlled from the remote web browser interface.

The ReadyNas might be overkill if all you want to do is share your iTunes Library on your network, but if you like the sound of the other features, it's well-specified and reasonably priced. Just remember to budget for an additional hard drive if you want to take advantage of the automatic back-up.

WESTERN DIGITAL MYBOOK WORLD EDITION

Price £150 (£128 ex VAT) for 1TB
Contact Western Digital + *westerndigital.com*

The MyBook World Edition is part of Western Digital's popular range of MyBook storage devices. However, it's not supported on the Mac. It should work with Mac OS X 10.4.10 or later, by connecting using SMB, but if you have a Mac, you're better off with one of the other options here.

The MyBook World Edition is stylish in a white casing that when placed on a shelf looks like a book. It has a circular capacity gauge on the rear which is a handy way of judging how much space is left without having to check on your PC. It's available in capacities of 500GB, 750GB, and 1TB and connects to your network using gigabit Ethernet. There's also a USB port to allow you to plug in a USB hard drive for additional storage.

There's no wireless option and no media or iTunes server. But if you want an elegant, reasonably priced Nas to store your iTunes Library on, the MyBook World Edition could be it.

MASTERCLASS
Create a speech autocue using QuickTime Pro

Use QuickTime Pro to produce a speech autocue for your iPod…

Kit required QuickTime Pro + iTunes + TextEdit and a video iPod
Time 15 minutes
Goal To use an iPod as a handheld autocue device
Skill level Intermediate

For most of us, public speaking doesn't come easily. Professionals, whether TV presenters or politicians at annual conferences, have the benefit of an autocue to help them deliver their lines confidently and appear relaxed at the same time. Why not use your iPod to give yourself the same advantages?

QuickTime Pro is useful for all sorts of things. You can join together several short movie clips, create a chapter list, create picture in picture effects, record and add a voiceover to a movie and subtitle video using a text overlay. This Masterclass shows you how to use a text track in QuickTime Pro to produce vertically scrolling text, which you can then download to a video iPod to turn it into the perfect handheld

autocue, ideal for every public speaking event, from work presentations to weddings.

QuickTime Pro is an optional upgrade to QuickTime and costs £20. To upgrade you need a licence key, which you can buy from the Apple website. It's a sound investment, though, as it unlocks some great features. Some software applications, such as Apple's Logic Studio, include a QuickTime Pro Licence. If some of the menu items on the QuickTime player are greyed out and have a Pro tag next to then, you need to upgrade.

Technology can be great, but it can also run out of power just when you need it most. If you're making a presentation then don't forget to cover yourself and carry a paper backup, just in case…

INTERFACE

First, write your speech and save it as a .txt file using a text editor such as TextEdit.

QuickTime Pro converts the text, adding descriptors to automatically format it. You can edit this file in TextEdit.

Finally, export the file for playback on your iPod.

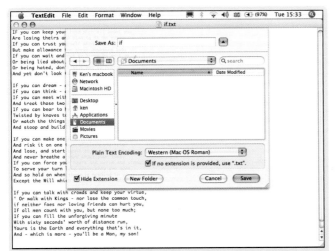

▲ **STEP 01 CREATE THE TEXT** Launch TextEdit and write your speech, this is the hardest bit and not something we can help you with. Save the speech as a .txt file. If the save dialog box doesn't provide .txt as an option, open Preferences and check the Plain Text radio button on the New Document panel, create a new document, paste your text into it and save it.

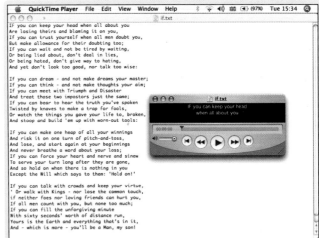

▲ **STEP 02 IMPORT TO QUICKTIME** Launch the QuickTime Player and select File > Open File to import the text file, then click on the play button. QuickTime automatically formats the text to play as a slideshow, with each slide displayed on the screen for two seconds. The text track is in vector format so you can resize the movie window without pixellating the text.

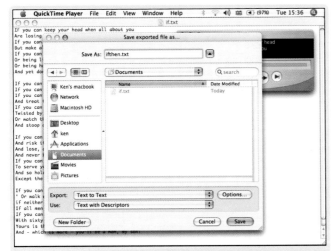

▲ **STEP 03 EXPORT FROM QUICKTIME** Text appearance is determined by descriptors in the text file. You can edit these to change the formatting, for example to change the font attributes, change the slide duration, or make the text scroll. First, you export the text from QuickTime. Select Export and choose Text to Text from the menu and Text with Descriptors from the Use menu.

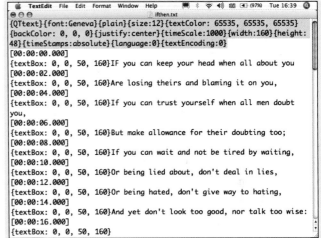

▲ **STEP 04 BACK TO TEXTEDIT** Open the exported file in TextEdit. Most of the formatting descriptors that QuickTime Pro added to display the text as a slideshow are reasonably self-explanatory. The first couple of lines define the file as a QuickTime text track, set the font attributes and set the movie size.

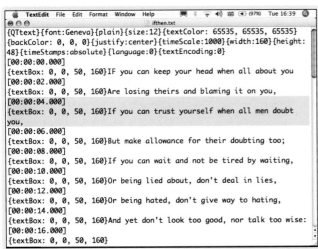

▲ **STEP 05 SLIDE SPLITTING** The remaining lines split the file into slides. The TextBox descriptor puts each block of text into a 50 x 160 box, which will appear in the top left of the screen if the text track is placed over a larger movie track. The line above each textbox is the time, from the beginning of the text track, that the 'slide' is displayed.

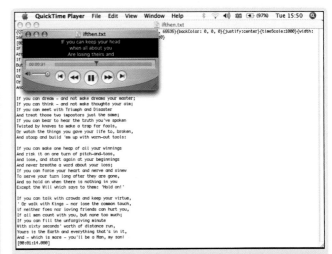

▲ **STEP 06 REPLACE THE SLIDES** We're going to scroll the entire speech in one text block, so delete everything between the [00:00:00.000] start marker and the [00:01:14.000] end marker and paste in its place the original speech text. Save the file and reopen it in the QuickTime player.

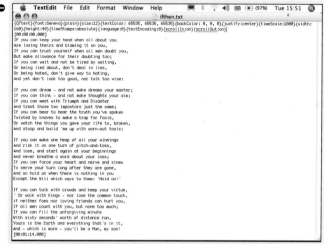

▲ **STEP 07 SET THE SCROLL** Only the first three lines of text are now displayed – there isn't room for the rest and we haven't yet added the commands to scroll the text. Return to the edited text file in TextEdit and add the following after *{textEncoding:0}*:
{scrollIn:on}{scrollOut:on}

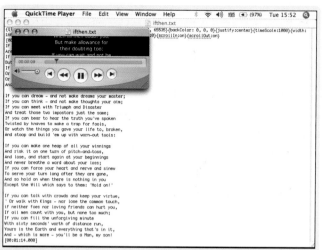

▲ **STEP 08 TEST PLAY** Save the file and reopen it in the QuickTime player. The entire speech should now scroll vertically from beginning to end. The speed of scrolling is determined by the amount of text and the length of the text track. To slow down the scroll speed, we need to lengthen the track duration marker in the last line of the text file.

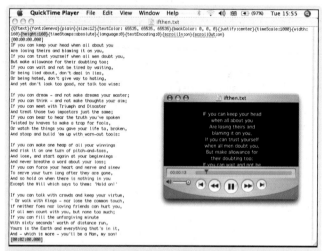

▲ **STEP 09 SLOWER SCROLLING** The track duration marker is currently set to [00:01:14.000], or 1 minute and 14 seconds. Change it to [00:02:00.000] to extend the length to 2 minutes and slow the text scrolling to about half the speed. While you're at it change the {height} value to 160 to display more lines of text. Save the text file and open it in the QuickTime player

▲ **STEP 10 EXPORT THE MOVIE** Select Export from the file menu and choose Movie to Mpeg-4 from the Export pull-down menu. If you choose Movie to iPod the text won't display as there is no video track. Only choose movie to iPod if, for example, you're using text as a subtitle track for a movie. And finally click on Save.

▲ **STEP 11 DELIVERY** Launch iTunes and drag the exported mp4 file into your library then sync with your iPod. If things get ahead of you, for example if you need to pause more than you anticipated for bouts of prolonged laughter, applause and the odd standing ovation, just press the pause button on your iPod until you are ready to continue.

▲ **STEP 12 PREVIEW** Text overlays can be used for more than speaking engagements. You can subtitle movies and caption slideshows. Text descriptors allow you to position text anywhere on screen and you can make it scroll horizontally as well as vertically. For a list of all the available text descriptors, go to *apple.com/quicktime/tutorials/textdescriptors.html*.

#1 for power and ease of use
3D Software That Fits

CINEMA 4D
RELEASE 10.5

If you're the type of person who likes to forget your surroundings and conjure up images from your imagination, then try CINEMA 4D.

Renowned for its ease of use and powerful 3D toolset, CINEMA 4D has everything you need to create the highest quality pictures and animations of whatever you can imagine. From a fantasy chair to motion graphics to a sun-kissed hotel complex.

With unrivalled support for Photoshop, Illustrator, After Effects, Final Cut Pro, Shake and more, CINEMA 4D makes it easy to combine 3D with your other artwork. But don't take our word for it. Try the CINEMA 4D demo at www.maxon.net.

- **Unrivalled power and ease of use**
- **Supports Photoshop, Illustrator, After Effects, Final Cut Pro, Shake, …**
- **Superior render quality**
- **Outstanding value for money**

MAXON | 3D FOR THE REAL WORLD

www.maxon.net

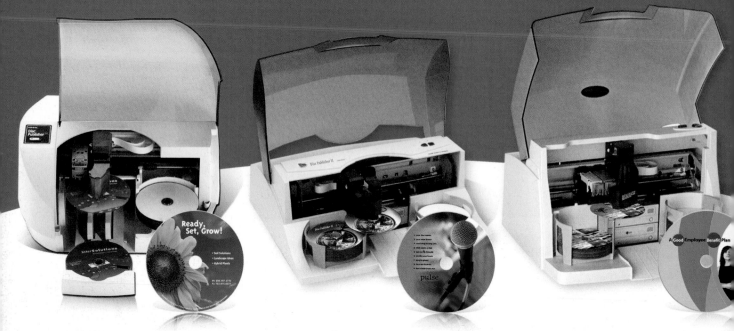

Features

112 Podcasting for profit

116 DJing with your iPod

120 Who really created the iPod?

126 iPod timeline

130 Back to the future for the iPod

132 Old vs new

134 Best iPod websites

138 iPod Q&A

140 Troubleshooting

144 iPod glossary

Podcasting
for profit

Podcasting is the rebellious child of radio. It's kids in their bedrooms telling us about skatepark life, it's sex-crazed couples revealing their most intimate secrets, and it's so-called experts holding forth on subjects about which they know very little. Or at least it was.

First, the BBC saw the potential of putting its radio programmes online, replaying *In Our Time* and *From Our Own Correspondent* through our iPods. Then the Americans caught on, bringing National Public Radio to a worldwide audience. The trouble was, it didn't pay. Enter London talk station LBC, the world's first media outlet to make money from its podcasts. To see how they did it, we caught up with David Lloyd and Dave Walters, the two men heading the most revolutionary take on radio since the switch to FM.

▲ **LBC's David Lloyd (left) and Dave Walters.**

David Lloyd bought an MP3 player recently. His first one, and all he'll say about it was that it wasn't an iPod. Nothing extraordinary about that, you may think, until you realise that he's recently become one of the most important players in the booming world of podcasts.

He spends his days running LBC, London's only commercial talk station, from a converted brewery in a well-heeled London borough. A relative newcomer to a place where some of the on-air staff can boast 20 years behind the same set of mics, Lloyd was brought in from parent group Chrysalis Radio's music stations to broaden its appeal and bring in the cash without busting the budget.

Where talk is concerned, that's no simple task, for while the likes of Capital, Absolute or Forth One can play a library of familiar tracks cycled week in-week out, LBC has nothing but the skill of its staff and the wit of its callers.

'You can't hide behind jingles and music,' Lloyd tells us, explaining where much of his budget is spent, and comparing LBC's output to an equivalent 24-hour breakfast show, the most expensive programme on any station's roster. 'The presenters are the one commodity on which the station can sell itself, and so we have to pay premium fees to attract premium talent.'

Yet these are lean times for the broadcast media. There are now more than 200 digital stations in the British Isles, and many times that number operating on the grace of an analogue AM or FM licence. They're competing with an ever-expanding number of low-grade satellite TV networks, websites and magazines for a viable share of a national advertising budget that, when split so many ways, gets smaller every year.

From the moment Lloyd arrived to build on LBC's past financial success, it was clear he could no longer rely solely on advertisers to stump up the cash.

Enter Dave Walters. For the last eight years, he's been Chrysalis' technical manager, running the studios of its expanding radio empire. When Lloyd decided it was time to supplement LBC's existing free 'best of' downloads service with a premium-rate podcast experiment, he turned to Walters.

There were no guarantees in those earliest days, and no one could predict what the financial impact might be. The station's emerging channels team had put together a proposal, accompanied by an unsustainable list of costs that made for grim reading. Hosting, billing, staffing... and combined they far outweighed even the most optimistic revenue projections.

Lesser teams might have given up at that point, but Walters had the support of a dynamic manager. 'Chrysalis is a good company to work for,' he explains, recalling the initial discussions. 'There's a real desire to move forward with good ideas like this, and you often find things are well funded just so we can work out what the business model will be, even if in the long run it means we pour money down the drain.'

The problem was, no one was really sure before it got off the ground how – or if – you could charge for an online duplicate of something that was available free of charge to anyone with a £10 tuner or a basic Sky box.

And then Lloyd had a brainwave: tangents. 'It's a bit like the way in which ITV1 shows a programme, and then ITV2 shows a behind-the-scenes documentary immediately afterwards,' he explains, outlining his vision for successful premium-content webcasting that supplements rather than duplicates what's already available free to air.

The station had already been outputting free 20-minute best-of podcasts that soared in popularity – so it was this simple tweak of an already proven format that brought about such success. But things hadn't always been quite so formalised. Although the premium podcasts were launched with plenty of notice and on-air advertising, the free-to-web highlights had appeared out of the blue.

Broadcast news

The original announcement that LBC would be moving into podcasts came as a surprise to many, not least for the station staff themselves. Phil Riley, divisional chief executive for Chrysalis' radio operations, made the announcement at an industry dinner in September 2005, when he explained to fellow diners that LBC would be putting out its debut podcast by the end of the week. The first his staff knew of these plans was when they arrived at work the next morning. Undaunted, they went away and put his plans into action, and indeed had podcasts up and running by the very next afternoon.

It was a quick fix, highly staff-intensive, that relied on the station's producers to record and re-edit the raw output before uploading it to the web. This was fine; it worked, and it fulfilled a promise, but it was clear that it wouldn't work as a long-term fix. If it was to podcast on a bigger and better scale than anyone else, it would have to implement an automated – or at least semi-automated – system, to reduce the potential workload on its staff.

The solution was a bespoke in-house application to interface with the Burli and PowerLog software that already recorded the station's news and programme output. This in-house answer, World of Podcasts, would read in not only the broadcast audio, but also all the actions performed on the mixing desks, such as opening and closing the mic faders, or switching to travel and ads. Any non-programme content, such as weather reports and station promos could then be quickly identified, based on the state of the faders and automatically stripped out, leaving the producers with a clean audio file ready for upload to the server.

The result is a 64Kbits/sec MP3 stream that should – technically – be of slightly better quality than the station's Mpeg 2 DAB output, although whether the untrained ear could discern this is open to debate.

Premium podcasting was under way, and although it may have started as an experiment, listener reaction has been better than Lloyd could ever have hoped for. In just five days of promoting the service on air, it had clocked up more than 80,000 premium, paid-for downloads. At least part of the credit for that must go to the free best-of

PODCASTING?

Podcasting was declared 'word of the year' by the *New Oxford American Dictionary*, a spin-off from the *New Oxford Dictionary of English*. Many associate it almost exclusively with the iPod, although some sources claim that the 'pod' half of the term was first coined in September 2004 by Doc Searls to denote 'personal option digital', while a month later 'podcast' in full was being used to denote personal on-demand broadcast.

LONDON'S BEST CONVERSATION

LBC is owned by the Chrysalis Group. It broadcasts in London on 97.3FM, online at *lbc.co.uk* and on Sky Digital, channel 927. It held the first-ever live radio phone-in show hosted by a serving British Prime Minister, Tony Blair. It was the UK's first legal commercial radio station, launched on 8 October 1973, and has been bought and sold many times since then, eventually passing to Chrysalis in 2002. Its call sign stands for London Broadcasting Company, although one presenter once famously changed that to I'll Be Seein' You (LBCing you). The parent company started out as Chrysalis Records – the name based on its two founders, Chris Wright and Terry Ellis. Founded in 1969, it has since published Carter USM, Blondie and Billy Idol among others. Chrysalis Records was sold to EMI in 1991.

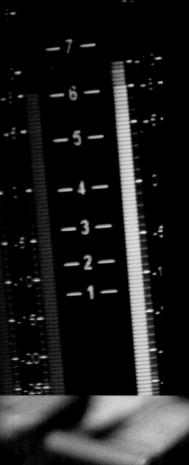

streams that had been running for the previous four months, and clearly done much to prepare the ground. They had regularly topped the iTunes podcast charts, with the station serving 45% of its million-plus downloads through iTunes. The station switched hosting companies four times before it found one with the resources to meet its needs.

The demand was seemingly insatiable, and extended far beyond the narrow group of young, middle-class urbanites we'd usually call the 'iPod Generation'. Lloyd has kept an email from one listener, a 70-year-old Londoner, who bought an iPod specifically to listen to the service, but subscribed for just a three-month trial in case she didn't live to see the end of the project's first year.

Others are slow to follow her lead, a fact Lloyd understands only too well. LBC's audience is fairly unusual; infinitely diverse and unpredictable, attracted by the lure of its general-interest non-news, non-sport output, which makes it almost unique in UK radio. It was the first legal commercial station in the country, and many of the listeners have been with it since day one: 8 October 1973.

From launch, then, an alternative to the iPod was a requirement, not an option, satisfied by the inclusion of a Flash player on the station's own site. For the same reason, it was important to talk about each podcast's content rather than the delivery mechanism, with LBC selling them on the merits of the presenters putting them out – comedians Iain Lee and Jenny Eclair, *Big Breakfast* co-host Paul Ross and others – and it's paid off. '£1.60 a month [if you sign up for six months] isn't bad at all for unrestricted access to Clive Bull, Steve Allen, Jenny Eclair, Iain Lee, James O'Brien and Anna Raeburn,' writes LBC subscriber

Rajesh Joshi who signed up when he found that the best-of feeds were too brief to give him a proper LBC fix every time he strayed outside the broadcast area.

Now that Chrysalis has proved revenue-generating podcasts are a possibility rather than an optimistic theory, it's all but certain that other broadcasters will follow, although once again this is a bandwagon that Apple seems reluctant to leap on with any kind of enthusiasm.

'Apple was good when we were having trouble getting things listed on the podcast directory,' Walters explains. 'But they didn't seem interested in getting premium content sorted out. iTunes is the ideal place [for feeding podcasts] because it already has a charging mechanism, but it doesn't have a model to fit [precisely] what we are doing now.'

Lloyd echoes his thoughts: 'I suspect that if Apple could put something in its software to let people charge for podcasts, then it could be very successful.'

It's as well, then, that LBC finds itself in an enviable position – as a side-effect of spending so much on producing 100% speech-based output, it has a rights-free revenue stream from owning copyright on all its products. A music station might find it difficult to copy this proven model, and would have to reassure the record companies that what could be a money maker for the broadcaster won't sap the artists' incomes as the unprotected MP3 streams are copied and handed around.

The lack of controls in iTunes' podcasting model could see it shunned by premium podcasters unless Apple starts to take them seriously. 'iTunes supports podcasting, which is great,' says Walters. 'But it doesn't support any kind of premium podcasting and if we need to protect our podcasting with Windows Media, then that doesn't fit with the iTunes model, so I'm not entirely sure that iTunes has a future in this.'

Whichever channel ends up as the delivery mechanism, the winner will be the listener, even if that listener has no access to an iPod, iTunes or a broadband connection. 'The podcasting experiment is a good testing ground as it's free from broadcast regulation,' says Lloyd, outlining how it's being used to trial new and innovative ideas that may not work on live radio.

Those ideas that prove themselves in a podcast will most likely find their way into the station's mainstream FM, DAB and Sky broadcasts, opening up to listeners in London – and beyond – fresh and innovative content that might otherwise never have made it to air.

DJing with your iPod

The Beastie Boys may have summed up DJing as two turntables and a microphone, but now those turntables are under threat as the iPod gains popularity in nightclubs.

It's not surprising really as a fully loaded iPod can store thousands of tracks and even the burliest of DJ isn't going to be able to lug that volume of vinyl around. And as musical tastes become more eclectic, with clubs nights often varying widely from house, to hip-hop with reggae and funk in between, only a digital DJ can handle such a musically diverse crowd.

However, DJing with an iPod isn't as straightforward as it might seem – there are several hurdles that digital DJs will need to overcome. But as we'll see new technology is starting to come to the rescue.

► The Numark iDJ was one of the first iPod mixing decks.

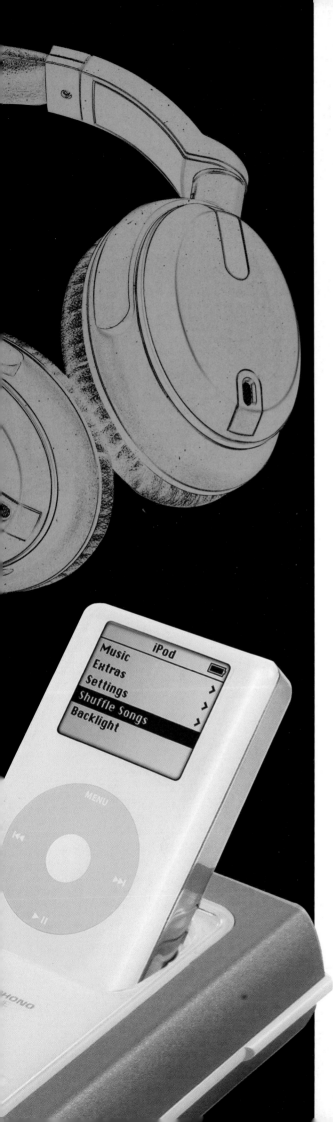

Whoever put the 'i' in iPod obviously felt that Apple's little white box of tricks was destined to be a lone listening experience, much like Sony's Walkman, which was in many ways the iPod's spiritual predecessor. However, the iPod was born into a world that had become obsessed with the cult of the DJ, thanks to the massive popularity of dance music. Given these cultural conditions it seemed that the iPod was always destined to get dragged into the world of DJing and that's exactly what has happened.

In the beginning, people started using their iPods to pump out music at private parties. All that was needed was a simple audio lead to connect the iPod's headphone socket to the input on the music system, then once you picked a playlist your iPod acted as the DJ for the night.

It was only a small step from here to actually DJing with an iPod rather than just relying on it to play a selection of tracks. During 2003 and 2004 club nights such as NoWax and Playlist started springing up in London. The clubs didn't have any official DJs. Instead punters could just turn up with their iPod, add their name to a list and wait their turn before getting the chance to DJ for 15 or 20 minutes.

'We liked the feeling of subverting a personal technology into becoming a social and connected thing that everyone could share,' says Jonny Rocket, co-founder of the Playlist night that has run in various venues around London.

The fun thing about these nights was that everyone could have a go – there was no need to spend hours practising in your bedroom to learning how to beat mix or scratch. As a result these clubs drew a broad cross section of music lovers. 'Goths, indie kids, grime enthusiasts, all kinds of music fans would turn up and give it a go,' says Rocket. 'Many of them found it as addictive as karaoke.'

By now even more 'normal' DJs were starting to take notice. They found that it was easy to connect an iPod to a DJ mixer and use it to cue in tracks along side those being spun from vinyl or CD decks. However, this change was also being driven by a change in the way dance labels were starting to distribute promotional copies of their releases.

Smaller labels used to send out exclusive mixes of tracks to DJs on either an acetate or a white label. An acetate is a reference disk cut by a producer or sound engineer. It can be played on a standard record deck, but is more fragile than vinyl and will wear out quickly. A white label is a vinyl 12inch produced as a small run and supplied in a white sleeve without any artwork – hence the white label tag. Pressing acetates and vinyl is relatively expensive and as most records are now recorded digitally it seemed ludicrous to distribute them via an analogue medium.

This is why many labels stopped sending out acetates and vinyl and instead started emailing tracks directly to DJs. In this way a producer could finish a track at 6pm and a DJ could be playing it out to a live crowd by 9pm. However, it also meant that DJs needed to add an MP3 player, such as the iPod, into their arsenal of mixing technology.

As a result of these changes even big name DJs have now started to wean themselves off their vinyl addiction. Pete Tong, for example, says that most of his vinyl collection is in storage now and when he DJs it is usually with digital tracks in MP3 format.

Of course, the iPod was never designed as a tool for DJs, so those using it to mix tunes have had to adapt. Early on most DJs connected it to the audio line-in on their mixing desks. They could then cross-fade between the iPod and vinyl or CD decks using the mixer. Some even replaced their decks completely and just used two iPods. However, this was less than ideal as it involved messy cabling and no matter how user friendly the iPod's scroll wheel and buttons are for picking out tunes, they're small and fiddly to use in a club. Luckily manufacturers of DJing equipment caught on to the craze and started producing products with built-in iPod docks. One of the first examples was Numark's iDJ. This had twin iPod docks, large backlit buttons and a separate touchwheel for moving through your iPod's menus. Gemini, another famous DJing brand, released a similar product, the iMix 1000, which lacked external buttons, but did have twin iPod docks and a lower price. Naturally there were two big problems with these products. The first was that you needed two iPods, making the set-up pricey. The second was that the speed of the tracks could not be controlled, so they couldn't be used for beat mixing – the process of matching the beats between two tracks before seamlessly mixing between them.

However, this issue was solved on the second generation of mixers, such as the Kam iMix 100. These had built-in signal processing chips that allowed DJs to adjust track speed in real-time using sliders, just as they would when working with vinyl decks. Nevertheless, the problem of needing to use two iPods remained.

Thankfully the third generation of iPod mixers has finally solved this problem. These devices treat your iPod as an external hard drive and pull the audio files directly from the drive rather than using the audio output from the headphone socket or dock connector. The means they can stream two tracks at the same time from a single player.

When you plug in your iPod, it scans the contents and indexes all the tracks based on their ID3 tags. Your library is shown on the mixer's large screen so you can select the tracks you want to cue up and play using the large backlit buttons and touch wheels. Naturally, they also have signal processing onboard to allow you to control the speed of the playback using pitch sliders, much like those found on vinyl DJ decks. You can even scratch tracks in real-time using the touch wheels.

At the moment the only device on the market with all these features is the dMix-300 from Cortex, which we've reviewed here, but this will be joined shortly by a similar system from Numark called the iDJ2. With these mixers opening up the market, the iPod has truly come of age as a DJing tool.

▲ The dMix-300's jog wheel can be configured to allows DJs to do some serious beat mixing.

► The Numark iDJ2 is the next generation of iPod mixers.

DJ MIXER

Cortex dMix-300

★★★★★

PRICE £499 (£424 ex VAT)

CONTACT Cortex 0870 870 0880 + *cortex-pro.com*

The dMix-300 allows you to mix two tracks using just a single third-generation or above iPod, including nanos. It has a USB port for playing tracks from a hard drive or flash drive, and you can connect a set of record decks to the phono sockets.

When you first slide your iPod into the dock, the mixer scans it and indexes all the songs based on their ID3 tags. You can then select tunes using the large screen and D-pad buttons at the top of each mixer channel. Both channels also have a large jog wheel. This can be configured to work either as a pitch control for beat mixing, a scratch wheel for hip-hop, or search control for cueing up your tracks.

The mixer feels exceptionally sturdy and thanks to the large buttons and big bright screens it's a delight to use when mixing. One thing to be aware of, however, is that it only plays tracks in MP3 format, so tunes ripped or downloaded in AAC won't work.

TIPS FOR ASPIRING DJS

1 THE CHEAP OPTION If you just want to be able to crossfade between tracks and aren't that worried about beat mixing, you can just hook up two iPods to a cheap mixing desk via a pair of phono cables.

2 PERFECT YOUR PLAYLISTS Work up an idea of the tracks that you might want to play at your party or club night and collect them together into a single playlist. Having tracks grouped together in playlists on your iPod makes it much faster to flick between them when you're DJing and will

help you to avoid any embarrassing silences as you search for the next track.

3 RIGHT TOOLS FOR THE JOB If you want to get into beat mixing (and what DJ doesn't?), you'll need an iPod mixing deck such as the iMix 100 or dMix-300, because they have pitch controls to allow you to speed up and slow down tracks.

4 BABY STEPS TO BEAT MIXING When learning to beat mix, it's best to start with dance tunes that use simple

four-to-the-floor drum beats – you'll find them easier to match up. Also stick to tracks that have roughly the same beats per minute.

5 CUT THE BASS, SMOOTH THE MIX A good tip when mixing two tracks together is to use the mixer's EQ to turn down the bass of the track that you're about to add into the mix. Then, as you crossfade it into the mix, gradually increase its bass frequencies again. This helps to stop the bottom end of your mix sounding too cluttered.

DJ MIXER
Gemini iTrax

★★☆☆☆

PRICE £100 (£85 ex VAT)
CONTACT Gemini 0870 870 0880 + *geminidj.com*

The iTrax from Gemini was one of the first DJ mixers available that was designed exclusively for use with the iPod. Unlike the dMix-300, it can't stream two tracks at the same time from a single player, but instead you need to slide two iPods into the twin docks at the top of the mixer.

Selecting and cueing tracks has to be performed directly on your iPods, as there's no screen or cueing buttons built-in to the actual mixer. This does, however, make it quite tricky to use in the dimly lit conditions you'll be presented with in most clubs. Also, as it doesn't have pitch controls, you can't use it for beat mixing.

What you do get with the iTrax is a smooth slider for crossfading between the output of your iPods, plus a three-band EQ for controlling high, mid and bass frequencies. There's also a microphone socket on the front of the mixer that you can use for a bit of MC-ing over the top of your selection of tracks.

In truth, the iTrax is a fairly basic iPod mixing deck that will only really appeal to those who want a simple way of crossfading between tracks during parties. Real DJs will need to look elsewhere to get their kicks.

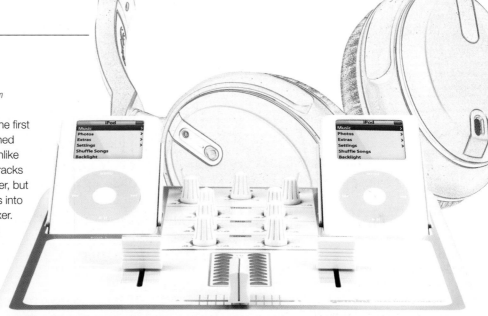

▲ The Gemini iTrax is a fairly simple mixer that lacks the depth of control of its rivals.

▼ Featuring twin iPod docks, the Kam iMix provides advanced controls for digital DJs without the high price tag.

DJ MIXER
Kam iMix 100

★★★★☆

PRICE £179 (£152 ex VAT)
CONTACT Kam 01582 690600 + *kam.co.uk*

The Kam iMix 100 represents a halfway house between the dMix-300 and iTrax models. You need two iPods to use it, but it also has the more advanced features that real DJs crave.

The crucial tool for any beat mixer is a pitch control slider, and thankfully that's present here. To use it, you first select the degree of pitch control you want – 16%, 32% or 90% – and then you start pushing the slider in the required direction to slow down or speed up the track.

The mixer also has large chunky buttons for cueing tunes or moving through your iPod's menus and, because many of these are backlit, they'll be easy to see in darkened nightclubs. Although we found the crossfader a little too light to the touch, its action is at least smooth and you do get connections for a pair of vinyl decks and a microphone input.

The iMix 100 is a good example of a mixer that takes the twin iPod approach, but these models are now being superseded by the likes of the dMix-300. If you have two iPods already, it's a decent option, but most serious DJs would find the dMix-300 much more convenient and satisfying.

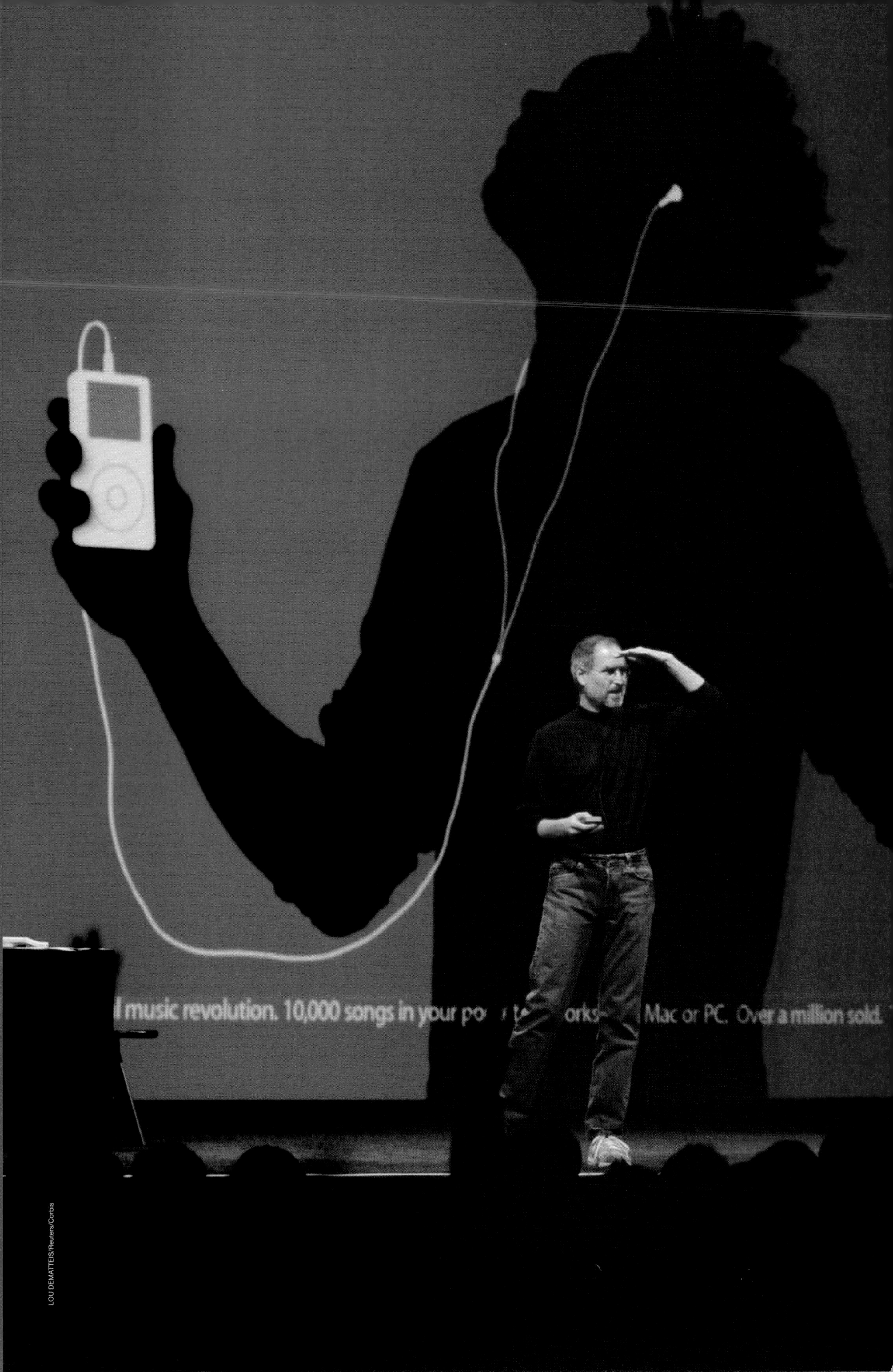

LOU DEMATTEIS/Reuters/Corbis

THE IPOD IS WITHOUT DOUBT THE ACE card in Apple's deck right now. It's the poster boy for all that is cool and great about the coolest, greatest company in the Valley. It has captured the market for portable music players and usurped the iMac and Power Mac as the first things most people think of when they hear the name Apple Computer, and it has also marked a big turnaround in the way the company does business.

Apple was always known for its snobbish attitude, often ignoring technologies that did not originate in its own labs, and in doing so producing a series of proprietary products priced higher than the market average. Many claimed this end-to-end control of how its products were made and what they did provided the best platform for fuss-free computing the world has ever seen; one that was all-but guaranteed to work without a glitch, 24/7/365.

The iPod was a turning point. It wasn't a traditional Apple product. It wasn't Apple from the ground up. Even the idea didn't originate from inside Apple's Cupertino offices. The iPod is a bought-in idea, built using bought-in technology,

'desirable' PDAs – and, most surprisingly of all, the iPod.

It was while working as an independent contractor that Fadell came up with the brainwave of taking a regular MP3 player and combining it with a Napster-style music service, and using the two as the focus of a dedicated company.

According to MLAgazine, he pitched the idea to both Philips and RealNetworks, neither of whom were interested. It was `a bit like the time Derek Rowe of Decca Records turned down The Beatles – and Fadell's next stop was Apple.

Fortunately, Apple saw the potential in this music player, just as EMI had seen the potential in that music-making foursome. The company then approached PortalPlayer to make the iPod hardware on its behalf.

PortalPlayer had been working with several manufacturers at the time, and was even developing a far more complex and impressive player for IBM, which featured Bluetooth connectivity – something that has been mooted for the iPod for some time. Apple's approach, though,

WHO REALLY CREATED THE iPOD?

The iPod is seen as the definitive Apple product – a triumph of Apple innovation – but you'll be shocked to discover that the company didn't even create the hardware or software for the device, let alone come up with the original concept. So, who actually created the world's most sought-after music player?

accompanied by bought-in software. Apple's involvement – in the early days at least – was little more than administration and co-ordination. And deciding how loud it should play.

For Apple, it has been a massive success but for many of those who contributed to its development, growth and worldwide domination, it has been a far from happy tale. So this is the inside story of how the iPod was conceived.

TONY FADELL WAS AN ENTREPRENEUR FROM an early age. At eight, he was selling eggs to neighbours in his home town of Rochester, New York, and by 15 had moved across the country to sell china and crystal in Dallas.

He graduated from the University of Michigan with a BSc in Computer Engineering in 1991, by which point he had attended no fewer than 11 schools, and went on to start up six different businesses.

Fadell worked for the likes of Philips, RealNetworks and General Magic, and then went on to invent both the Velo – one of the first truly

was clearly so compelling that for a time it became PortalPlayer's primary client.

Fadell also had his own vision of the iPod's potential impact. In a 2004 interview in *Wired* magazine, Ben Knauss, once a senior manager at PortalPlayer, explained how Fadell had told the PortalPlayer developers that he believed the iPod was 'going to remold Apple and 10 years from now, it's going to be a music business, not a computer business'.

Apple's computer business is still profitable, but many are starting to wonder whether this forecast might not turn out to be correct in the long run. To date, the company has released five generations of iPod and supplemented them with the mini, shuffle, nano and video variants, shipping more than 10 million players and close to half a billion iTunes Music Store tracks. Fadell's business plan clearly had legs.

As such, PortalPlayer's original device was a fast-track route for Apple to bring Fadell's plans to fruition. It still didn't have all of the features we

recognise as being standard for the iPod today
– playlists, for example, couldn't be any longer
than 10 entries – but with an operating system
and a basic design, it was more than halfway there.

Apple added the features it wanted, including
support for FairPlay digital rights management, and
although the project almost failed when the engineers
had trouble extending the battery life beyond three
hours (even when switched off), it eventually made
it to market on 23 October 2001. Knauss left
PortalPlayer shortly before the iPod shipped.

You'll find very little mention of the iPod on
PortalPlayer's site (*portalplayers.com*) and Apple
doesn't even appear in its list of customers.

ANOTHER HARDLY ACKNOWLEDGED PLAYER IN
the iPod's success is Pixo, the company behind
the Apple Newton's operating system. Pixo wasn't
an altogether random choice. It was local to Apple,
so the in-house team could keep a close eye on
what was going on, and it employed several
ex-Apple staffers.

Working with Jeff Robbin of Apple's resident
iPod firmware team, the Pixo engineers merged
their company's interface library to the PortalPlayer
firmware to create something close to today's
familiar interface.

Remarkably, the first version was ready just two
weeks after Apple made its first approach, largely
because Pixo had already been working on interface
software for mobile phones sold by Nokia and
Samsung, and so had considerable experience of
developing easily navigated software for use on
small screens.

Speaking to the *San Francisco Chronicle* in
August 2004, Paul Saffo, director of Menlo Park's
Institute for the Future, believes Pixo's involvement
indicates Apple had tried to produce a no-nonsense
interface itself and failed – probably on the time and
money front – but the newspaper's approaches to
Apple yielded nothing more than an admission that
Pixo had contributed 'a piece of technology in
the iPod's development'.

If Pixo's involvement really is as crucial as we
are lead to believe, then this seems more than a
little ungracious. Stereophile, a high-end audio site,
carries a comment attributed to Mike Neil, former
architect of the Pixo OS, that outlines more clearly
how his company was involved in the development of
the iPod's user interface: 'PortalPlayer was not the
company that developed the operating system that
drives the UI for the iPod, Pixo was... Additionally,
while Pixo was heavily involved in the design and
implementation of the original iPod, Apple did
most of the actual visual design of the UI...
Apple engineers provided many of the software
components and, since the 1.0 product, have been
doing all of the core software development.'

Pixo is no longer credited on the iPod's About
screen, although it was there on the first release in
2001, along with PortalPlayer.

Visiting *pixo.com* today redirects you to Sun
Microsystems' Java pages. Pixo was acquired when

01

Reuters/CORBIS

02

Alexandra Buhl

GENERAL MAGIC

Had it not been for Apple CEO John Sculley's belief that third-party companies were not interested in Apple products, General Magic would never have come about.

When Marc Porat started working for Apple in 1988, it was with a simple brief: come up with something revolutionary. And he did – a personal intelligent communicator. Designed not only to pass voice calls, it would also send faxes and short texts called telecards, and look up useful information, much in the vein of Sherlock.

Sculley saw that it had potential, but didn't believe anyone would support it if it came out of Apple, so spun off General Magic two years later and gave Porat free reign to recruit pretty much whoever he wanted. Soon the staff roster looked like a *Who's Who* of Apple history: Bill Atkinson, Susan Kare, Andy Hertzfeld.

So excited were potential investors by the potential for Magic's phone product that they invested heavily in the company, but Apple, which owned 16.5%, was getting concerned by the number of employees on the verge of defecting, so set up a division to produce its own competing product, the Newton.

General Magic perhaps embodies the stereotypical hippiness of Silicon Valley more than any other. Employees worked insane hours, slept at the office, kept pet rabbits in their working spaces, and adopted magical job titles. Tony Fadell, a diagnostic software engineer, was officially known as a 'Silicon Sorcerer'.

01 Apple CEO Steve Jobs models a first-generation iPod.

02 Original iPods credited PortalPlayer's involvement.

03 Apple's Cupertino HQ where the infamous Panic meeting took place.

04 Steven Frank waits in Apple reception for a meeting to discuss the future of Audion.

05 SoundJam, the predecessor to iTunes.

Sun saw the potential that could be gained through adding Pixo's payment and electronic distribution system to its portfolio. Why? Nothing to do with digital music, apparently. Rather, Pixo had developed a means of handling transactions through Java-based mobile devices and Sun looks set to dominate Java once and for all.

It is now Apple who develops the iPod's operating system.

WHAT ABOUT ITUNES, THOUGH? THE SECOND half of Fadell's business plan called for a music download service, and this would have been thwarted without the iTunes player. This is another area in which the development trail has been wiped fairly clean.

iTunes evolved from SoundJam, but if you try to find a download location for its predecessor, you'll most likely fail. The *soundjam.com* domain seems to be lying empty, and links through VersionTracker and other download sites are turning up blanks, pointing to Casady & Greene, the software's now defunct publisher.

SoundJam was developed by Jeff Robbin, Bill Kincaid and Dave Heller. Kincaid, an ex-Apple employee, was the driving force. He first heard about MP3 on the car radio one day, and was intrigued by talk of something called a Rio, which as we all now know was one of the first solid-state music players. When the presenter signed off with a comment that Mac users shouldn't get themselves too excited because it wouldn't work on anything other than Windows PCs, he decided he had to do something about it. He quit his job and hooked up with Jeff Robbin, also at the time an ex-employee of Apple, and together they learned all they could about MP3 and how it worked.

The first public showing was at the Apple Worldwide Developer Conference, and it was released just a couple of weeks before Audion, Panic's now retired, yet still iconic software player.

With hindsight, it looks as though Audion may itself have once been destined to become what we now know as iTunes. In June 2000, when Apple was showing the world its latest beta builds of Mac OS X it contacted the developers at Panic to talk about 'the future direction of Audion', but as they were already in negotiations with AOL, the Panic developers thought it only fair that it was a three-way discussion.

The AOL execs were tied up for the foreseeable future and the meeting never took place. 'They couldn't make it – at all,' writes Panic co-founder Cabel Sasser in his story of the development of Audion. 'Those crazy business people, I tell you! All those Palm Pilots and not a pixel of free time on the calendaring screen.'

It was to be some months – after the launch of iTunes and Audion 2.0 – before the AOL execs would find out what the meeting would have been about.

The AOL deal fell through and a second meeting was set up. In the meantime, Apple launched iTunes 1.0 at the Macworld Expo. It wasn't nearly as complex and accomplished as Audion, but it was clear that it was, in effect, a ported version of SoundJam, Audion's primary competitor. The guys from Panic – Sasser and Steven Frank – were in the audience, and after the keynote in which Apple CEO Steve Jobs introduced iTunes to the world, Sasser approached him on the show floor. He relates their brief discussion line by line:

'Hi Steve, it's Cabel, from Panic.'

'Oh, hey Cabel! Nice to meet you. So tell me, what'd you think of iTunes?'

'Well, I think it looks great! You guys have done a great job with it. But, you know, I still feel we'll do alright with Audion.'

'Oh, really? That's interesting, because honestly I don't think you guys have a chance.'

'Well, Steve, I really think it'll still find an audience. We've got a lot of higher-end features that you guys probably won't ever add.'

'Yeah? Like what?'

'Well, umm… you can keep a count of how many times you've played a song, or you can even rate your songs by popularity…'

'Why the hell would anybody want to do that?'

'Well, maybe you want to sort your playlist by your favourite songs.'

'You've got to understand, this is just 1.0, of course. You can only imagine where we'll be by the time we release 2.0!'

A week later, the meeting continued in the boardroom at Apple HQ. 'It's like you guys are a little push-cart going down the railroad tracks, and we're a giant steam engine about to run you down,' said Jobs, before asking Sasser and Frank to join the company. They turned him down.

In the face of iTunes' success, Audion is no longer actively developed. Panic describes it as 'retired', being available for free download, but no longer supported.

However, what of SoundJam, the product that morphed into iTunes? The actual deal is a complicated one, and was complicated still further by a period of extended silence from its publisher, Casady & Greene, which was, according to various sources, forbidden to talk about the deal for two years.

In July 2003, the company closed its doors once and for all, after 19 years of software publishing, by which time the staff had been working without pay for a full year. There's no link to Apple as the contact point for SoundJam customer queries – another link to a piece of key iPod development that has been all but erased from history.

Mac rumour site, Think Secret, recites the chain of events from an unnamed source: 'The deal… was for Apple to obtain SoundJam's rights from C&G. Jeff Robbin, the lead developer of SoundJam and Conflict Catcher, was an operating system engineer at Apple while developing those products on the side, doing so years before SoundJam was purchased by Apple. For iTunes, no developers were "bought" from C&G, since the company was a marketer and distributor, and didn't employ any developers. When

▼ ▶ **Key to Apple's financial security, every newcomer to the iPod range is given the full keynote address treatment.**

Apple purchased SoundJam, Jeff Robbin was already working there.'

In short, Apple seems to have circumvented the software's publisher and obtained the rights from the developers directly.

THE IPOD IS MORE THAN JUST AN ICONIC MUSIC player, and is the architect of Apple's upturned fortunes. It's an indication of how the company has changed in recent years, shrugging off some of its former arrogance.

Most likely, the iPod has been a learning experience for the company. When Jobs returned as interim CEO, one of his first acts was to spike the Newton. Many saw this as a move designed purely to spite former CEO John Sculley, who had championed the project since he'd seen the potential of General Magic. However, at the same time, it concentrated Apple's focus once again on traditional computing products – products used on a desk or a lap.

The arrival of the iPod, then, could be seen as the first aberration in that course, and this perhaps explains why Apple was so willing to partner with third-party developers and hardware manufacturers to bring the product to market before someone else captured the majority share.

It was a gamble that paid off, and looks set to influence the company's future direction. The first iPods were expensive – about the same as a cheap computer, and many times higher than most of their less-attractive competitors – but over the years their price tags have been reduced to more palatable figures. We're now seeing this trickle through into the rest of Apple's product line, with the low-end Power Mac G5 far more pocket-friendly than it once was, and the new Mac mini actively encouraging end users to integrate non-Apple peripherals with their Apple-badged hardware.

For the companies that were lost along the way, this will seem little consolation. However, for those of us set to benefit from greater integration and co-operation, and the price reductions this could bring about, the future looks bright.

FURTHER INFO

The True Story of Audion, including those Apple quotes
panic.com/extras/audionstory

Steven Frank's (half of Panic Inc) personal website
http://stevenf.com

San Francisco Chronicle
sfgate.com

Apple's iPod pages
apple.com/uk/ipod

Details of Pixo's involvement in developing the iPod OS
stereophile.com/digitalsource reviews/934/index6.html

Inside Story on the Birth of the iPod from *Wired*
wired.com/news/mac/0,2125, 64286,00.html

Forbes report on how the iPod is benefiting PortalPlayer
forbes.com/markets/2005/03/15/03 15automarketscan04.html

iPod timeline

The iPod is currently the best selling portable digital audio player on the market. It seems you can't walk down any high street anywhere without seeing somebody plugged in to a pair of white earphones or fiddling with a click wheel. Here we take a look at how this extraordinary phenomenon came into being.

March 1998
MPMan F10

The first MP3 playing portable audio device sprang from Asia in 1998 in the form of the Saehan Information Systems MPMan F10. This device had 32MB memory and faded into oblivion without making much of an impact. The company is still selling MP3 players, though.

December 1998
Rio PMP300

The second MP3 player to market did a better job of raising an interest in portable digital music players. The Rio PMP300 from Diamond Multimedia measured 3.5in x 2.5in had a click wheel for navigation and an LCD display for finding tracks. Again the memory was sparse by today's standards at 32MB, but users could upgrade this by adding their own SmartMedia card to the device. Demand from consumers was high and the device came to prominence when the Recording Industry Association of America unsuccessfully sued Diamond Multimedia. The publicity pushed the idea of digital music into the public consciousness, made portable digital devices officially legal, and the technology expanded.

January 2001
iTunes 1

iTunes 1 launched nine months before the iPod at the Macworld Expo in San Francisco and at the time was simply a front-end for music stored on a Macintosh. The software wasn't written by Apple but was simply an updated version of the SoundJam MP software Apple had purchased from Mac developer Casady & Greene. It would be another two years before the combination of these two Apple offerings exploded into the global phenomenon they are today.

October 2001
First generation iPod

It took Apple three years from the introduction of the MPMan and Rio PMP300 to enter the market. With typical Apple bravado it introduced the iPod on October 2, 2001 as 'a breakthrough MP3 music player that packs up to 1000 CD-quality songs into an ultra portable, 6.5 ounce design that fits in your pocket.' Steve Jobs claimed that 'with the iPod, listening to music will never be the same again.' The original iPod had a 5GB hard drive and a built-in FireWire port for syncing directly with iTunes. The device, Apple claimed, had a battery that could last for ten hours and had a 20-minute buffer for jog protection. It was the advertising slogan 'a thousand songs in your pocket' that grabbed the attention of the buying public even if the eye-watering £350 price tag didn't.

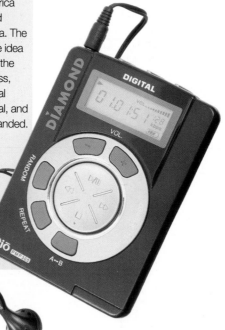

January 2004
iTunes 4

Version 4 and its various iterations was by far the most important version of the software to date. Though there were updates and improvements to the iTunes software it wasn't until version 4 launched to work in conjunction with the third generation iPod that it became more than a digital jukebox. The iTunes Music Store allowed users to download songs for 99 cents. When it launched in the United States the store had a library of 200,000 songs. A week later Apple reported it had already sold over 1 million tracks. Perhaps the most important release of iTunes ever, though, was version 4.1. This included support for Microsoft Windows users. Version 4.9 saw the inclusion of a podcast directory to further cement Apple's position as number one audio download provider.

February 2004
Fourth generation iPod

By the time the fourth iPod was launched the world had caught on to the mania surrounding it. iPods had taken the market by storm. The touch-sensitive buttons were gone, to be replaced by the same wheel/button arrangement of the recently launched iPod mini. Announced in February 2004 the fourth generation iPod was more transitional than revolutionary.

June 2004
AirPort Express

The AirPort Express was the first sign that pointed at Apple's intention to move towards complete domination of the home entertainment market. The wireless base station interacts directly with iTunes to stream your music around your home. Plug the device into a wall socket, connect it to your stereo and you can listen to your music collection anywhere there's a pair of speakers.

October 2004
iPod photo

Originally the iPod 'Photo', but quickly renamed the iPod photo with a lower case 'p', this was the first iPod with a colour screen. Launched in October 2004 the screen was capable of displaying Jpeg, BMP, Gif, Tiff and PNG image formats on its 220 x 176 pixel screen. This fed the flames of rumour and speculation that it would only be a matter of time before Apple released a video-capable iPod. At the same time Apple announced the special edition U2 iPod. This themed device had a black body and red click wheel. The rear was etched with the signatures of the band.

January 2005
iPod shuffle

Apple introduced a flash-based iPod in January 2005, which in typical Steve Jobs style, went against all the perceived wisdom surrounding small flash memory-based MP3 players. It didn't have a screen or a radio or a user replaceable battery. The industry was sceptical that Apple's 'Life is random' tagline could convince people to go for what many saw as an obviously flawed product. Apple was right again, though, as the shuffle sucked up market share at a blistering pace. It would seem that size really isn't all that important, as the shuffle was available in what were fairly small 512MB and 1GB incarnations.

September 2005
iPod nano

September 2005 saw Apple dump the mini for the nano. The nano is based on flash memory rather than the hard drive technology used in other iPods. At just 0.27in (6.9mm) thick, the first nano was small and only weighed 42g – it came with either 2GB or 4GB memory. It featured a colour screen that can display photographs, and used USB 2 for transferring data and charging the battery. The nano marked a shift in the iPod colour scheme with both black and white versions available. Shortly after the nano hit the shelves Apple was hit with a class action lawsuit, which claimed that it scratched too easily. Apple tried to allay fears about a faulty product by going public with the news that a small batch of the first nanos was incorrectly manufactured. It began shipping the nano with a soft case included not long after that.

October 2005
iTunes 6

In October 2005 with the release of iTunes 6 Apple moved the whole iTunes Music Store a little closer to an entertainment hub with the inclusion of music video and television show downloads. To complement the fifth generation iPod and its video playback abilities Apple began offering television/video broadcasts for download. The basic design of the iTunes front end has hardly changed since version 1 of this player, but its capabilities have increased exponentially. Apple has by far the biggest market share in the legal download sector, and outsells other digital music player manufacturers by a huge margin.

October 2005
Fifth generation iPod

The fifth iPod offered the video capability that Steve Jobs had denied would happen. Thinner than previous iPods the device was launched in October 2005 shortly after the company announced it had sold just under 6.5 million iPods in the preceding three months. The iPod with video capability offered playback of Mpeg-4 and H.264 formats, and was launched simultaneously with iTunes 6.1. The screen size was increased to 2.5in and this had a resolution of 320 x 240 pixels. As with the launch of the iTunes store the collection of video downloads was fairly restricted, but Apple quickly expanded the number of shows available.

MENU

January 2007
iPhone

Steve Jobs announced the iPhone at Apple's annual new year keynote in San Francisco. Despite having been the subject of rumour and speculation for months, if not years, the product turned out to be better than anyone imagined and, when it went on sale that summer, quickly sold out. It incorporates a widescreen display for playing movies, and what Apple calls the best iPod the company has ever produced, complete with orientation-sensitive hardware that alternates between playlist views and album art, featuring the Cover Flow technology found in iTunes 7.4, allowing users to visually leaf through their music collections. Many saw it as the start of the end for the conventional iPod.

September 2006
iPod, iPod nano, iPod shuffle and iTunes 7

Apple updated its entire iPod range in September 2006 and released a new version of iTunes.

Visually, the biggest change was to the iPod shuffle which looks completely different, it was even smaller now and only comes in a 1GB version. The nano's look was updated with multiple colours available, and capacities including 2GB, 4GB, and 8GB. The plastic case was replaced by a sleek and tough anodised aluminium shell, which made it less susceptible to scratching than its predecessor. It also had a brighter screen and 24-hour battery life.

The iPod now came in capacities of 30GB and 80GB, had a brighter screen and played games like *Pac Man* and *Bejewelled*, as well as music, photos and videos.

The iTunes update added a neat new way to view cover art, gapless playback and a sleeker user interface – complete with an improved source list.

There was also a new iPod information display, the ability to back-up Libraries to CD or DVD and the ability to playback music from multiple libraries.

September 2007
iPod strikes back

Reports of the iPod's demise proved unfounded as Apple rolled out a spectacular update to the full range, with slimmer cases throughout. The nano is now squarer than it once was, and has video playback features, the full-size iPod is now the iPod classic, and a new member joins the family: the iPod touch. Slimmer than the iPhone, the two share many common features, including Cover Flow, orientation sensitivity, and wireless networking, allowing tracks to be downloaded directly from the iTunes Store. A deal struck with UK public wifi network The Cloud allows for Internet access in railway stations, coffee shops and airports, pushing the iPod line well beyond anything offered by any rival MP3 hardware manufacturer, cementing Apple's position at the top of the market.

Back to the future for the iPod

Knowing what sort of iPod to choose is tricky, especially when a much-hyped latest and greatest offering is just around the corner. But can the next generation of designs mean such a big difference for the nano, classic, shuffle and touch?

It's always dangerous to try and guess Apple's next move, particularly where the iPod is concerned. Before every new announcement rumour sites try to predict what CEO Steve Jobs may or may not announce, and while some occasionally get it right (with the help of some careful leaks), most are way off the mark.

Even those that get it right, though, do so only a few days before the announcement itself. They usually herald their discovery with a picture of the product in question – almost always blurred beyond recognition as it was taken in a hurry – which is quickly discounted by more reputable sites as being nothing more than a questionable 3D render.

The latest iPod nano is a case in point. Pictures of an orange version of the device in its retail packaging were leaked on various websites and quickly racked up impressive hits. Even the usually less cautious rumour sites were quick to point out that it could have been the result of a bored graphics undergraduate with an evening to spare and a copy of Photoshop to hand, but in the end they turned out to be spot on.

The best way of guessing what the next iPod will look like, then, is to scour the web in late summer, as Apple traditionally

unveils new models in early September to give them plenty of time to rack up good sales in the run up to Christmas. Think carefully before putting too much faith in any apparent leaks that appear in early summer, winter or spring.

But of course that doesn't give you much notice of what the next iPod will comprise. So what can we expect Apple's genius engineers to come up with in the next few iterations, and is it worth your while hanging off buying a new device to see whether something better is just around the corner?

Our advice is the same where iPods are concerned as it is for any other gadget: if you want it now, and you can afford it, then buy it now. Your device may eventually be superseded by something slimmer, faster and more capacious, but the functions in your iPod device will carry on as before, and if they were good enough for you on the day you bought them, why should they not be any good just because something better has appeared?

If you are determined to always have the latest, greatest offering, but still want to invest in an iPod today, then our advice would be to steer clear of the iPod nano and iPod classic, and instead buy either a

shuffle or a touch. The shuffle boasts exactly the same features today as it did when it was first launched, except for a higher capacity and a more attractive casing. It may get cheaper and be able to store more tracks in the future, but unless Apple is going to add a screen, which would be difficult on a device of its size, it's not going to be possible to add much in the way of new features. What you buy today, then, will always be a close approximation of the best you can get.

The iPod touch is the exact opposite. Apple has already released several

Genius didn't appear on existing iPod nano and classic models, you shouldn't expect the new ones to benefit from new features over time. You should therefore only buy a nano or a classic if you are sure that the current feature set meets your needs and will continue to do so in the future.

Over time Apple will continue to shrink its music players, although it is difficult to see how it can make the touch or nano any thinner than they already are. Certainly the touch's big selling point – apart from its wireless connectivity – is its 3.5in screen, and so we can't expect that to get much smaller, as it will be impossible to type on. However, the nano could shrink still further if the multi-touch interface found on the touch, iPhone and some Apple notebooks was extended to its screen. This would have to be fairly rudimentary and restricted to simple track skipping, playlist navigation and volume controls unless Apple was happy to compromise on the size and make the screen physically larger.

Future classic and nano models would benefit from the addition of wireless networking, but full-blown Internet features would be impossible to implement on such small screens. Browsing web pages would be very uncomfortable on either, and unless you were willing to dial out each letter of your email they would not be good communication devices either. However, the addition of wifi networking would enable you to download tracks direct from the iTunes Store without first connecting the iPod to your Mac or PC and synchronising from there.

As the iPod line matures, Apple will find it very difficult to introduce new features that add real value to the line. This was obvious for the latest updates, which added little in the way of improvements beyond capacity increases, size reductions, price cuts and new colours. That could mean it has trouble sustaining the impressive sales record that has seen it capture over 70 per cent of the market for portable music players, in comparison to Microsoft's 2.6 per cent.

At the same time, though, it must resist the temptation to add new features for the sake of it. The reason that the iPod has enjoyed so many years of success is that it is simple, easy to use and focused on one key goal: playing media to the masses. The iPod touch's manifold abilities were something of a gamble. Fortunately for Apple they paid off, and it had been able to test the waters in advance with the iPhone. Whether it can repeat such a move remains to be seen.

screen, adding extra external buttons or new hardware-focused updates, such as GPS, the current iPod touch will likely be able to keep up-to-date with revisions to the line through software updates alone.

You will, of course, have to pay for these updates to the iPod touch firmware, as the business model Apple operates on that device is very different to the one it uses for the iPhone, which uses almost exactly the same operating software, and can be updated free of charge. This leaves us with the mid-range products: the iPod nano and iPod classic.

The primary revisions to these products over the last two iterations are further slimming down of the players' bodies while software updates add the Genius playlist feature. Although Apple ships firmware updates for all of its iPods from time to time, these do not usually add new features to each model, and so just as

software revisions for its top-end music player, keeping its feature set roughly in line with the iPhone – barring the camera, and GPS and calling features.

When it announced Genius, the new software in both iTunes and the fourth-generation iPod nano, sixth-generation iPod classic and second-generation iPod touch, it was an optional add-on to the original iPod touch for a nominal fee and a software download. Until Apple gets around to increasing the resolution of the

OLD VS NEW

If you are looking to buy, sell or simply update your iPod why not take a look at the secondhand market? It's bursting with choice and there are plenty of bargains to be snapped up too.

A NEW iPOD LIFE

Just as iTunes has become a byword for digital music stores, the iPod is now the default portable music player. Revolutionising the digital music player market upon its launch in 2001, it has defined a generation, and has been hailed as a modern design classic. With a new generation appearing almost every year, and the range now stretching from the screenless iPod shuffle to the all-singing all dancing iPod touch, what should you look for in a secondhand model? And, if you want to upgrade, how should you prepare your current iPod for sale, and how much can you expect to sell it for to offset the cost of a shiny new one?

RESETTING YOUR iPOD

Before sending your iPod on its way to a new life with a new owner, it needs to be reset and all music stored on it deleted. Content must be cleared from any iPod before selling, because if not you could find yourself in trouble with worldwide recording industry associations. Sharing music and selling your iPod without the removal of content is a violation of copyright laws not only in the UK, but also Europe and the US, and there are heavy penalties to pay.

Whichever iPod you have, the resetting and wiping process is an easy one. iTunes can be used to restore your model's original factory settings, erasing the disk at the same time. Connect the iPod to your computer when iTunes is open, and wait for it to appear under the 'Devices' panel. Then click on the 'Settings' tab at the top of the screen, and click the 'Restore' button in the version section. While the iPod is connected to the computer, and when the restore process is complete, the iTunes Setup Assistant window will appear asking you to not only name your iPod, but also to choose your syncing preferences in a similar way to when you first connected your iPod to both your computer and iTunes.

SELLING YOUR iPOD

What makes your iPod different from the other 100 million around when you come to sell it? Not very much, but generally speaking, as with other items, if it's in good condition, it's more attractive to potential buyers. By far the most popular way of disposing of your used iPod is to employ the services of Internet auction sites such as eBay (ebay.co.uk). Listing is easy, doesn't take long, and should you sell it successfully, can be highly effective in earning you a

decent amount of money to offset the cost of the shiny new device which will replace it.

HOW MUCH WILL IT GO FOR?

The value of your pre-loved iPod depends very much on which particular model it is. Of course, the recently-unveiled new range covers more bases than that of, say, 2006, but even back then there were still various models to choose from.

The simplest model from the 2006 range is the 1GB shuffle; it can sell from around £14, rising to as much as £23. There seems to be no variation in price for any particular colour, either, such is the popularity of the clip-on iPod. Surprisingly, the undeniably less fashionable but still capable, first-generation shuffle from 2005 commands the same price, so it makes sense to buy the newest model you can; it may well be a case of style isn't everything. Brand-new shuffles have a recommended retail price of £32 for the 1GB version, and £45 for one with twice that capacity. The 2008 models do no better than those from 2006, so the cheapest prices could represent a good-value £9 saving.

The next rung up the iPod ladder is the nano. It's available in 2GB, 4GB, and 8GB in its 2006 second-generation form, compared

to the 8GB and 16GB versions of today. The smallest-capacity models can fetch anything from £30 to £55, while the average price of a 4GB machine is in the region of £65.

Top-end second-generation 8GB nanos can go for as much as £90. However, an interesting point to note is that we saw a first-generation 1GB nano for £33.

Third-generation 4GB nanos with video-playing features from 2007 start from £60, with 8GB models going for upwards of £80. New fourth-generation nanos start at £109 for the 8GB version, and apart from the more stylish aluminium case, taller screen and accelerometer, are quite similar to their forebears. Again, it's a case of choosing what you can afford.

The large-capacity 30GB and 80GB fifth-generation iPods hit the streets in late 2006. The smaller-volume model kicks off at around £75, rising to £110, which is where prices start for its higher capacity sibling.

The iPod classic arrived in 2007 in 80GB and 160GB flavours, building on the video-playing qualities of its predecessor. Prices for the 80GB models can start at £90, while 160GB versions kick off from around £150. As with the smaller shuffles and nanos, colour seems to make little difference. New iPod classics are only

available in 120GB (30,000 track) form, and ship for around £179, so a late older model, higher-capacity classic seems to be a good-value buy.

Hot on the heels of the iPhone, the super-sleek iPod touch with its 3.5in widescreen multi-touch display arrived to a rapturous reception in the autumn of 2007, in 8GB, 16GB, and later 32GB flash-drive forms. The lowest-capacity used models start at £120, with a typical average price of £140. Mid-range 16GB iPod touch versions sell for around £150, with a few undercutting that at the same price as its smaller 8GB brother. At the other end of the scale, full-fat 32GB models command anything from £150 to £220 and beyond. A brand-new iPod touch in 8GB flavour costs £169, a 16GB version £219, and a top-end 32GB £289, and without much difference between old and new, there are savings to be had by buying a used model.

BUYING SECONDHAND

Selling your old iPod may get you a good price to offset a new one, but if you don't need anything in a brand new one, is there anything to watch out for when buying a used iPod? Rather obviously, check that the iPod being offered for sale isn't faulty, in

need of repair, or even non-functional. Sellers who advertise such models usually state that there is something wrong with them, but it still pays to check the description carefully.

Another thing to look out for is engraved iPods. While it might have been a good idea to proclaim your love for your partner at the time of giving an iPod as a gift, or wishing that close friend a happy birthday, it may not be such a wise move when it comes to selling time. To potential buyers, it's personal to the seller, so they may not spend their readies on your model, going for that clean, impersonal one instead. And of course, check that the iPod you are thinking of buying has had all of its music files and other content removed, otherwise you could fall foul of those international copyright laws.

A used iPod can give as much satisfaction and pleasure as a brand-new model. And, whether you're selling an old shuffle to raise funds for a new nano, or simply to buy a secondhand model, it's wise not to purchase any iPod with a view to making money from it.

iPods are there to be enjoyed, so whatever model you have you can be safe in the knowledge that you own the most stylish MP3 player on the market.

Best iPod websites

There are many websites dedicated to the iPod, from fan sites to support forums. Here, we take a look at those websites that we have found indispensable when playing with our iPods.

Apple's iPod pages

apple.com/itunes

Apple's iPod pages are the only official source of information about its line of ubiquitous music players. So long as you bear in mind the fact that their ultimate goal is to extract some money from your pocket by selling you one, you'll find that they are an invaluable, unrivalled authority on all things iPod, iPhone and iTunes.

But this site is about much more than just iPods. It also rolls in Apple TV, the latest additions to the iTunes Store and accessories from Apple and third-party developers, and it could arguably be the only online stop you need to make to get all the information you could ever possibly use.

The speed at which Apple updates the site is impressive, on account of the fact that it is the only organisation to have advance notice of what the next breed of iPod will look like and when it will be available. One thing you won't find here, though, is any kind of rumour, and barring the very rare occasion when someone has hit the publish button a day early, you don't get advance announcements here, either, so it'll be no good if you're trying to decide whether or not now is the right time to be buying a new iPod. Why? Because as far as Apple is concerned it's always a good time to be buying one.

This is also the only place from which you can legitimately download a copy of iTunes if you're not using a Mac and updating regularly through Software Update.

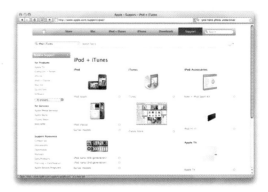

Apple Support Forums

apple.com/support/ipod

Apple's support forums are second to none, regardless of the product that's causing you problems. The iPod area is sectionalised neatly to cover both current models and those that have been superceded. If you do have an old iPod, then it helps to have an idea of what has replaced it over time. Pioneering owners of the first hard-drive based iPods, for example, need to know that to diagnose their own particular problems they need to click on the 'Earlier models' entry beneath iPod classic, and not the 'Earlier models' link below iPod nano.

Fortunately each section is illustrated by a photo of the latest addition to the range, and supplemented by other areas for iTunes, the iTunes Store, iPod Hi-Fi, Apple TV and the Nike + iPod Sport Kit.

Clicking on a particular iPod range lets you view its specs, download its manuals and check its compatibility with your system. However, of more interest is the Discussions section within each one, where you can talk through your problem with other users. What sets this apart from third-party websites with discussion boards, though, is the fact that Apple employees also dive in and help out with the discussion.

As a result, the chances are that if your particular problem has already been discussed in the past any solutions published on the boards are more likely to be authoritative and accurate than they would have been had Apple itself not been involved.

Cult of Mac *cultofmac.com*
One of the most-read blogs on the subject of Macs in general (and Apple culture) is Wired's Cult of Mac. Written by a small team of contributors and updated daily, the site is a great place to turn to get not only low-downs on possible upcoming products, but also analysis of the current state of the Mac and iPod market.

Despite being entitled Cult of Mac, it's not sycophantic. It takes a very level-headed view of things and isn't afraid to criticise Apple, its management, its direction or its products when it feels it's justified. Neither is it unwilling to recommend non-Apple products when they're better alternatives than the Cupertino company can produce itself.

The one slightly disappointing thing about the blog, considering it's got the backing and resources of such a big and impressive brand as Wired, is the fact that it attracts relatively few comments considering its potential.

So, if you've always fancied sounding off on the subject of Apple, perhaps this is your chance to be heard. Read what Cult of Mac has to say, and wade in on the comment link with your own thoughts on the subject. As one of just a few voices rattling around at the foot of the post, you can't fail to be seen.

How Stuff Works
electronics.howstuffworks.com/ipod.htm
If you've not yet come across How Stuff Works, you're in for a treat. The site is a massive repository of information about – literally – how stuff works. Of course, in this case we're not interested in how dogs perceive time, how special effects artists make films more zingy or how car salesmen manage to up-sell you every time you walk on to a forecourt, but how an iPod works.

The six-part article covers the inner workings of the iPod (complete with photos of a dissected iPod classic) and what it is inside the click wheel that senses and interprets what you're doing with your fingers as you wipe them around its surface.

At the time of writing, the article could have done with a minor refresh as it didn't cover much beyond the fifth-generation full-size iPod. However, a handy set of links to related articles gives you quick access to information on bits and bytes, digital rights management, how podcasting works, and a range of iPod hacks if you want to enable your iPod to do more than Apple ever intended.

Elsewhere on How Stuff Works, a dedicated iPods library draws together all of the site's information on this and other media players. It can be found at *electronics.howstuffworks.com/ipod-media-player-channel.htm*.

MacUser *macuser.co.uk*
If you'd rather have your iPod news in context, then check out MacUser (or its sister site for PC users at *pcpro.co.uk*). This general-interest Mac news site covers all the latest updates to the iPod line-up, and the software that helps them run.

Its news feed is written just for the site, but much of the rest of the content is drawn from *MacUser* magazine, meaning you have access to all of the reviews and labs tests published in its printed edition, with all the resources at the editorial team's disposal.

By covering more than just the iPod, iPhone and iTunes, the site can give you a more rounded overview of the iPod ecosystem, putting each device into a context that helps you judge when best to upgrade to the latest, greatest model.

Its lively forums are the place to discuss the latest iPod developments and general Mac news, and with a heritage stretching back almost quarter of a century, you know MacUser is a brand you can trust.

iPod flea

video.google.com/videosearch?q=ipod+flea

Apple's iconic iPod ads have spawned countless imitators. Most consist of little more than the dancing silhouettes re-cut to a new tune. iPod flea, though, is a whole lot more inventive. Put together by Scott Kelby (better known for writing Photoshop how-to books) the iPod flea commercial highlights an imaginary product, the smallest iPod ever (not) created: the iPod flea.

Looking suspiciously like a Tic Tac, it holds one track and plays for an hour, comes with Bluetooth in the form of Flea Control and can be transported in the handy, over-sized Flea Bag. As each one has capacity for just one track, if you want to take an album with you you'll have to carry more than one, which is where another great accessory, the Flea Collar, comes in handy.

With more flea-related puns than you can shake a nano at, this three-minute video is as funny today as it was the first time we saw it. Check it out, along with the spoof Microsoft iPod packaging design, below.

iLounge *ilounge.com*

One of the longest-running iPod-focused sites was originally called the iPod Lounge, until Apple started clamping down on the use of the trademarked name of its music players. The result, iLounge, is arguably far better – particularly as it means it can now cover all manner of i-prefixed devices, including the iPhone.

It is unapologetically fascinated with the whole iPod ecosystem, posting high resolution photos of new models being unboxed, racing to get news of accessories onto the web before anyone else, and spawning 14 international versions around the world.

It is logically organised, with sections covering software downloads, tutorials and lively visitor discussion forums. It is also totally platform neutral, with add-ons for Windows, Mac OS X and Linux users, and links to web apps for use on the iPhone.

It even has specific editions optimised for viewing on the iPhone and iPod touch.

Its dedicated Widgets for the Mac OS X Dashboard and Yahoo on both the Mac and Windows are sectionalised to keep you up-to-date with the latest iPod-related news, reviews and queries, while the site's links to Pricegrabber mean you'll be able to source the best prices for iPods, cases, iPhones, headphones and speakers. It's a shame, though, that all of the results are priced up in US dollars.

Microsoft redesigns the iPod box

youtube.com/watch?v=aeXAcwriid0

Another spoof, this time looking at how Microsoft would have tackled the tricky task of designing the iPod's packaging. Out goes the iconic underdesigned white packaging of the original hard drive-based player; in comes a cluttered mess full of bullet points and unnecessary stats.

The Microsoft-flavoured design is spot on, which is why we can quite believe stories that Microsoft itself put the movie together for its own internal purposes. The company is know for being able to laugh at itself, after all, as demonstrated by the videos Bill Gates and Steve Balmer used to put together once a year for big trade shows. Gates, memorably, dressed up as Harry Potter for one of them.

iPodnn *ipodnn.com*

A spin-off from the hugely-successful Macnn, iPodnn is an iPod-specific news site. Mixing in authoritative reporting, press releases, links to other news sources and an intriguing collection of rumours and hearsay, it provides a good mix of the actual and the possible where iTunes and the iPod are concerned.

As part of the Macnn network, it also has links to the Macnn podcasts, giving you regular updates on the latest Mac news, easily consumed using your iPod when you're away from your computer.

Its iPod forum also takes in iPhone and Apple TV topics to cover the whole i-related ecosystem, but its iPod world blog could do with a bit of love and attention. At the time of writing, the most recent posting to it was almost two years old and missing its embedded images.

Wordpress theme for iPhone and iPod touch
iwphone.contentrobot.com

If you want to create a site of your own, the easiest way to keep it regularly updated is to run it as a blog. There is a wide range of blogging software available, including Blogger and LiveJournal, but one of the most flexible is Wordpress – particularly if you have installed it on your own server.

By running your own server-based blogging platform, you can control everything from the order of your posts and the way the date is formatted, to the whole overall look and feel of your site. But did you know that you can run two styles together, side by side, with the browser choosing the most appropriate one for the device on which it's displayed?

Fortunately you don't need to design your site twice; this plug-in will make your WordPress blog automatically serve an iPhone and iPod touch-optimised version of your content for mobile browsers. It's a smart solution to a newly-arrived problem.

Myijump *myijump.com*

Considering how good the iPod touch's browser is, you would think there would have been more sites formatted specifically to take advantage of its features and abilities. While there are several application sites hosting online software that works well on its particular screen, there are very few news and information sites formatted that way.

One of the few is Myijump, which is localised for US or UK users, using iPhones or the iPod touch, with a French edition recently added. The layout is a simple top-down structure kept narrow to fit the devices' portrait-oriented screens, with tabs at the top for clicking between the homepage and four key sections: web applications, regular applications, games and 'free'.

Myijump is part of the thumblounge suite (*thumblounge.com*), which takes a lot of regular content from elsewhere on the web and reformats it for display on the iPhone and iPod touch, giving you a more attractive, and better-formatted interface for entry into sites like BBC iPlayer.

Can I use my iPod with anything other than iTunes?

Officially, no. iTunes and the iPod are designed to work seamlessly and exclusively with each other. However, while that's the official line, it's not entirely how things have worked out. By connecting your iPod to your Mac or PC and clicking its entry in the left-hand column of iTunes, you can enable it for hard disk use. This lets you use the iPod as a portable hard drive for storing and transporting files in any part of the disk or internal memory not used for movies, songs and podcasts.

If you connect to a Linux machine, you can also often access the device directly, allowing you to drag files onto and off it, and even access the music it contains without using iTunes.

Can I put my iTunes library on anything other than an iPod?

Again, the official answer is a resolute no, on account of the fact that iTunes refuses to recognise any device attached to your computer other than an iPod. However, the two main formats that it uses – AAC and MP3 – are industry standards, and so there is nothing to stop you from exporting the contents of your library, importing the results into an alternative music management

application and transferring them from there onto another device.

However, iTunes is the only application to use Apple's FairPlay digital rights management software, which wraps all tracks bought from the iTunes Store, other than iTunes Plus tracks in protective data. Without the key to unlock this data, no application can play the protected tracks, meaning that you will be unable to export protected tracks for use on anything other than an iPod or another authorised installation of iTunes.

It is worth considering whether you'll want to play your tracks on more than one device and what file formats that device can read before ripping your music to your library. If it can't handle AAC then encode rip your tracks as native MP3 files when you first import them into iTunes by hitting command -, to open Preferences and clicking the Import Settings button on the General tab. Change the Import Using setting to MP3 encoder and OK out of the dialogues.

Why don't the capacities and drive sizes of the various iPod match up?

Looking at the various iPods' specs, you might spot that some appear to make better use of their internal storage than others. At

first you might put this down to more efficient compression of the tracks you load on to them, but as that is controlled by iTunes, not the iPod itself, that can't be the case. What is actually happening, is that more advanced iPods like the iPod touch have a bulkier operating system, which eats up more of the internal storage than others in the range. As such, less advanced iPods like the iPod nano would appear, wrongly, to make more efficient use of their music-storage capacity.

Can I upgrade my iPod's software?

Apple delivers fixes and updates to the iPod's internal firmware every so often, and iTunes will automatically check to see when an update has become available. You can force it to check for updates by connecting your iPod and, in iTunes, clicking its entry in the left-hand column followed by the Check for Updates button.

Unfortunately this usually won't deliver the new features in each latest breed of iPods for use on older models, as they may not have the necessary hardware to make use of them (older nanos had no accelerometer for indicating which way up they were being used, for example), and Apple can use these new software-based features as a selling point. However, you can go further than this with the more flexible iPod touch and iPhone.

As well as checking for updates to the operating system you can install your own choice of applications in addition to the ones already in place. These are downloaded from the online App Store, usually through iTunes, although if the application in question is small – under 10MB in size – they can be downloaded directly to the iPhone or iPod touch.

Hardcore users who want to perform the ultimate upgrade can replace their iPod's operating system altogether. Several choices for running Linux on an iPod are offered by ipodlinux.sourceforge.net and others, although in many cases they work only on older machines, and they are most certainly not approved or supported by Apple, so you install them at your own risk.

These replacement operating systems add a range of features not found in a regular iPod, including new games and, in some cases, video playback – albeit in a very rudimentary form – on some of the oldest clickwheel iPods.

Can I replace my iPod battery?
It depends on the model in question. It was relatively easy to crack open many of the older models of iPod, as the seemingly welded-shut casing actually had a small notch between the silver back and white front. Third-party manufacturers exploited this fact by producing replacement batteries.

It is still possible to replace the battery in some iPods, but they are not designed to be opened up. However, the iPhone has an official battery replacement policy. The battery can be returned to Apple when it has significantly degraded and if it is still under warranty or you have taken an optional Apple Care policy to cover the device, this may be done for free. If not, you will be presented with a bill to cover parts and labour.

Why doesn't my accessory work with my new iPod?
If you have bought add-ons for your current iPod, there is no guarantee that they will work with the next generation when you upgrade. This is because from time to time Apple changes the Dock connector on the bottom of the device. Used by all official iPod and iPhone peripherals that don't plug in to the headphone socket, this connector carries both data and power in both directions to and from the iPod.

Apple licenses use of this connector through its Made for iPod accreditation scheme, and runs a similar scheme – Made for iPhone – for peripherals designed to work with the iPhone. Unfortunately there is no guarantee that devices designed to work with the iPod will work with the iPhone, despite the similarity between that and the iPod touch, so you should always choose any add-ons you buy with care.

When is the best time to buy an iPod?
Traditionally, the end of the year and the run-up to Christmas has always been a good time to buy an iPod. Apple makes key product announcements in January, summer and autumn. January is often a time when it updates its line-up of consumer computers and software; summer is often a time when it updates its professional computers; and autumn is the time it updates its range of iPods, to get them into the shops in time for Christmas. It may be worth holding off upgrading your existing iPod if you want to buy a new one in late summer, just in case new ones are around the corner.

However, the fact remains that as with any electronic gadget, the iPod you buy today will work just as well when it has been superseded. So, if you need one now and you're happy to be one step behind the crowd when the next one comes out, go ahead. Alternatively, wait a few weeks and either buy the next great release or use its appearance as an opportunity to buy the current model second hand – at a considerable discount – on eBay.

My new iPod classic's battery doesn't last as long as it should. I did the initial charge of several hours.

iPods that contain a hard disk have a feature called skip protection, and a small amount of memory (a cache) that's used to store the next few tracks to be played. The iPod is able to play several songs before it needs to start the disk up and refill the cache with more songs.

This feature's effectiveness depends on how much you've squashed your music down. On its default settings, iTunes imports CDs as AAC files at 128kbps, which takes up around 1MB per minute. If you've increased the bit rate to 192kbps to store music in better quality, then tracks will take up roughly 1.5MB per minute, while switching the format from AAC to Apple Lossless takes up around 5MB per minute. Apple's recommendation is to keep individual songs to under 9MB to get good performance out of the battery.

It's tempting to keep music in the highest quality possible when there's as much as 160GB of storage available, but the side effect is reduced battery life. The more space each track takes up, the fewer of them will fit in the cache at one time and the more often the disk will have to be spun up to refill it, consuming more power.

A few other factors can affect battery life, such as using the iPod when it is too cold, so let it warm up to room temperature if it's been exposed to the cold; try to keep it warm in an iPod Sock or similar case when using it outside in cold weather.

How you listen to music has an impact too, and skipping many songs in shuffle mode or in a Genius playlist will force the disk to spin up to refill the cache and consume even more power. Using the Equalizer also drains power more quickly, and it's best to refrain from using the Backlight's Always On option – choose a lower setting so that it turns off more quickly after you've selected a track.

I can't share music from my housemate's computer, even though the sharing options are enabled in iTunes' Preferences window.

The sharing features need to be able to talk to other computers over specific ports and your security software may be set to such a high level that it's blocking them. The steps you'll need to take differ depending on the firewall that you're using, so look at your firewall's documentation to find out how to open them. The ones that need to be opened are TCP port 3689 and UDP port 5353.

Also open Task Manager and look in the Processes tab for one called mDNSresponder.exe to check that it's running. This is part of Bonjour for Windows, a technology that iTunes uses to automatically detect compatible devices on the same network, such as a pair of speakers attached to an AirPort Express or an Apple TV. It also affects music sharing, and if it's running then also check that your firewall isn't blocking it.

Also check that Bonjour is still installed; it should appear in the Add or Remove Programs list in Control Panel, and the application (consisting of the .exe file and mdnsNSP.dll) are usually installed into c:\Program Files\Bonjour. If it's missing, or if you want to be sure that it's correctly installed and undamaged, then you don't need to redownload the whole iTunes package. Bonjour is available as a separate download from *http://tinyurl.com/2xqbw4* where you'll find separate links to download it for 32-bit and 64-bit versions of Windows, so make sure that you get the right one.

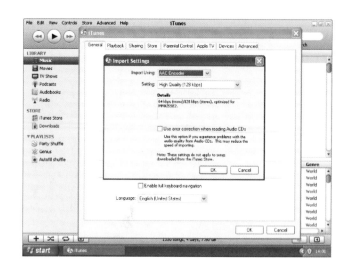

The latest version of iTunes won't install. Windows tells me that it's not a valid Win32 application.

This can crop up if Internet Explorer is unable to download the file correctly, so the quickest workaround is to get the iTunes installer from apple.com/itunes using a different web browser such as Firefox, if you have one installed. Otherwise open Internet Explorer and click the Tools button, then choose Delete Browsing History. In the window that appears, click the Delete files button next to Temporary Internet Files.

The problem might still crop up, so make sure there are no other copies of QuickTimeInstaller.exe and iTunesSetup.exe on your computer before downloading the installer again. If it still won't work, Try removing QuickTime from your computer and then download and reinstall the standalone version (that doesn't include iTunes) from *apple.com/quicktime/download/win.html*.

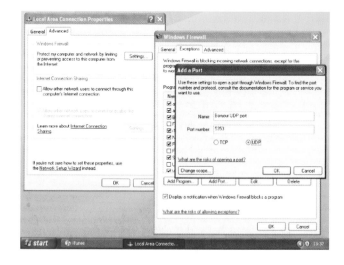

I can't get songs that I bought from the iTunes Store to play on my iPod. They'll only play on my computer, though songs imported from CD play on the iPod just fine.

Even though the songs play in iTunes, try to reauthorise your computer to play songs from your iTunes Store account.

If the problem only affects some but not all purchased songs then the problem may lie in those specific files, and you should restore them from a backup. Make sure you have a backup file, then remove the current copy from the library. Delete the file if you're offered the choice, then remove the track from your iPod and copy the restored version to it.

If that doesn't fix the issue, remove the non-playing tracks from the iPod again and choose Store > Deauthorize Computer and you'll be prompted to enter your account ID and password to confirm the change. To reauthorise your computer, find one of your purchased tracks in the library, play it and enter your account details when prompted. Now try copying the tracks back to your iPod.

If this fails, you may need to restore the iPod, but first copy any tracks that aren't on your computer back to it using a tool such as ephpod for Windows (*ephpod.com*) or Senuti on a Mac (*fadingred.org/senuti*), as well as any files you've copied to it in disk mode. Update iTunes to the latest version then plug in your iPod and select it in the sidebar. Click the Restore button to erase the iPod. Just copy a track from the iTunes Store to the iPod for now and try playing it.

Should the songs still refuse to play, try recreating the iTunes Library file. Instructions on how to do this can be found at *support.apple.com/kb/HT1451*. If that still doesn't help, you'll need to contact the Store's customer services at *apple.com/support/ itunes/store/browser*.

I've tried disconnecting and reconnecting my iPod shuffle and waiting a few minutes. It just won't appear in iTunes.

Check whether the computer can see the shuffle in Windows' Device Manager (in the Disk drives category) or under USB hardware in a Mac's System Profiler. It may even appear on the desktop despite not working with iTunes.

So long as the computer can see the shuffle, you can restore it on Windows XP or a Mac with the iPod Reset Utility, a piece of software that works exclusively with the iPod shuffle, both the original chewing gum-sized block and the newer models with a built-in clip. Download it from support.apple. com/kb/HT1238. Disconnect the iPod then run the utility, then reconnect the iPod directly to your computer, not through a hub or port on a keyboard.

Click the reset button on the utility - you need to be an administrator to use it, and you may be asked for your name and password again. Don't disconnect the iPod during the process. When it's finished, open iTunes and the iPod should appear. If it doesn't, try disconnecting and reconnecting it to your computer.

In the rare occurrence that the utility says "Can't mount iPod", contact Apple for support. Details are at *apple.com/uk/ support/contact*.

iTunes complains that there's a problem with my audio configuration and it refuses to open.

This is due to a problem with QuickTime for Windows. iTunes 7.7 or later more helpfully tell you this, but versions up to 7.6 either return the message about your audio configuration or more cryptically just give you a -200 error.

You'll need to reinstall QuickTime, but first you have to get rid of the old version. Open Control Panel and go into the Add or Remove Programs panel to remove it. Make sure that the files QuickTime.qts and QuicktimeVR.qtx have been removed from c:\windows\ system32 but be careful not to change anything else in the folder.

Download the latest version of QuickTime from *apple.com/quicktime/ download/win.html*. Even if you're running an older version of iTunes, for now just select the option that doesn't include it. Once the installer is downloaded, run it and try opening iTunes again. Should the same error occur, try removing QuickTime again.

This time, disconnect your computer from the Internet and your local network, temporarily switch off your anti-virus and anti-spyware software in case it is interfering with the QuickTime installer. Don't forget to switch them back on before reconnecting to the network though.

iTunes doesn't list my iPod touch under Devices.

iTunes relies on two things to work on Windows. First connect your iPod touch then click Start > Run and type devmgmt.msc. Click the plus sign next to Universal Serial Bus controllers and look for something that looks like an iPod – it may be called Apple Mobile Device USB Driver or Apple iPod touch. If it's there and tagged with a small yellow graphic that contains an exclamation mark, the driver isn't working properly. Right click it and select Properties, then go to the Driver tab and click the Update Driver button. The Hardware Update Wizard appears, and you should tell it not to look on Windows Update for a driver but to install the driver automatically, so that it will look for the driver that should have been installed as part of iTunes. If this fails, you should back up your iTunes library (File > Library > Export Library), remove iTunes and download and install the latest version from apple.com/itunes.

If the driver is installed correctly and the iPod still doesn't appear, go to the Add or Remove Programs list in Control Panel and look for Apple Mobile Device Support. Also check that the service is running by right-clicking on the Taskbar and choosing Task Manager. Look for AppleMobileDeviceSupport. exe in the Processes tab, as it needs to be running in the background to detect when an iPod touch (or iPhone) is plugged in.

With both the driver and service installed and working, there may be a conflict with other software. Errors may appear in the Application log with iPod Service listed in the Source column. Double-clicking a row will show you the error that occurred, but they can be tricky for inexperienced users to deal with, and it may be easier to try reinstalling iTunes.

Before doing so, back up your iTunes library by choosing File > Library > Backup Library to keep a copy of your ratings, then remove iTunes, QuickTime, Apple Software Update and Apple Mobile Device Support using the Add or Remove Programs list. Download and install the latest version of iTunes from Apple's website. Don't give up if this doesn't work first time as you can also try disconnecting from the Internet and temporarily disabling any security software such as anti-spyware before installing iTunes. Don't forget to turn it back on before you reconnect to the Internet.

Songs that I've imported from CD and bought from the iTunes Store are sorted on first name. I can put the surname in first when I import CDs, but then they display in reverse order.

iTunes actually has two groups of fields to record (Track) Name, Album, Artist Name, Album Artist, Composer and Show (for TV programmes). The first set contains the information as it will be displayed throughout iTunes and on your iPod, while the second set defines how the track is sorted. If no information is provided in the second set, iTunes falls back on the first one when sorting the library.

When importing a CD, the information that you provide is added to the first set, leaving the second set empty except in a few cases; right-click on a column name during import and you'll only see the regular fields, but do the same in the music library and you'll see a longer list with extra values for sorting. Unfortunately music from the iTunes Store doesn't come with the Sort fields completed either.

The good news is that iTunes does behave intelligently in a few cases. Enter a band name such as The Smiths or a track name such as 'A Little Less Conversation' into the regular fields and it automatically copies the text to the sort field and removes the first word. This causes the items to appear in the correct place when browsing the library.

However, it has no way to determine whether an act's name is that of a band or a person, nor which order the latter is in. Unfortunately you'll have to go through your library in small segments to comprehensively add the sorting information. It'll be hard work but it's worth it in the end, as details are presented in reading order but properly sorted in iTunes and on your iPod.

My iPod is frozen. The wheel and buttons wouldn't do anything while playing music.

You may need to recharge your iPod for at least 20 minutes before it'll turn back on. New iPods don't come with a mains charger but if you have one then connect the iPod to a wall socket. Otherwise connect it to a computer but make sure the computer doesn't go to sleep as the iPod charges.

My iPod nano only appears on the desktop but not in iTunes.

iTunes interacts with iPods such as the nano and classic in a different way to the iPod touch. Disconnect your iPod from the computer and click Start > Run and enter services.msc and look for iPod Service in the list. Right-click it and choose stop, then right-click again and choose Start, then reconnect your iPod.

Should the iPod still not appear in iTunes, back up your library (File > Library > Backup Library) and remove iTunes and QuickTime through the Add or Remove Programs list in Control Panel. Also remove iPod Updater if it's listed. Once you've uninstalled iTunes, go to the location where it was installed (usually in c:\Program Files) and delete the iTunes folder if it's still there, then empty the Recycle Bin to be sure that old and possibly damaged files are gone. Now try reinstalling iTunes.

If that fails, there may be a problem in the Registry that stops the iPod and possibly other USB hardware working. Try plugging a USB flash drive or hard drive into the port used for the iPod. If it doesn't appear then you'll find a technical guide on Microsoft's site at *tinyurl.com/4on4fj* for dealing with this, but make a complete backup of your computer's contents before following it.

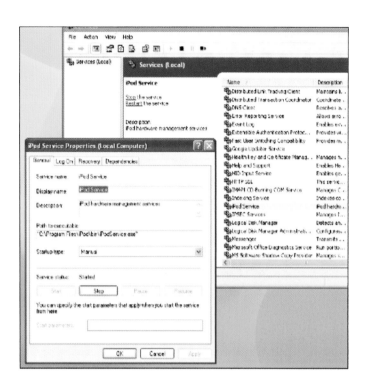

The Autofill button in iTunes sometimes fills my shuffle with long dance mixes. Is there a way to stop this?

A Smart Playlist will do the trick. Choose File > New Smart Playlist and set it to match a single rule where Time is less than 5:00, or whatever maximum duration you prefer. Tick the box to limit the length of the playlist, and choose it to fill to the nearest megabyte below the iPod's capacity, for example 964MB for a 1GB iPod shuffle, and tell iTunes to select the songs by random.

Click on the iPod under Devices and go to the Contents tab. Set it to autofill from your new playlist and tick the box to replace all items when autofilling. Whenever you want to change the tracks on the iPod, select the playlist then remove all of the tracks from it so that iTunes selects new ones for you, then go back to the iPod's Contents tab and hit the Autofill button. None of the tracks copied to the iPod will exceed the duration that you chose.

I recently bought a new iPod and my Universal Dock no longer plays video to my television.

When Apple introduced the iPod touch, it replaced the iPod Universal Dock with the similarly named Apple Universal Dock. The older dock doesn't work with the iPod photo, fifth-generation iPod, or any models introduced since 2007.

Similarly, you can't use the original iPod AV cable with models introduced since September 2007. You'll need to replace it with a new one called the Apple Composite AV Cable, or you can use the alternative component AV cable if your TV has the appropriate but rarer connectors.

Apple publishes a comprehensive guide to which iPods, docks and cables can be used together at *support.apple.com/kb/HT1454*.

I STILL HAVE A PROBLEM. WHERE DO I GO FROM HERE?
Apple provides a 5 R's of iPod troubleshooting for Windows at support.apple.com/kb/TS1369 and for Macs at support.apple.com/kb/TS1410. Once you've run through any extra tests there, you should contact Apple for support. Details for telephone support are at www.apple.com/uk/support/contact along with details of where to find your nearest Apple Store or an authorised service provider.

iPod Glossary

The world of iPods and iTunes is strewn with unfamiliar terms, phrases, contractions, abbreviations and acronyms. Fortunately, Apple makes things as simple to understand as possible when it comes to choosing a music player, but to really know what an iPod expert is talking about, it helps to be familiar with the terminology.

1G, 2G, 3G, 4G, 5G, 6G

Informal shorthand for denoting the 'generation' of an iPod, with 1G (First-Generation) iPods being the initial release.

AAC

Advanced Audio Codec (AAC) is the preferred format for music storage in iTunes and on the iPod. It is also the standard format for music tracks (although not Podcasts) downloaded from the iTunes Music Store.

AIFF

Audio Interchange File Format, developed by Apple in 1988 and most commonly use on its Mac computers.

ALBUM ART

Iconised versions of album and single covers downloaded automatically at the same time as music bought from the iTunes Music Store. This is displayed in a pane on the iTunes interface, and on the screens of modern (colour screen) iPods during song playback.

AUDIOBOOKS

Specially formatted audio files (not necessarily books) that allow for bookmarking. Stopping playback of an audiobook track at any point will save your position so that when you start to play the next time you will pick up at the same place. Bit rate means of expressing the number of audio samples processed in a set period of time, usually a second. See also KBPS.

CAPACITY

The amount of data (in megabytes or gigabytes) that can be held by your iPod. This will be slightly smaller than the stated capacity of the iPod itself due to the way capacities are measured.

CLICK WHEEL

Circular controller found on all current iPods apart from the shuffle. This has evolved over the years to include the audio control buttons themselves as well as the scrolling feature. Previous versions kept the buttons separate, either ranged around the edge of the wheel, or in a row just below the screen.

DOCK

Small brick-like device with a slot for the iPod to sit in. Inside the slot is a connector that exactly matches that on the end of an iPod data cable. Sitting the iPod in the Dock both charges it and updates its library. Newer docks include a remote sensor, while those for photo and video-capable iPods can include connectors for outputting video to an external display.

DRM

Digital Rights Management. A range of systems that control how music can be used and how many times it can be copied. It protects music creators' and publishers' copyrights.

FAIRPLAY

The DRM system used by iTunes and the associated Music Store. It is used to protect AAC-encoded audio files and, some say, it's the key to the success of the iPod, as only iTunes-compatible players such as the iPod can play back FairPlay-protected music tracks.

FIREWIRE

High speed data connection type used to link older iPods to Apple Macintosh computers and regular PCs. Now superseded in later iPods by the USB 2 connector. Its primary benefit is fast data transfer rates, which made it a common feature on video cameras.

GB

Gigabyte. Roughly one billion bytes, where one byte is equivalent to a single character, such as the letter 'a' stored on a disk. It is a measurement of data capacity, and is the terminology used when describing the capacity of the iPod and iPod nano devices.

H.264

High quality digital video format that allows videos, such as those downloaded from the iTunes store, to be highly compressed while retaining as high a quality as possible.

iPHONE

All-in-one communications and entertainment device from Apple, produced as a follow-up to its phenomenally successful iPod line of portable music players. It was developed amid utmost secrecy, and finally revealed to the public in January 2007, following massive blog and media speculation. As well as regular telephony features, it incorporates an address book, music and video player, mapping application and full-blown email client, with push-email services similar to those found on a Blackberry.

iPOD

As well as a generic term used to describe Apple's range of portable music players it is, more specifically, how Apple described the full-sized, top-end player in its range, now called the classic.

iPOD MINI

A now superseded player that was available in five colours and two capacities (4GB and 6GB), and had a monochrome screen. It was the most successful iPod model of all time, but was replaced by the iPod nano in 2005.

iPOD NANO

The smallest iPod ever to feature a screen, it ships in two capacities: 8GB and 16GB. Hugely successful and now capable of handling video as well as audio.

iPOD SHUFFLE

The smallest iPod ever, it is little more than a memory stick with audio control buttons and a headphone jack. It does not feature a screen, and comes in two small capacities: 1GB or 2GB.

iPOD TOUCH

Touchscreen iPod that shows many common features with the iPhone, including wireless Internet browsing and wide-screen video playback.

iTUNES

Apple software for both PCs and Macs used to download, store and play back music, interact with its own online music store and transfer tracks to an iPod.

KBPS

Kilobits per second. A measurement of the number of audio samples that go to make up each second of music in a digitally-encoded track. The higher this number, the smoother and more CD-like the file will sound.

LOSSLESS

Level of compression that has no discernable impact on the sound quality of the audio file being compressed.

MB

Megabyte: one million bytes, where one byte is a single character, such as the letter 'a'. Used to measure the capacity of a device,

such as the iPod shuffle, which has a capacity of 1024 or 2048 megabytes.

MINIJACK

Port for connecting headphones to an iPod. In older models this was accompanied by a second connector that allowed the iPod to be controlled by external devices, such as a remote control on the headphone cable, but this has been phased out in all current iPods and was never a part of the iPod shuffle.

MOBILEME

Online service run by Apple to provide a range of features of use to Mac and PC owners, including email, online storage, calendar synchronisation across multiple machines and basic backup tools. On a Mac it appears as a connected drive, and on all platforms it can be used as an online storage area for personal files and folders. Its email service is Imap-based, meaning that users' mail accounts will always be in the same state, reflecting the same read and unread messages, on any device used to access the service. It replaced the ageing .Mac service that was compatible with the first iPhone. Subscription costs £59 a year.

MP3

Dominant form of audio compression, and the name that people give to files compressed in this way. Unpopular among many recording industry executives as it is difficult to impose copyright preservation measures on this format. This is the most common format for podcasts, and can be played by the iPod and iTunes.

MULTITOUCH

Name given to Apple's technology for implementing on-screen actions by moving fingers around a seemingly inflexible display, such as that found on the iPod touch.

ON-THE-GO

Special type of playlist that is defined on the iPod itself while away from your PC.

PLAYLIST

List of tracks drawn from one or more albums that will be played either in sequence or a random order, or burned to disc through the iTunes interface. Playlists can be copied between iTunes and the iPod, allowing you to take 'virtual' albums on the move.

PODCAST

Non-live radio style broadcast downloaded through the iTunes podcast directory in the Music Store. Quality is highly variable. However, the likes of the BBC and Penguin Books are now seeing the benefit of podcasting, which means a wide range of high quality material is now available.

POP3

Post Office Protocol 3; the predominant technology for email delivery used by most consumer Internet service providers.

PUSH EMAIL

Technology by which emails are sent from the central server that holds them to a client device, such as a mobile phone or Blackberry, without the owner having to manually instigate a retrieval. This is implemented on the iPod touch in partnership with Yahoo! Mail.

QUICKTIME

Video format developed by Apple. Closely tied in to iTunes software, and shipped with all Macintosh computers. It is required by iTunes to play back videos, and is a popular format for professional video production.

REMOTE

Device for controlling the iPod without using the buttons on the device itself. Older models of iPod were bundled with a remote control half way up the headphone cable. Newer video-capable models can be controlled by an optional remote control when plugged into a suitable Dock with an infra red sensor.

RIP

To extract audio from a CD for digital playback from a computer, or portable device such as the iPhone or iPod.

SYNC

Contraction of synchronise. To copy tracks from iTunes to an iPod, and pass other data back to the computer, such as the number of times a track has been played from the iPod.

USB 2.0

Hi speed connection method used to link modern iPods and either PCs or Macs. This replaced the FireWire cables used to connect older models of the player, serving to make them more universally compatible.

VBR

Variable Bit Rate. Used to describe compression in which the number of samples per second (see Kbps) is varied according to the complexity of the audio waveform being digitised. This has the dual benefit of saving on space when you might otherwise use too high a sample rate for less complex waveform sections, and maintaining quality in those more varied parts of a file that would suffer if too coarse a sample rate was applied.

WIFI

Once colloquial, but now generally-accepted term for wireless networking. It embodies several standards, of which the four most common are 802.11a, 802.11b, 802.11g and 802.11n. The 802.11a and 802.11g can each achieve a maximum data throughput of 54megabits per second, while 802.11b runs at 11megabits per second. 802.11n, the fastest standard at 248megabits per second, is as yet unratified, although draft standards have allowed it to be built into many wireless devices already, giving it good overall industry support. The iPod touch uses 802.11b and g.

WIRELESS ACCESS POINT

Hardware device that connects to your network or broadband connection and replicates the features of wired networks in a wireless form to provide network and Internet access to wifi devices such as the iPod touch.

WMA

Windows Media Audio. Another dominant, although proprietary media format, this time developed by Microsoft. It is well supported, with a wide range of media available in this format, but it is incompatible with the iPod and iTunes.